DEFENDERS
OF FORTRESS EUROPE

RELATED TITLES FROM POTOMAC BOOKS

Brassey's D-Day Encyclopedia:
The Normandy Invasion A–Z
by Barrett Tillman

Guderian:
Panzer Pioneer or Myth Maker?
by Russell Hart

Hitler's Ambivalent Attaché:
Lt. Gen. Friedrich Von Boetticher in America, 1933–1941
by Alfred M. Beck

Hitler's Headquarters:
From Beer Hall to Bunker, 1920–1945
by Blaine Taylor

DEFENDERS
OF FORTRESS EUROPE

*The Untold Story of the German Officers
During the Allied Invasion*

SAMUEL W. MITCHAM JR.

POTOMAC BOOKS, INC.
WASHINGTON, D.C.

Library of Congress Cataloging-in-Publication Data
Mitcham, Samuel W.
  Defenders of fortress Europe : the untold story of the German officers during the Allied invasion / Samuel W. Mitcham, Jr. — 1st ed.
    p. cm.
  Includes bibliographical references and index.
  ISBN 978-1-59797-274-1 (alk. paper)
  1. World War, 1939-1945—Campaigns—France—Normandy. 2. Germany. Heer—Officers— Biography. 3. Soldiers—Germany—Biography. 4. World War, 1939-1945—Biography. 5. Atlantic Wall (France and Belgium) I. Title.
  D756.5.N6M4958 2009
  940.54'21421092243—dc22
                                        2009002660

Printed in the United States of America on acid-free paper that meets the American National Standards Institute Z39-48 Standard.

Potomac Books, Inc.
22841 Quicksilver Drive
Dulles, Virginia 20166

First Edition

10 9 8 7 6 5 4 3 2 1

CONTENTS

ILLUSTRATIONS

Photographs

Maps

PREFACE

The purpose of this book is to be a history of the defenders of Fortress Europe—the German military leaders who met and sought to defeat the great Allied invasion of Western Europe.

Battles are fought and directed by men. I have always felt that, to understand history, one must read biography—especially the biography of leaders. This is the story of the men who defended Normandy. It differs from other books in that it focuses on the German generals of all levels—not just the field marshals but also the colonels commanding regiments or divisions. In attempting to show their strengths and their weaknesses, I hope to add depth to our body of knowledge of this, one of the most important battles of history.

The life of each man covered in this book is divided into three parts: his early career, his part in the Normandy campaign, and his life after Normandy, if he had one. The third part is covered in chapter 13.

I hope that *Defenders of Fortress Europe* enlightens and entertains and that the reader enjoys it.

I would like to thank a number of people for their help in the preparation of this book. First and foremost, I would like to thank my long-suffering wife, Donna, and my children, Lacy and Gavin. I would also like to thank Melissa Mathews, the chief of the interlibrary loan department at the University of Louisiana at Monroe. Thanks also go to the late Theodor-Friedrich von Stauffenberg, who left me his papers and the 201 Files (personnel extracts) of many of the officers discussed here. Thanks also go to Paul Moreau and Dr. Donny Elias, MD, for their assistance along the way.

Dr. Samuel W. Mitcham Jr.
Monroe, Louisiana

Map 1. General Regions of the Third Reich

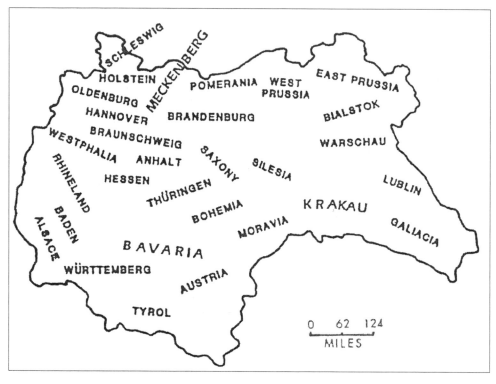

Map 2. The Wehreise, 1939

Map 3. Major Cities of the Third Reich

Map 4. The Eastern Front

Map 5. The Western Front

1

The Atlantic Wall

After Germany conquered France and the mainland of Western Europe in 1940, virtually no thought was given to defending the area for two years. Control of the relatively few occupying forces in France, Belgium, and the Netherlands was given to the commander in chief, Army Group D, which evolved into OB West, the German abbreviation for Oberbefehlshaber West, a term referring to the commander in chief, West, or his headquarters. The first OB West was Field Marshal Erwin Job Wilhelm Georg von Witzleben.

✦

Erwin Job Wilhelm Georg von Witzleben was a salty old Prussian infantry officer and the scion of an ancient German military family. Born in Breslau, Silesia (now Wroclaw, Poland), on December 4, 1881, he was educated at the cadet schools of Wahlstatt and Gross Lichterfelde (Germany's West Point), and was commissioned *Leutnant* (second lieutenant) in the 7th Grenadier Regiment of the Imperial Army on March 22, 1901. (See appendix 1 for a table of comparative ranks.) He remained with his regiment at Leignitz, Lower Silesia (now Legnica, Poland), for seven years before being named adjutant of Area Command Hirschberg in late 1908. He was promoted to first lieutenant in 1910. Meanwhile, in May 1907, he married Else Kleeberg, who bore him a son and a daughter.

Witzleben was adjutant of the 19th Reserve Infantry Brigade when World War I broke out but took command of a company in the 6th Reserve Infantry Regiment in October 1914. He spent the war on the Western Front, and by the time of the Battle of Verdun (1916), he was a captain. He was named battalion commander in the 6th Reserve in the spring of 1917. He also fought in Champagne and Flanders, earned both grades of the Iron Cross, and was wounded in action. Selected for the abbreviated General Staff at Sedan (which lasted three months instead of the normal three years), Witzleben was on the staff of the 108th Infantry Division on the Western Front at the end of the war.

1

After the war, Witzleben returned to Germany and held various General Staff and command assignments. His career was characterized by steady but unspectacular advancement: commander of the 8th (Machine Gun) Company, 8th Infantry Regiment at Frankfurt/Oder (1921–22); Staff, Wehrkreis IV (IV Military District) at Dresden (1922–25); Staff, 12th Cavalry Regiment, also in Dresden (1925–26); General Staff, Infantry Command III in Berlin (1926–28);[1] and commander, III Battalion, 6th Infantry Regiment (which was abbreviated III/6th Infantry) (1928). He was then chief of staff of Wehrkreis VI at Münster (1929–31), commander of the 8th Infantry Regiment back at Frankfurt/Oder (1931–33), and commander of Army Command Hanover (1933–34). He was promoted to major (1923), lieutenant colonel (1929), and colonel (1934). On February 1, 1934, he was promoted to major general and, despite his relatively low rank, was given command of the Wehrkreis III—the extremely important Berlin military district. Meanwhile, his friend and predecessor, General of Artillery Baron Werner von Fritsch, was named commander in chief of the army.

Witzleben was chosen for this important post because Nazi Party–army relations were near the breaking point, and, a tough and experienced Prussian officer, he had pledged that he was perfectly willing to use his troops against the Brownshirts (SA) if Hitler would not or could not control them. Witzleben, indeed, hated the crude and perverted stormtrooper leaders and would have ordered his men to fire on them in a minute if called on to do so. This turned out not to be necessary, however; in the Blood Purge of June 30–July 2, 1934, Hitler got rid of them himself with the aid of the SS, Gestapo, and other party and state agencies. When he first heard that the leading Brownshirts were being executed, Witzleben was delighted and wished aloud that he could be there to watch it. Later, however, he learned that the Nazi death squads had also murdered retired General of Infantry Kurt von Schleicher and retired Major General Kurt von Bredow during the bloodbath, and his attitude changed completely.[2] He demanded a military inquiry into their deaths and became a fervent opponent of the Nazi regime until the day he died.[3]

Witzleben was promoted to lieutenant general on December 1, 1934, and to general of infantry on October 1, 1936. When Fritsch was dismissed from his post in late January 1938 on manufactured charges of homosexuality, Witzleben advocated overthrowing the Nazi government by force. He even proposed shooting Adolf Hitler, if need be. Hitler, however, was successful in removing Fritsch and replacing him with his puppet, Colonel General Walter von Brauchitsch.

As part of a deal with the Führer, Brauchitsch immediately purged the army of its principal anti-Nazi elements, and Erwin von Witzleben was near the head of the list. Witzleben was forced into retirement in early February 1938. Later that year, however, the Sudetenland crisis neared the boiling point. In August, as Hitler pushed the world to the brink of war, Witzleben returned to active duty as commander of the 1st Army on the Franco-German border. Meanwhile, the anti-Hitler conspirators decided that—rather than allow him to embroil Germany in another hopeless world war—they would overthrow him and his regime. They selected General von Witzleben as the military head of the conspiracy because he was willing to act—with or without the consent of Brauchitsch or the vacillating chief of the General Staff, General of Artillery Franz Halder.[4]

The coup planned in the fall of 1938 was the best plan ever devised by the anti-Hitler conspirators. It had a fatal flaw, however, because it depended on Hitler coming to Berlin, where Witzleben was able to assemble sufficiently large forces to execute his plan, which was to arrest Hitler and have him committed to a lunatic asylum. A variation of the plan, which Witzleben approved, called for Major Friedrich Wilhelm Heinz, the commander of Witzleben's assault squad, to personally assassinate the Führer. Unfortunately, neither of the variations could be carried out because Adolf Hitler had the survival instincts of a rat. In the late summer and fall of 1938, he hopped around Germany like a flea but avoided Berlin like the plague. He did not return to the capital until after the British and French signed the Munich Accords, giving the Sudetenland to Germany and ending the crisis in favor of Hitler.

The outbreak of the war took Erwin von Witzleben by surprise. He still favored a coup, but neither Brauchitsch nor Halder had any more interest in it. Witzleben's 1st Army continued to guard the Siegfried line during the German conquest of Poland. The general, however, was tired and sick (he suffered from severe hemorrhoids) and took little pleasure in his promotion to colonel general on November 1, 1939. He led the 1st Army against the Maginot line during the western campaign of 1940 and surrounded the French Army Group 2 near the end of hostilities. As a result of this, coupled with his seniority, his integrity, and the high esteem with which he was held throughout the army, he was promoted to field marshal on July 19, 1940.

Witzleben and his 1st Army were on occupation duty in France for the next year. As the main German armies moved east for the planned invasion of the Soviet Union, he was named commander in chief of Army Group D (and simultaneously Oberbefehlshaber West) on May 1, 1941. His command included the much-reduced 7th and 15th armies, disposed along the Atlantic coast from Antwerp to the Spanish frontier, and his former command, the 1st Army, which was headquartered in Paris and occupied the interior of France.

✦

Unlike the vast majority of the German generals in the spring of 1941, Witzleben had the strategic vision to see that things would not end well for the Third Reich. He realized that one day the Western Allies were likely to attempt to return to the mainland of Europe and that Germany should begin at once to prepare for this contingency. In other words, he foresaw the D-Day invasion more than three years before it occurred and took steps to meet it—and he was the first German general to do so. Naturally, however, he received no help from Berlin or Zossen, the seat of the High Command of the Army (Oberkommando des Heeres, or OKH). When he attempted to secure the French coast from the invasion by constructing permanent defensive installations, OKH refused to give him a single construction battalion. He therefore ordered his subordinate units to begin the project themselves—each German infantry division, generally speaking, had one combat engineer battalion—but not much was accomplished with these limited resources. (Construction engineer battalions and combat engineer battalions are very different animals, with very different jobs and capabilities. Also, France was then in the process of becoming a giant hospital and recuperation center for units decimated on the Russian Front. The officers and men, including the generals, occupying the Atlantic Wall were interested in recovering, living again, and preparing to return to Russia—not in working on construction projects.)

In March 1942 Field Marshal von Witzleben went on leave to undergo a hemorrhoid operation. Hitler seized on this pretext to retire him again on March 21, 1942, and he was never reemployed. Witzleben retired to the Lynar estate at Seesen, a few miles south of Potsdam, where his health continued to deteriorate. Hitler, however, had not heard the last from this man of courage and integrity, although his place on the stage of OB West was taken over by lesser men.

Karl Rudolf Gerd von Rundstedt succeeded Witzleben as OB West.

✦

Karl Rudolf Gerd von Rundstedt was born at Aschersleben in the Harz Mountain region on December 12, 1875. The descendant of an old Prussian Junker family from Mecklenburg, he could trace his lineage back to 1109. His father (also called Gerd) was a hussar (light cavalry) officer who rose to the rank of major general. Young Rundstedt entered the junior cadet school at Oranienstein in 1888, at age twelve, and graduated from Gross Lichterfelde in 1892. He entered the army at the age of sixteen as a senior officer cadet and was commissioned second lieutenant in the 83rd Prussian Infantry Regiment at Kassel in June 1893. (He would have much preferred a cavalry unit, but his father—who had three other sons—could not afford it.) Hitler was three years old at the time, Erich von Manstein was six, and Erwin Rommel was in diapers.

Rundstedt was well educated and early in life adopted the sophisticated manners of an Old World gentleman—characteristics he exhibited throughout his life. His tact and consideration, his finesse in dealing with both individuals and problems, his diplomatic aplomb, and his general bearing certainly impressed his superiors, who looked on him as more mature and intelligent than his peers. His family background and the fact that his father was a general did nothing to impede his advancement, nor did the fact that he never disagreed with his superiors and obeyed all orders without question.

Leutnant von Rundstedt served as a battalion and regimental adjutant until 1902, when (after ten years' service) he was promoted to first lieutenant. That same year he married Luise "Bila" von Götz, the daughter of a retired major. They had one son, Hans Gerd, who broke with family tradition and became a historian. (Lieutenant Dr. von Rundstedt served as his father's aide from 1943 on.) Also in 1902 Rundstedt took his required Wehrkreis exam. Those officers who scored in the top 15 percent on this exam were sent to the War Academy in Berlin to undergo General Staff training. Even then, the road to the General Staff was extremely hard. Only about a third of the 150 men selected to attend the War Academy each year ever graduated and were allowed to wear the red stripes of a General Staff officer. Rundstedt did well, however, and became a member of the General Staff on April 1, 1907—six days after he was promoted to captain.

Rundstedt spent three years (1907–10) attached to the Greater General Staff in Berlin, followed by two years on the staff of the XI Corps (1910–12), before becoming a company commander in the 171st Infantry Regiment. When World War I broke out in August 1914, he was named operations officer (Ia) of the 22nd Reserve Division and fought on the Western Front (including in the Battle of the Marne) until November 1914, when he was promoted to major and was assigned to the staff of the general government of Belgium.

Even though he was fluent in English and French (his mother was a Huguenot and his nanny was British), he spent most of World War I on the Eastern Front. In the spring of 1915 he became Ia of a division serving in the Baltic States, and he took part in the drive to Narev. At the end of the year, he was assigned to the staff of the general government in Warsaw. In 1916 he was sent to Hungary as a corps chief of staff and apparently did a brief tour of duty with the Turkish General Staff in 1917 before he returned to the northern sector of the Russian Front that fall. He served as chief of staff of the LIII Corps in the Lake Peipus battles. After Moscow sued for peace, Major von Rundstedt returned to France as chief of staff of the XV Corps, a post that he held when the war ended in November 1918.

When the Reichswehr was formed in 1920, Rundstedt was promoted to lieutenant colonel and was named Ia of the 3rd Cavalry Division at Weimar in Thuringia. Promoted to colonel in early 1923, he became chief of staff of Wehrkreis II and the 2nd Infantry Division in Stettin, western Pomerania (now Szczecin, Poland), in October. He was transferred in early 1925 to Paderborn, Westphalia, where he commanded the 18th Infantry Regiment until September 1926.

Rundstedt continued his rapid postwar advancement on October 1, 1926, when he became chief of staff of the Group Command 2 at Kassel. He was promoted to major general on November 1, 1927, and assumed command of the 2nd Cavalry Division in Breslau, Silesia, in November 1928. A promotion to lieutenant general followed on March 1, 1929. He was briefly commander of Wehrkreis III and the 3rd Infantry Division (1932) before assuming command of Army Group 1 (1933–38). All three of these units were headquartered in Berlin. He was promoted to general of infantry on October 1, 1932, and to colonel general on March 1, 1938.

Rundstedt was a nonpolitical general whom the Nazis found very useful. Hitler was impressed with his aristocratic manners (although he did not care for most of the German nobility) and apparently felt slightly inferior to Rundstedt socially (which he was—but more than slightly). Erich von Manstein later recalled that Rundstedt "had a charm about him to which even Hitler succumbed. The latter seems to have taken a genuine liking to him. . . . What probably attracted Hitler was the indefinable impression the general gave of a man from a past which he did not understand and to the atmosphere of which he never had access."[5]

In early 1938, when Defense Minister Werner von Blomberg and Colonel General Werner von Fritsch, the commander in chief of the army, were forced to retire, Hitler seriously considered giving Fritsch's old job to General of Artillery Walter von Reichenau, the most qualified pro-Nazi officer available. Rundstedt (together with Colonel General Ritter Wilhelm von Leeb) blocked the appointment, telling Hitler that the army would "never" accept Reichenau. The position went to General of Artillery (later Field Marshal) Walter von Brauchitsch instead.[6]

Command Group 1 temporarily became 2nd Army during the Sudetenland crisis of 1938. Rundstedt was among those who opposed war with Czechoslovakia because he feared that the Wehrmacht could not defeat Prague's allies, Great Britain and France. He did advise the new army commander in chief not to object too strenuously to Hitler's aggression, however, because he was afraid the Führer would fire Brauchitsch and replace him with Reichenau. At this time Rundstedt was first approached by dissident officers and asked to join the anti-Hitler conspiracy. His reaction was distinctly negative—as it continued to be for the next six years. He did not, however, inform the Nazis about the plot. His attitude was basically that he would join it if it succeeded. When Field Marshal Rommel approached him in 1944, his reaction was, "You, too?!" He then told the the field marshal, "You are young. You know and love the people. *You* do it!" Rommel tried. Rundstedt never lifted a finger to help.

Rundstedt retired in November 1938 and was simultaneously named honorary colonel of the 18th Infantry Regiment. To be named an honorary colonel of any regiment was great honor in the German army and a distinction Rundstedt cherished above all others. From then on, Rundstedt wore his regimental commander's uniform exclusively (with his field marshal's insignia on his shoulder boards) and was often mistaken for a colonel by the lower ranks. When this happened, Rundstedt only laughed.

General von Rundstedt was recalled to active duty in May 1939 and was placed in charge of Working Staff Rundstedt, which played a major role in planning the invasion of Poland. Most of the work, however, was done by his chief of staff, Lieutenant General Erich von Manstein, and Günther Blumentritt, his chief of operations.[7] Until August 1939 Rundstedt remained at his home in Kassel where the 18th Infantry was based. This was typical of Rundstedt's leadership style. He never concerned himself with the nuts and bolts of an operation and always left that to his subordinates. (Fortunately for him, most of these men were extremely talented, especially until the end of 1941.) He remained aloof, almost above the fray, rarely visited the troops, and spent virtually all of his time at his headquarters, which one general said was characterized by "incredible idleness."[8] He also had a love for cheap detective novels, which he frequently read on duty. This passion embarrassed him, so he always read them with a desk drawer open, so that he could quickly hide them when a visitor entered his office.

Working Staff Rundstedt was upgraded to Headquarters, Army Group South, in August 1939, and Rundstedt commanded it in the Polish campaign the following month. After Warsaw fell, he was briefly commander in chief, East, but was soon transferred to the Western Front, where his headquarters was redesignated Army Group A. Here his chief of staff—Manstein—came up with the plan that led to the conquest of France in a brilliant six-week campaign. Rundstedt approved the plan, but when Brauchitsch and the chief of the General Staff, General of Artillery Franz Halder, rejected it, Rundstedt did not "go over their heads" and submit the concept directly to Hitler. Manstein had to do that personally with the help of Hitler's army adjutant, Lieutenant Colonel Rudolf Schmundt. Meanwhile, Rundstedt did nothing to help Manstein when Brauchitsch transferred the uncomfortably brilliant general away from the center of action to the command of an infantry corps then forming in Stettin.

The Manstein Plan worked exactly as its creator said it would. Between them, Army Group A and Army Group B (under Fedor von Bock) destroyed the best French and British divisions in Belgium. Although he later denied it, Rundstedt made a major mistake in May 1940, when he advised the Führer to halt his panzer in front of Dunkirk, rather than to capture the city by armored assault. As a result, more than 300,000 British and French troops escaped via naval evacuation. The gravity of this mistake, however, was not recognized at the time, and after the fall of Paris, Rundstedt was promoted to field marshal on July 19, 1940. He had, meanwhile, moved his headquarters to Bastone and then to a luxurious hotel at St. Germain on the Seine, a few miles downriver from Paris.

In 1941 Rundstedt's command was renamed Army Group South. Together with Army Group Center (Bock) and Army Group North (Leeb), it invaded the Soviet Union on June 22, 1941. Here, Rundstedt played a part in winning some of Nazi Germany's greatest tactical and operational victories. The strain of the campaign resulted in his first heart attack (a mild one) in November 1941. Rundstedt, however, remained in command. Hitler sacked him for the first time on November 30, 1941, two days after Rundstedt ordered a retreat from Rostov. The field marshal had opposed capturing the city in the first place and had already signaled Führer Headquarters that he would take Rostov but did not have the strength to hold it. On November 28, in the bitter cold of a Russian winter, his depleted 1st Panzer and 17th armies were under heavy Soviet counterattack. To avoid a disaster, Rundstedt ordered a general retreat to the Mius. Two days later the dictator signaled the field marshal to halt the withdrawal and hold his positions at all costs. Rundstedt, who had a temper, signaled back to Führer Headquarters that Hitler's order was "madness" and that, if Hitler insisted that the order be obeyed, he should find someone else to carry it out. Rundstedt was relieved of his command that evening. His successor, Field Marshal von

Reichenau, initially tried to obey the order but reversed himself within twenty-four hours. He resumed the retreat on December 1.

Later, after SS General Josef "Sepp" Dietrich convinced the Führer that he had done Rundstedt an injustice, Hitler recalled Rundstedt to duty as OB West on March 10, 1942. (Rundstedt later referred to Dietrich as "decent, but stupid.")

✦

As OB West, Rundstedt adopted a laissez-faire attitude. Unlike Rommel, he did not believe that the Allies could be halted on the invasion beaches and did little to prepare the Atlantic Wall for defense. He believed that the decisive battle should be fought in the interior of France and was, in fact, preparing for a 1941-style battle in 1944. He did not realize that the Allies' aerial superiority had rendered the great blitzkrieg victories of the past impossible. His strategy was to establish Panzer Group West under the command of his personal friend, General of Panzer Troops Baron Leo Geyr von Schweppenburg. He planned to allow the Allies to land and advance inland, out of the range of their navies' big guns. Then Geyr would attack and defeat them with his ten panzer and panzer grenadier divisions. He took no interest in the details of Geyr's plan; instead, he retired to his headquarters with his brandy and cigarettes, and left the details of planning the battle to others. Unfortunately, his former chief of staff, Manstein, had long since been replaced by the much less capable Günther Blumentritt, so the actual leadership of the German army in the West devolved on Geyr von Schweppenburg and Erwin Rommel, who became commander of Army Group B (7th and 15th armies and Wehrmacht Command Netherlands) in December 1943. Also unfortunately for the Wehrmacht, they found it impossible to unite on a common strategy.

✦

Baron Leo Geyr von Schweppenburg—who was called "von Geyr"—was born in Potsdam, an ancient garrison town near Berlin, on February 2, 1886, the descendant of an old Württemberger military family. He entered the service as a *Fahnenjunker* (officer cadet) in 1904 and was commissioned in the family regiment, the 26th Light Dragoons (2nd Württemberg Dragoons) in 1905. He was appointed to the War Academy in 1911, graduated in 1914, and went to war with his regiment in August. He was, however, soon transferred to the staff of the 9th Cavalry Division. Promoted to captain in 1915, he served on both the Eastern and Western fronts and in the Balkans, where he was a liaison officer to the Bulgarian army. He also served tours of duty as Ia of the 30th Infantry and

26th Landwehr divisions on the Western Front. (See appendix 2 for a list of the German staff positions; appendix 3 shows German units, with their normal strengths and the normal ranks of their commanders.) Geyr was also wounded at least once, although the details of the injury are lacking. After the war, he helped suppress civil unrest in Stuttgart and the Ruhr, and he spent the 1920s alternating between cavalry and General Staff assignments. He commanded the Prussian-Mecklenburg (Preussisch-Mecklenburgisches) 14th Cavalry Regiment at Ludwigslust from 1931 to 1933. He had been promoted to first lieutenant in 1913, *Rittmeister* (captain of cavalry) in 1915, major in 1925, lieutenant colonel in 1930, and colonel in 1932. Promotions to major general (September 1, 1935), lieutenant general (October 1, 1937), and general of cavalry (April 20, 1940) followed. (Geyr formally changed his rank to general of panzer troops on June 4, 1941.)

A sophisticated and urbane person, bright, articulate, and well educated, and possessing great social skills, Geyr represented Germany as military attaché in London, Brussels, and the Hague from 1933 to 1937 and was an excellent military dip-lomat. Seeing that the future belonged to the panzer branch, he befriended Heinz Guderian and transferred to the tank arm in 1937. He commanded the 3rd Panzer Division (October 12, 1937–February 15, 1940), XXIV Motorized (later Panzer) Corps (February 15, 1940–January 7, 1942), XXXX Panzer Corps (July 9–October 1, 1942), LXXXVI Corps (February 21–April 1, 1943), and LVIII Reserve Panzer Corps (August 5–December 31, 1943). He was assigned to OB West in July 1943 as commander-designate of Panzer Group West, a headquarters roughly equal to an army, which he led from January 24 to July 2, 1944. (Panzer Group West was, in fact, redesignated 5th Panzer Army on August 5, 1944.)

Meanwhile, in December 1943, much to Rundstedt's dismay, Field Marshal Erwin Rommel arrived in Western Europe to conduct an inspection tour of the Atlantic Wall.

✦

Erwin Johannes Eugen Rommel was born in Heidenheim, Swabia, a district of Württemberg, in southwestern Germany, on November 15, 1891. The son and grandson of schoolteachers, he grew into a serious, innovative, and self-reliant young man. Despite the lack of military background in his ancestry, he joined the army as a Fahnenjunker in the 124th (6th Württemberg) Infantry Regiment on July 19, 1910, at the age of eighteen. He was admitted to the War School at Danzig, West Prussia (now Gdansk, Poland), in March 1911, graduated, and was commissioned second lieutenant in January 1912.

An official photograph of Field Marshal Erwin Rommel, the Desert Fox (USAMHI).

Until World War I broke out, Rommel's career had been about average. The battlefield, however, transformed him into a warrior of the highest order. Brigadier General Desmond Young later wrote, "From the moment that he first came under fire he stood out as the perfect fighting animal: cold, cunning, ruthless, untiring, quick of decision [and] incredibly brave." A fellow officer recalled, "he was the body and soul of war."[9]

In 1914 and 1915 Rommel fought in Belgium and France, at Verdun and the Argonne. He was wounded in late 1914 but returned to the trenches in early 1915 as a company commander. Promoted to first lieutenant in September 1915, he became a company commander in the elite Württemberg Mountain Battalion, with which he served in Romania and in the Italian Alps. Here he proved to have an uncanny instinct for tactics and improvisation. In October 1917, during the struggle for Monte Matajur, he captured nine thousand Italians and eighty-one guns during a forty-eight-hour period. For this incredible feat of arms, he was awarded the Pour le Mérite. A promotion to captain followed shortly thereafter. Much to his disgust, he spent the rest of the war in staff or backwater assignments.

From 1919 to 1939 Rommel was employed in infantry or training assignments. He commanded a security company during "the war after the war," as the Germans called the Communist insurrections of 1919 and the early 1920s, which the army and *Freikorps* (Free Corps, right-wing paramilitary organizations) put down with the utmost severity. Rommel's fighting took place in Westphalia. In 1920 he was accepted into the Reichswehr, as the armed forces of the Weimar Republic (1920–33) was called.[10] He assumed command of a machine gun company in the 13th Infantry at Stuttgart that same year and remained with this regiment until 1929, when he was sent to the War School at Dresden. The son and grandson of teachers, he proved to be an excellent instructor. He was promoted to major on October 10, 1933.

Erwin Rommel was named commander of the III Battalion, 17th Infantry Regiment, a mountain unit at Goslar. After this successful command, he was promoted to lieutenant colonel and in 1935 became a course director at the War School at Potsdam. He was promoted to colonel on August 1, 1937, and was named commandant of the War School at Wiener-Neustadt (in Lower Austria, twenty-eight miles south of Vienna) in November 1938.[11]

In the late 1920s Rommel wrote a book about his experiences, *Infantry in the Attack*, which became a bestseller in Nazi Germany and led to temporary duty assignments at Führer Headquarters in 1938 and 1939. He commanded the Führer's Bodyguard Battalion in the occupation of the Sudetenland, the occupation of Czechoslovakia, and the Polish campaign; then he used his high standing with Hitler to obtain command of the 7th Panzer (formerly 2nd Light) Division on February 5, 1940.

The 7th Panzer was one of the worst-equipped armored divisions in the Wehrmacht. It had only three tank battalions instead of the standard four, and it was outfitted mainly with captured Czech T-38 tanks, which weighed only nine tons, as opposed to the twenty-three-ton Panzer Mark III (PzKw III), which was becoming the standard main battle tank. Rommel nevertheless threw himself into the task of bringing the 7th up to par, and when the invasion of France and the Low Countries began on May 10, 1940, it was ready. In six weeks the division suffered 2,594 men killed, wounded, or captured—more than any other German division in the campaign. In the process it took 97,468 prisoners, captured 277 guns, 67 antitank guns, 458 tanks and armored cars, 4,000 to 5,000 trucks, at least 1,500 horse-drawn vehicles, and tons of other supplies and equipment. It also captured the commander of the French Atlantic Fleet, four other admirals, and at least seventeen generals.[12]

After the fall of France, Rommel and his "Ghost Division" were stationed in the vicinity of Bordeaux, southwestern France, as part of the army of occupation. In early February 1941 he was suddenly summoned to Führer Headquarters. Here, on February 6, Hitler promoted him to lieutenant general (to date from January 1, 1941) and named the surprised Swabian commander of the Afrika Korps (DAK), which consisted of the 15th Panzer and 5th Light (later 21st Panzer) divisions. Later he commanded Panzer Group Afrika (1941–42), Panzer Army Afrika (1942–43), Army Group Afrika (1943), and Army Group B in northern Italy and then France (1943–44). In the process, he won a spectacular series of victories against tremendous odds. His exploits in the desert are legendary. Disobeying the orders of Brauchitsch and Halder, he assumed the offensive within a few weeks of arriving in Libya. He captured Benghazi, overran Cyrenica, beseiged Tobruk, and pushed to the border of Egypt while crushing a British corps in the process. When the British tried to liberate the Tobruk garrison in Operation Brevity (July 15–17, 1941), Rommel (although outnumbered more than 2 to 1) smashed their relief forces and destroyed or captured more than a hundred tanks, against a loss of twenty-five of his own. Hitler was so pleased that he promoted the Desert Fox (as he was now called) to general of panzer troops, effective July 1, 1941, and named him commander of Panzer Group (later Panzer Army) Afrika. He even let Rommel form a new division, the 90th Light. Unfortunately for Nazi Germany, this was all the reinforcement Rommel would get, except for the 164th Light Afrika Division and a small parachute brigade, until the war in Africa was lost.

In the second half of 1941 the British air and naval forces operating out of Malta, Gibraltar, and Alexandria, strangled Panzer Group Afrika. In November Rommel received only 15 percent of his required supplies. When the British 8th Army launched Operation Crusader on November 17, 1941, Rommel had only 249 panzers and 146 nearly useless Italian tanks against 748 Allied tanks. He was also extremely short of fuel. Under his inspired leadership, the Germans fought like Tigers, but the Siege of Tobruk was finally broken on December 5, after 242 days, and Rommel was forced to retreat to Tripoltania on December 8. He had only twenty-six panzers left.

The British generals were now convinced that the war in North Africa was as good as won. German morale, however, remained unbroken. Erwin Rommel had some undefinable quality that enabled him to get more out of his men than they thought they could give, and they loved him for it. He was also quite likely to turn up in person anywhere and at anytime—often on the front lines. He was extremely brave and energetic and liked to joke or talk in the Swabian dialect with his enlisted men, who had boundless confidence in him.

As the British built up for their final drive on Tripoli, an Italian supply convoy finally made it past Malta and off-loaded fifty-five panzers in early January 1942. On January 21 Rommel—whom everyone thought was beaten—launched a surprise counteroffensive, smashed the British 1st Armoured Division and 201st Guards Brigade, captured an Indian brigade, recaptured Benghazi, and pushed 8th Army back to the Gazala line. A happy Führer promoted him to colonel general on January 30, 1942.

After the second Cyrenican campaign, a lull descended on the North African Front, as both sides built up their supplies. They were in a race to see who could launch an offensive first and naturally Rommel won it. He struck on May 26, 1942. He was outnumbered almost 3 to 1 in tanks (excluding the nearly worthless Italian tanks), 10 to 1 in armored cars, and 8 to 5 in artillery. He nevertheless won the Battle of the Gazala Line and on June 21 captured Tobruk, along with thirty-two thousand British, South African, and Indian prisoners. A jubilant Führer promoted him to field marshal the next day. Rommel remarked that he would rather Hitler had given him one more division.

Tobruk was the high water mark of Rommel's career. After the battle, Rommel had only forty-four operational panzers left. He nevertheless invaded Egypt but was checked in the First Battle of El Alamein, only sixty miles from Alexandria.

Rommel was now a very sick man. Exhausted by a year and a half in the harsh environment of the Sahara Desert, he suffered from desert sores, chronic stomach problems, intestinal catarrh, circulatory problems, liver trouble, and symptoms of exhaustion. On September 20 he handed command of Panzer Army Afrika over to General of Panzer Troops Georg Stumme and left for Semmering, a mountain resort near Vienna.[13] Apparently Hitler intended to allow him to recover, and then he would give Rommel a command in Russia; however, on October 23, Keitel telephoned the Desert Fox. Could he return to Egypt right away? Panzer Army Afrika was under heavy attack, and General Stumme was missing. (Later Stumme was found dead. He had suffered a heart attack while under Australian machine gun fire.)

The Allied superiority in the Second Battle of El Alamein was overwhelming. They outnumbered the Germans 4 to 1 in men, 5 to 1 in tanks, 5 to 1 in artillery, 3 to 1 in antitank guns, and 4 to 1 in operational aircraft. (The Italian units were now incapable of offering prolonged resistance.) Rommel nevertheless checked the British for more than a week. Finally, on the night of November 2–3, with the Afrika Korps down to thirty-five tanks, he admitted defeat and ordered a general retreat. Much to his surprise, Hitler refused to allow it, commanding him to "stand fast, yield not a yard of ground, and throw every gun and every man into the battle."[14] Although Rommel retreated against orders on November 4 and Hitler reversed himself after the fact, the delay cost Rommel the Italian X Corps and the Ariete Armored Division, as well as much of what was left of the Afrika Korps. Up until this time, Rommel's relationship with Adolf Hitler had been good. From then on, when he visited Führer Headquarters, he was subjected to the same scenes as Wilhelm Keitel and some of the other generals: temper tantrums, charges of defeatism, screaming fits, violent outbursts of hatred, unreasonable orders, irrational demands, and other pathological behavior. Eventually, Rommel joined the anti-Hitler conspiracy.

Erwin Rommel's retreat from El Alamein was brilliant. He eventually escaped to Tunisia, where he commanded Army Group Afrika from January 1 to March 9, 1943. Because of his constant demands that North Africa be abandoned, Hitler relieved him of his command and sent him home. He was recalled to Führer Headquarters in early May 1943, as the Axis front in Africa was collapsing. "I should have listened to you," Hitler confessed.[15] It was too late now, however; Germany lost 130,000 men. The civilians in the Third Reich called the debacle "Tunisgrad."

Rommel's last command was Army Group B, which he took over in September 1943. Initially a headquarters without troop units, it had been seriously depleted on the Eastern Front. Rommel commanded it in northern Italy until late November 1943, when it was withdrawn to Germany. While deciding on Rommel's future employment, Hitler sent him on an inspection tour of the Atlantic Wall.

◆

When the Führer sent Rommel on his inspection tour of OB West, he, Keitel, Jodl, and the other generals, assumed that Rundstedt and the field marshal would not get along. (Rundstedt had already asked Keitel if Rommel was earmarked to replace him as OB West.) The men of Führer Headquarters, however, underestimated Gerd von Rundstedt's abilities as a military politician. (He had not reached the rank of field marshal because he did not understand such things.) When they met, he made every effort to charm Rommel and experienced some success. The two men even developed a faint liking for one another, and

Rundstedt suggested that Rommel work for him. Rundstedt offered to place 7th Army, 15th Army, and the Armed Forces Netherlands under Rommel's Headquarters, Army Group B. This suited the daring Swabian "right down to the ground," as the Germans say. These were OB West's strongest armies, and Rommel would almost certainly be in tactical command of the German forces that would meet the Allied invasion. Hitler and his cronies were somewhat shocked by this turn of events. The Führer did not like the idea at all but had little choice but to go along with it. The stage was set for great events. (Map 6 shows Army Group B's area of operations in early 1944.)

Rommel's three principle subordinates were Friedrich Christiansen, the commander of Armed Forces Netherlands; Colonel General Hans von Salmuth, commander of the 15th Army in Belgium and northern France; and Colonel General Friedrich Dollmann, commander of the 7th Army, which was stationed south of the Seine and charged with defending Normandy and Brittany.

◆

Map 6. The Area of Operations, Army Group B, 1944

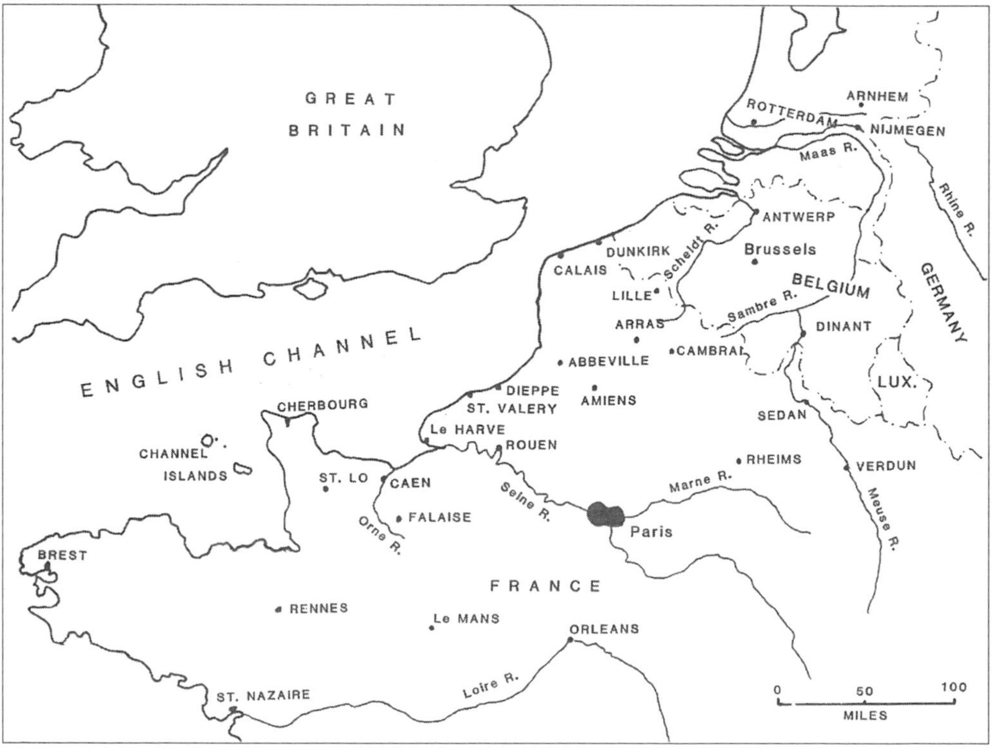

Field Marshal Erwin Rommel (far right) inspecting a motorized field artillery unit, France, 1944 (Bundesarchiv).

Friedrich Christiansen was born in Wyk, on the island of Föhr, on December 12, 1879. (Föhr is part of the Friesian Island chain on the North Sea coast of Germany, in extreme northwest Germany The western part of the chain belongs to the Netherlands.) The son of a captain in the merchant marine, he followed in his father's footsteps and, at the age of sixteen, became a sailor in the merchant marine. Initially, he was a cabin boy on a five-masted sailing ship. Christiansen remained in the merchant marine from 1895 to 1901 and from 1902 to 1914. In 1901 he began a one-year voluntary enlistment in the Imperial Navy, where he served in the torpedo boat branch. He remained in the reserve until 1914, when World War I began and he was called up for active duty. In 1913 he had begun flight training at the Central Aviation School at Holtenau, near Hamburg.

Christiansen spent the first six months of the war as a flight instructor at Holtenau. He spent the rest of the war as a pilot, squadron, and wing commander in Flanders, flying seaplanes, some of which were fighters. He and his men patrolled the North Sea and English Channel, bombed ports in England and Belgium, and attacked British shipping. Christiansen himself shot down twenty-one enemy aircraft (some sources place this total as high as twenty-seven) and an airship, and he was awarded the Pour le Mérite in December 1917. (He was one of only three naval aviators to receive this decoration. The other two flew land-based aircraft; Christiansen was the top float plane ace of the war.) He was commissioned ensign (Leutnant) of reserves in 1916, lieutenant j.g. (*Oberleutnant*) of reserves in 1917, and lieutenant (*Kapitän der Reserve*) in September 1918. He was discharged from the navy in March 1919 and promptly joined the Freikorps, which was engaged in enforcing law and order (which had largely collapsed when the kaiser fell) and in putting down communist insurrections throughout the country. Christiansen was part of the famous III Marine Brigade under Capt. Wilhelm Friedrich von Loewenfeld. He returned to the merchant marine in 1920 and became a captain in 1923.

On March 3, 1933, Christiansen—who was a Nazi—became a *Ministerialrat* (senior civil servant) in the Reich Air Ministry, the forerunner of the Luftwaffe. He was commissioned colonel on January 3, 1934, and initially served as inspector of (secret) Luftwaffe schools. He became commander of Luftwaffe schools in March 1935, just after Hitler announced the existence of the German air force (March 9) and renounced the Treaty of Versailles (March 16). Later that year, on December 1, he became a major general. He was promoted to lieutenant general on August 1, 1937, and a general of fliers on January 1, 1939.

On April 20, 1937—Hitler's birthday—Christiansen was named *Korpsführer* of the National Socialist Flying Corps (NSFK), a paramilitary organization charged with providing primary flight instruction to members of the Hitler Youth and thus a reservoir of trained personnel for the Luftwaffe. The NSFK also trained glider pilots, navigators, radio operators, and other future airmen. Christiansen, who had a talent for training, thus provided a real service for the Third Reich. He held the post until June 26, 1943, when Colonel General Alfred Keller replaced him. Meanwhile, on May 28, 1940, he was named Wehrmacht commander of the Netherlands, a post he held until the last month of the war. Christiansen also commanded the 25th Army in the Netherlands from November 10, 1944, to January 28, 1945.

It is generally conceded that Christiansen was not qualified for his post as Wehrmacht commander, Netherlands, and owed his appointment solely to his friendship with Hermann Göring—although the fact that he was a Friesian islander may have been a factor in his appointment. His incompetence for higher command was partially alleviated by the highly capable Luftwaffe Lieutenant General Heinz-Hellmuth von Wühlisch, a veteran army General Staff officer who served as his chief of staff from January 12, 1942.[16]

♦

Hans von Salmuth was born in Metz, then a German garrison town, on November 21, 1888, the son of Anton von Salmuth, who retired as a captain.[17] Hans entered the service as an officer cadet in 1907 and was commissioned in the 3rd Grenadier Guards Regiment in 1909. During World War I he fought in Belgium and France and served as a battalion adjutant and then as a General Staff officer. He joined the Reichswehr and was a company commander in the Prussian 1st Infantry Regiment at Königsberg (1920–22). He then served on the General Staff of the 1st Infantry Division at Königsberg (1922–23), on the General Staff of Artillery Command I (1923–24), and as a company commander in the elite Prussian 9th Infantry Regiment (1927–30). He returned to the Staff, 1st Infantry Division (1930–33), and became Ia of the 2nd Infantry Division in Stettin, Pomerania, on December 1, 1933. Later he became chief of staff of Wehrkreis II (also in Stettin) (1934–35) and was chief of staff of Army Group 1 from 1937 to 1939. He served as chief of staff of Army Group North (later B) during the invasions of Poland and France (1939–40). He was promoted to general of infantry on August 1, 1940. Earlier he had been promoted to first lieutenant (December 1914), captain (August 1916), major (1928), lieutenant colonel (1932), colonel (1934), major general (1937), and lieutenant general, to date from August 1, 1939. Later he became a colonel general (January 1, 1943). Salmuth commanded XXX Corps (1941–42), 17th Army (April–June 1942), 4th Army (June–July 1942), 2nd Army (July 1942–February 1943), and 4th Army again (June–July 1943)—all on the Eastern Front. A skillful and tough tactical commander, Salmuth was unjustly relieved of the command of the 2nd Army in February 1943 for failing to obey one of Hitler's impossible "not one step back" orders. The Führer and the Nazis thus earned Salmuth's undying hatred, for he was not a forgiving man.

The Nazis certainly thought more highly of Salmuth than he did of them. After briefly allowing him to command 4th Army in Russia for a second time, Hitler appointed Salmuth commander of the 15th Army in northern France and Belgium. He assumed command on August 1, 1943. This was a position of great responsibility, for it was generally assumed that the Allies would land somewhere in Salmuth's area of operations—probably in the Pas de Calais sector. He would thus initially have primary responsibility for defeating the D-Day invasion.

◆

In the zone of the 15th Army, little was done to prepare the Atlantic Wall for defense. Rommel visited the area in late 1943 and ordered Salmuth to lay hundreds of thousands of mines along the coast. When he returned in January 1944, he was not satisfied with the progress being made. He visited Salmuth at his headquarters—a luxurious chateau near Tourcoing—and ordered him to increase the amount of time each soldier in 15th Army spent laying mines, even if training time had to be reduced. Salmuth, who apparently looked down on the field marshal as a Swabian commoner who had gotten lucky, loftily informed Rommel that he wanted to go into battle with well-trained and well-rested soldiers. His condescending manner made it clear that he thought he knew more about military matters than Rommel and considered himself superior in everything but rank.

"Evidently you don't intend to obey my orders," Rommel snapped.

Salmuth scoffed and told Rommel that his program could not possibly be carried out in less than a year. Anyone who said differently was either trying to flatter the field marshal or was "a pig idiot."

Rommel was clearly annoyed by Salmuth's attitude, but he said nothing at all. It seemed apparent that Salmuth had gotten away with it and would continue to direct operations in his sector as he saw fit, regardless of the field marshal's views. When it was time for him to depart, however, Rommel pulled the colonel general aside, shut the door, and gave Salmuth the dressing down of his life. When they emerged, Salmuth's face was red and his manner had changed completely. Rommel acted as if nothing had happened.[18]

Colonel General Friedrich Dollmann, who commanded 7th Army in Normandy until his death on June 29, 1944 (USAMHI).

"He is a thoroughly rude fellow," Rommel remarked to Admiral Friedrich Ruge, his naval adviser, "and has to be treated the same way!"[19] But the message had been delivered. Either Salmuth would obey Rommel's orders or his replacement would. Mine laying and construction of the Atlantic Wall immediately picked up with vengeance throughout the zone of the 15th Army.

✦

Friedrich Dollmann, the commander of the 7th Army, was a large and physically impressive officer who showed great political skill and adaptability throughout his career. Born in Würzburg on February 2, 1882, he joined the Bavarian army as a Fahnenjunker in 1899. Commissioned in the Bavarian 7th Artillery Regiment, he served with this unit until October 1909, when he began General Staff training at the Bavarian War Academy. During World War I, he served as adjutant of the 1st Bavarian Field Artillery Brigade in Lorraine, on the Somme, at Artois, and at Verdun. From 1916 to late 1917 he commanded the Bavarian 7th Field Artillery Regiment on the Somme, on the Plateau de Californie, and in Champagne. After briefly serving as second General Staff officer (Ib or chief supply officer) of the 6th Bavarian Infantry Division on the Western Front, Dollmann joined the Staff, 6th Army, in January 1918 and remained there until the end of the war.

Dollmann served in staff positions from 1919 until late 1927, when he assumed command of the I/7th Artillery Regiment in Munich. He became chief of operations of the 7th Infantry Division in Munich on October 1, 1929, and commander of the 6th Artillery Regiment on February 1, 1931. He was promoted to Artillery Leader VII and deputy commander of the 7th Infantry Division in Munich on October 1, 1932. He then relocated to Berlin and was inspector of artillery in the Defense Ministry (1933–34). After commanding the Service Depot at Kassel (1934–35), he assumed command of Wehrkreis IX (1934–39), the main component of which became IX Corps on mobilization on August 26, 1939.

As commander of Wehrkreis IX, Dollmann immediately adopted a strongly pro-Nazi attitude. He even allowed political speakers to address the troops, but only as long as they were "politically non-biased National Socialist officers."[20] He was also personally friendly to any Nazi official and endorsed the party's anti-Semitic attitudes. This led to his promotion to the command of the 7th Army after the Polish invasion.

Dollmann commanded the 7th Army from October 1939 to 1944, but prior to D-Day had seen action only once in World War II—and on a secondary sector at that (fronting the Maginot line, 1939–40). He had commanded an army of occupation in France since 1940 and had never faced the Allies in battle.

✦

A political animal and a survivor, Dollmann did not require the same attention from Erwin Rommel that General von Salmuth had received. Dollmann realized that there were formal and informal chains of command and that the dominant influence in the West was now Field Marshal Rommel. All Rommel had to do, therefore, was to let Dollmann know what he wanted done and Dollmann would try to do it. Although four years had been wasted, obstacle construction, flooding of low-lying areas, and mine laying multiplied in 7th Army's zone almost as soon as Rommel arrived.

Unfortunately for the Germans, one of the measures Dollmann took back-fired in a major way. To keep his subordinates on their toes, he ordered a major map exercise be conducted at Rennes (not the 7th Army Headquarters at Le Mans) and was to be attended by every division commander in the army, as well as by two regimental commanders per division. Some of these men left their headquarters early on the evening of June 5; others waited until early morning on June 6. In any case, many of 7th Army's most important commanders were absent on D-Day.

On the German side, the great strategic debate of 1944 dealt with the question of how the Allied invasion could best be defeated. Rundstedt favored letting the Allies land in France virtually uncontested. The decisive battle, he felt, should be fought by Panzer Group West (ten panzer and panzer grenadier divisions) in the interior of France, out of the range of the big guns of the U.S. and Royal navies. Unlike Rommel, Rundstedt had never experienced the overwhelming might of the Allied air forces. The field marshal believed that the invasion had to be repelled on the beaches and within seventy-two hours of the Allied landings; otherwise, Germany would lose the war. Hitler compromised by giving Rommel three panzer divisions (the 2nd, 21st, and 116th), letting Rundstedt retain four under Panzer Group West (the 1st SS Panzer, the 12th SS Panzer, the 17th SS Panzer Grenadier, and the Panzer Lehr), and turning over the other three (the 2nd SS, the 9th Panzer, and 11th Panzer) to Army Group G in southern France. In short, he adopted neither strategy, and the compromise did not please anyone. History has proved that Rundstedt was wrong but has not proved that Rommel was right. (Map 7 shows the dispositions of OB West on June 5, 1944.)

An aristocratic snob, Geyr found it difficult to get along with Erwin Rommel, who was below Geyr socially (or so he felt), even though Rommel was superior to him in rank. Their disagreement over the use of the panzer divisions also contributed to their inability to get along, and Rommel made it clear that he would sack Geyr if he had the power. Their relationship improved considerably after the invasion began, when they developed a grudging admiration for each other.

Meanwhile, a diverse group of General Staff officers worked feverishly to prepare the Atlantic Wall and Fortress Europe for defense. They would play a disproportionately significant role in German operations on D-Day and included Günther Blumentritt, chief of staff of OB West; Alfred Gause and Hans Speidel, chiefs of staff of Army Group B; Rudolf Hofmann, chief of staff of the 15th Army; and Max Pemsel, chief of staff of 7th Army.

✦

Günther Blumentritt, who was promoted to general of infantry on April 1, 1944, was born in Munich on February 10, 1892. He joined the army in 1911 and was commissioned in the 71st Infantry Regiment the following year. He spent most of the war with his regiment, fighting in Belgium (1914), East Prussia (1914), Poland (1914–15), and France (1915–18), including in the Battles of Verdun, the Somme, and Ypres. Blumentritt served as adjutant of the III Battalion (late 1914–January 1918), regimental adjutant (1918), and adjutant of the 205th Infantry Brigade. He was wounded in the fall of 1918.

After the Armistice, Blumentritt served as a company commander in the Freikorps and was admitted to the Reichswehr in 1920, serving mainly with the 15th Infantry Regiment in Kassel in northern Hesse, although he did spend a year as Ia of the 6th Infantry Division at Bielefeld in the eastern Westphalia-Lippe area (1926–27) and two years as a company commander in the 19th Infantry Regiment in Munich (1930–32). From 1933 to 1935 he underwent clandestine General Staff training. He served as Ia of Wehrkreis VII in Munich (1935–37); commander of the I/19th Infantry Regiment (1937–38); chief of the training branch of OKH (1938–39); Ia of Rundstedt's Army Group South during the Polish campaign (1939); Ia of Army Group A (also Rundstedt) (1939–40) in Belgium and France; chief of staff of 4th Army (late 1940–early 1942), mainly on the Russian Front; and chief of operations of OKH (January–September 1942). He was dismissed from this post when Hitler abruptly sacked Franz Halder as chief of the General Staff and replaced him with Kurt Zeitzler. Blumentritt was immediately reemployed by his friend Rundstedt and served as chief of staff of OB West from September 24, 1942, to September 9, 1944, except for the period January 3 to June 26, 1943, when he was recovering from injuries suffered in a railroad accident. He was promoted to general of infantry on April 1, 1944.

Map 7. Dispositions, OB West, June 5, 1944

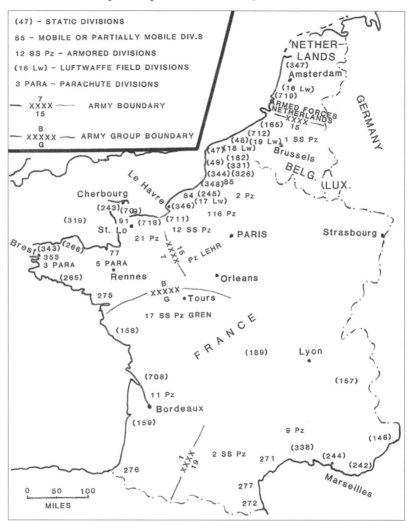

He had earlier been promoted to first lieutenant (1918), captain (1926), major (1933), lieutenant colonel (1936), colonel (1938), major general (January 16, 1942), and lieutenant general (December 1, 1942).

◆

Like Rundstedt and Geyr, Blumentritt supported the concept that the fate of the invasion should be decided by a large tank battle in the interior—not on the beaches. He also believed that the Allies would land at Pas de Calais, not Normandy. On D-Day he mistakenly concluded that the Allied paratroop drops were a diversion. He ended up supporting the Nazis during the attempted anti-Hitler putsch of July 20, 1944. His efforts to keep Army Group B supplied during the hedgerow fighting was ineffective, but given Allied air superiority, he cannot be criticized for this, since no one else could have done much better.

After Normandy, Hitler and his cronies decided to replace Blumentritt with Lieutenant General Siegfried Westphal, who had just recovered from a nervous breakdown during the Battle of Rome.[21] Rundstedt protested vehemently, but the German generals in the West (as well as all objective observers I know about) concluded that Westphal was a better chief of staff than Blumentritt.

Rommel, meanwhile, had come to suspect that Normandy (and the 7th Army) might be the actual target of the invasion. Consequently, he thickened the region's defenses. (Maps 8 and 9 show the defense of Normandy in April and June 1944 and show the larger units that Rommel moved into the area.)

✦

Josef Johann "Max" Pemsel was born in Regensburg, Bavaria, on January 15, 1897, and entered the army as a war volunteer in the 11th Bavarian Reserve Infantry Regiment in the spring of 1916. He spent most of the rest of the war

Map 8. Normandy, April 1944

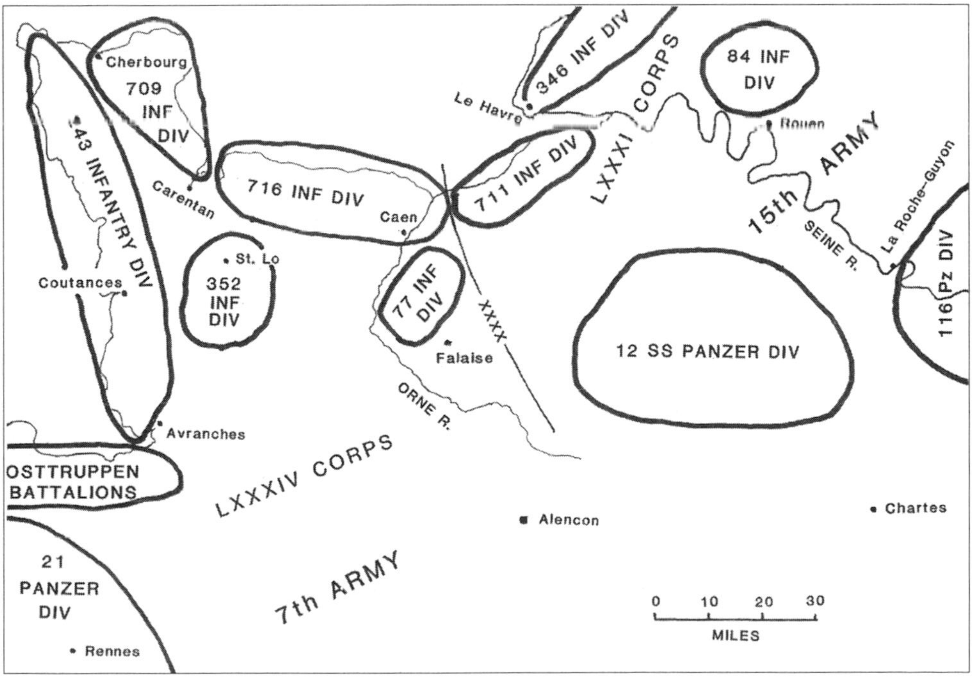

Map 9. Normandy, June 1944

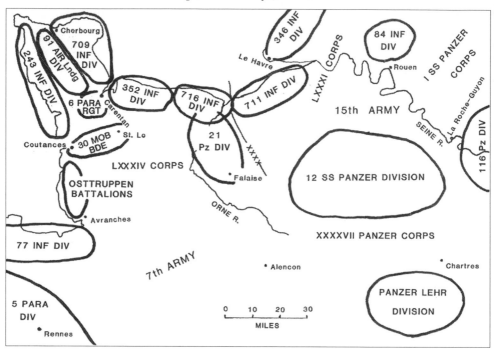

with his regiment, fighting on the Somme and the Meuse, and in other battles. He attended the Fahnenjunker course at Grafenwöhr from October 1917 to January 1918 and was commissioned second lieutenant in April. Pemsel served as a deputy battalion adjutant, deputy battalion commander, and company commander in 1918. He was deputy regimental adjutant in 1919. Pemsel assisted in the suppression of civil unrest in central Germany, was accepted into the Reichsheer, and spent 1920–30 with the Bavarian 20th Infantry Regiment in Regensburg. An enthusiastic and proficient skier, he was later awarded the German Olympic Games Decoration, 2nd Class, but won no medals. He passed his five-day Wehrkreis examination in the upper 15 percent in the spring of 1930 and was selected for secret General Staff training. He graduated in 1933. The following year he returned to Regensburg for a year's troop duty as a company commander. He then joined the mountain troops branch and was Ia of the 1st Mountain Division when World War II began. After the Polish campaign, he became chief of operations of the XVIII Mountain Corps and in late 1940 became the corps chief of staff. He held this post until April 19, 1943, and fought in France, Greece, and Lapland (the Far North sector of the Eastern Front). After a leave, he joined the 7th Army as its chief of staff on June 1, 1943. He had, in the meantime, been promoted to first lieutenant (1925), captain (1933), major (1936), lieutenant colonel (1939), and colonel (1941). He was promoted to major general on September 1, 1943.

Pemsel was somewhat slower than his counterpart at 15th Army in concluding that the invasion had come, but fifteen minutes after speaking with General Erich Marcks, the commander of the LXXXIV Corps in Normandy, at 2:00 a.m., he put 7th Army on full alert. He could not, however, convince General Speidel that the Allies were about to land.

Pemsel's commanders, General Dollmann and SS General Paul Hausser, made several major mistakes during the Battle of Normandy. What part Pemsel played in them is difficult to determine, but his overall performance was uninspiring and mediocre at best. He was sacked by Field Marshal Günther von Kluge on July 28 and was replaced by Baron Rudolf-Christoph von Gersdorff, who was clearly his superior as a chief of staff.

◆

Rudolf Hofmann was born in Würzburg on September 4, 1895. He entered the army in August 1914 as an officer cadet in the 9th Bavarian Infantry Regiment and served with it throughout World War I, fighting in Lorraine, the Battle of the Somme, and Flanders, where he was severely wounded in November 1914—the first of three wounds. He returned to the field as a platoon leader in the 1st Machine Gun Company in July 1915 and was promoted to second lieutenant on August 12. He assumed command of the company in June 1917 and led it for the rest of the war, except for temporary duty assignments. After the war, he remained in Reichsheer machine gun units until January 1921, when he became a platoon leader in the 21st Infantry Regiment at Nuremberg—a post he held until 1924. Meanwhile, he was promoted to first lieutenant in 1923. Hofmann began his clandestine General Staff training at Münster (the home of Wehrkreis VI and the 6th Infantry Division) in 1924. He finished this course in Berlin in 1928 and was assigned to the organizations branch of the Defense Ministry. Later he transferred to the training branch. In May 1932 he was sent to Munich as a company commander in the 19th Infantry Regiment. A year later, in October 1933, he returned to the staff as a General Staff officer with Area Command Ulm and spent the rest of his career in General Staff positions. In October 1935 Hofmann assumed the post of Ia of the 5th Infantry Division in Stuttgart. This was followed by assignments as Ia of Wehrkreis XIII in Nuremberg (October 1937), Ia of XIII Corps (August 26, 1939), chief of staff of the XIII Corps (February

1940), and acting chief of staff of the 9th Army. Meanwhile, he fought in Poland, Belgium, and France, and at Brest-Litovsk, Bialystok, Minsk, Gomel, Kiev, and Rzhev on the Russian Front. He reported himself ill on January 14, 1942, but returned to active duty as chief of staff of the 15th Army in northern France and Belgium on May 1, 1942. He still held this post on D-Day. Meanwhile, he was promoted to captain (1928), major (1934), lieutenant colonel (1937), colonel (January 1, 1940), major general (April 1, 1942), and lieutenant general (April 1, 1943).

Rudolf Hofmann was a superior General Staff officer and an excellent chief of staff. On June 5 he was one of the first on the German side to predict that D-Day would be the next day. Based on the Allied parachute landings and an intercepted dispatch to the French Resistance, he put the entire 15th Army on full alert around 10:00 p.m. His commander, General von Salmuth, did not agree with Hofmann but decided not to overrule his chief of staff. Salmuth was, in fact, busy with a card game and was not much interested in what his chief of staff did. Fortunately for the Allies, the High Command of the Armed Forces, OB West, and Army Group B did not pay much attention to Hofmann either.

◆

Alfred Gause was born in Königsberg, East Prussia, on February 14, 1896. He entered the army as an officer cadet in the 18th Engineer Battalion in March 1914 and was commissioned in 1915. He spent World War I with the 18th Engineers, fighting on the Western Front, where he was wounded several times. He was promoted to first lieutenant in October 1918. He was stationed in East Prussia from the end of the war until 1927 (mainly with the 1st Engineer Battalion), when he passed his Wehrkreis exam near the top of his class and began his General Staff training. He graduated in 1931. He was sent to Stuttgart, where he served in the 5th Infantry Division and later became Ia of the V Military District. Gause was promoted to major (1934), lieutenant colonel (1936), colonel (1939), major general (June 1, 1941), and lieutenant general (March 1, 1943). In 1937 he was sent to Berlin, where he headed the important Armed Forces Office in the War Ministry.

On February 4, 1938, Hitler established what essentially became the German command structure for the next war. He dismissed Colonel General Werner von Fritsch, the commander in chief of the army, forced the war minister, Field Marshal Werner von Blomberg, into retirement, named himself Supreme Commander of the Armed Forces, abolished the war ministry, and replaced it with the High Command of the Armed Forces (Oberkommando des Wehrmacht or OKW), under Colonel General (later Field Marshal) Wilhelm Keitel.[22] Theoretically, OKW directed the High Command of the Army (OKH), the High Command of the Navy (Oberkommando der Kriegsmarine, or OKM), and the High Command of the Luftwaffe (Oberkommando der Luftwaffe, or OKL), but Hermann Göring, the commander in chief of the Luftwaffe, quickly informed Keitel that the Luftwaffe would be independent of OKW, and there was nothing Keitel could do about it. The navy also maintained its corporate independence, although its commander in chief, Grand Admiral Erich Raeder, expressed himself in more diplomatic terms than Göring. Also established on February 4 was the High Command of the Army under Colonel General Walter von Brauchitsch. By 1942 OKH would be responsible for the Eastern Front and OKW would have hegemony over all other sectors.

Gause remained with OKW until late 1939, when he was named chief of staff of X Corps and took part in the invasions of Belgium and France. He joined to the staff of OKH in 1940 and, after briefly serving as chief of staff of XXXVIII Corps in France, was sent to Libya as chief of the German liaison staff to the Italian High Command. This staff was quickly taken over by Rommel, whom Gause served for the next three years. In September 1941 Gause became chief of staff of Panzer Group (later Panzer Army) Afrika. He was severely wounded during the Battle of the Gazala Line on June 1, 1942, but returned to duty in North Africa late that same year. He was named chief of staff of Army Group Afrika on March 1, 1943, but was sent back to Europe just before the army group surrendered in May.

That same month Gause became chief of staff of Rommel's Army Group B, which he served on in northern Italy and in the West. He and Rommel had a falling out in April 1944 (started by a spat between their wives), and Gause was placed in Führer Reserve. Rommel tried to have Gause placed in command of a panzer division, but the assignment fell through. On June 15, 1944, however, Gause was named chief of staff of Panzer Group West (later 5th Panzer Army), serving under Geyr, Heinrich Eberbach, and Sepp Dietrich. Dietrich took Gause with him when he was named commander-designate of the 6th Panzer Army in September 1944, but when Gause was relieved on November 20, 1944, Dietrich did nothing to help him.

◆

Hans Speidel was born in Metzingen, Württemberg, on October 28, 1897. He joined the army as an infantry officer cadet in the 123rd Grenadier Regiment in late 1914. He fought on the Western Front in World War I, served in the

Reichsheer, and was Ia of the 33rd Infantry Division (1937–39), Ia of the IX Corps (1939–40), Ia of Army Group B (1940), chief of staff to the Military Governor of France (1940–42), chief of staff of the V Corps (1942–43) on the Eastern Front, chief of staff to the German general with the Italian 8th Army in Russia (1943), chief of staff of the 8th Army in Russia (1943–44), and chief of staff of Army Group B (April 15–September 9, 1944). A lieutenant colonel when World War II began, he was promoted to colonel (1941), major general (January 1, 1943), and lieutenant general (January 1, 1944). He was fluent in French and English.

✦

During Rommel's absence on D-Day, Speidel performed poorly. He dismissed the reports of Allied parachute landing as just another rumor. Lieutenant Colonel Helmut Meyer, the 15th Army's intelligence officer, reported that his section had intercepted a signal to the Free Forces of the Interior (French Resistance, or FFI) at 9:15 p.m. on June 5, stating that the invasion would begin during the next forty-eight hours. Speidel also dismissed this report as a rumor.

Shortly after midnight, on the extreme left flank of the 15th Army, near its junction with the 7th Army, two British paratroopers landed on the lawn of the headquarters of the 711th Infantry Division and were captured by the divisional intelligence officer. The division commander, Major General Josef Reichert, was playing cards with members of his staff at the time. Unlike Salmuth, however, Reichert drew the correct conclusions and informed 15th Army Headquarters immediately. The message was relayed to LXXXIV Corps at 2:06 a.m. Twenty-one minutes earlier, dispatches arrived from Colonel Hamann, the acting commander of the 709th Infantry Division, stating that his men had taken prisoners from the U.S. 101st Airborne Division. (Hamann was in charge because Lieutenant General Schlieben, the division commander, was on his way to Rennes to attend General Dollmann's map exercise. So many German generals were away from their posts on D-Day that Adolf Hitler ordered the Gestapo to investigate whether the British Secret Service had anything to do with it.) Meanwhile, Major General Wilhelm Richter, the commander of the 716th Infantry Division, reported that enemy paratroopers had landed east of the Orne. Marcks immediately put his LXXXIV Corps on the highest state of alert and telephoned Major General Max Pemsel and told him that the invasion had definitely begun. Since he could not contact General Dollmann, Pemsel immediately put the entire 7th Army on full alert and telephoned General Speidel at La-Roche-Guyon. Speidel, however, was convinced that the Allies would land at Pas de Calais and would not come in horrible weather. He told Pemsel that he was falling for a diversion and should sit tight. Then he hung up.

A few moments later General von Salmuth called for Field Marshal Rommel and was put through to Speidel. Salmuth had just spoken with General Reichert. Over the telephone wires, Salmuth could clearly hear machine gun fire: the men of the 711th Infantry Division were clashing with Allied paratroopers very near division headquarters. The 15th Army commander was now alive to the danger. Speidel listened politely but—even now—refused to believe that the invasion had come. Speidel went back to bed. He did not think it necessary to telephone Field Marshal Rommel in Germany.

Huge Allied bomber forces blasted LXXXIV Corps, as well as German airfields, supply depots, rear area installations, and bridges. Even more seriously, Panzer Group West and the vaunted German panzer divisions—which should have been ready to move as soon as the Allies landed—were not placed on alert.

In Paris Field Marshal von Rundstedt and General Blumentritt agreed with General Speidel—the Allies were attempting to divert their attention from the zone of the 15th Army. Luftwaffe Field Marshal Hugo Sperrle, the commander of the 3rd Air Fleet, suspected the truth, but he had long since lost all influence at OB West and with Führer Headquarters. To pacify General Marcks—who continued to hotly insist that the invasion had come—they took the 91st Air Landing Division and the mobile elements of the 709th Infantry Division out of reserve and gave them to LXXXIV Corps. Marcks quickly ordered these units, which were located in the western part of the Cotentin Peninsula, to attack American paratroopers. In the meantime, Eisenhower's great invasion force crossed the English Channel and prepared to land on the shores of France, unhampered by the German navy.

2

D-Day

The Allied invasion began in Normandy on June 6, 1944. The first force with the mission of attacking the invasion forces was Naval Group West, which was commanded by Admiral Theodor Krancke.

◆

Theodor Krancke was born in Magdeburg on March 30, 1893, and entered the Imperial Navy as a cadet (*Seekadett*) aboard the heavy cruiser *Victoria Louise* in 1912. Commissioned in 1913, he spent World War I serving in the IX Torpedo Boat Flotilla. After the war, he was selected for the Reichswehr and was on the staff of Naval Station North Sea (1920–21), commander of the minesweeper *M-52*, commander of the torpedo boat *V-2*, instructor at the Torpedo and Signals School (1925–27), torpedo officer of the battleship *Schleswig-Holstein* (1927–29), and chief of the 4th Torpedo Boat Half Flotilla (1930–32). Krancke was on the staff of the High Seas Fleet (1932–35) when Hitler assumed power. He was on the staff of the Defense Ministry (1935–37), commandant of the Naval Academy (1937–39), chief of staff to the head of security, Naval Group North Sea (1939–40), naval adviser to OKW on the invasion of Norway and chief of staff to the Commanding Admiral Norway (1940), before becoming the captain of the surface raider (pocket battleship) *Admiral Scheer*. He distinguished himself in this post and sank 113,233 tons of Allied shipping from October 1940 to April 1941. In June 1941 he became chief of the Quartermaster Division of the naval staff, and in January 1942 he was named naval representative to the Führer—a difficult job indeed, even for the pro-Nazi Krancke. (Hitler became highly excited and emotional anytime the fleet was at sea and often verbally attacked Krancke, who was the senior naval officer immediately available.) No doubt to his relief, Krancke was given command of Naval Group West on April 20, 1943. In this post, he commanded all torpedo boats, S-boats (*Schnellboote* or fast boats), minesweepers, patrol boats, and others.[1] Krancke was promoted to lieutenant j.g. (1917), lieutenant (1922), lieutenant commander (1930), commander (1935), captain (1937), rear admiral (1941), vice admiral (1942), and admiral (March 1, 1943).

The decision made by the Allied commander, Gen. Dwight D. Eisenhower, to launch the invasion in spite of the marginal weather conditions took Admiral Krancke by surprise. He was so sure that the Allies would not come in such foul weather that he canceled the sea patrols scheduled for the night of June 5–6. The Allies thus had the English Channel to themselves. The Allied naval commander, British admiral Bertram H. Ramsay, reported that the sea passage had an "air of unreality" because of the total absence of a German reaction of any kind.[2]

✦

Wilhelm Falley was born in the German city of Metz, Elsass (now Metz, Alsace, France), on September 25, 1897. He joined the Imperial Army in December 1914 as a war volunteer in the Prussian-Saxon 93rd Infantry Regiment. He earned a commission as second lieutenant of reserves and was sent to the field in August 1915. He fought in the Battles of Loos, the Somme, and Artois. In late 1916 he was transferred to the staff of the 7th Guards Infantry Regiment as a mortar officer and later served as an ordnance officer and gas warfare officer. He was also wounded at least once. After the war he became an active-duty second lieutenant, and was accepted into the Reichsheer, where he spent nine years (1919–28) with the 29th Infantry Regiment at Crossen on the Oder (now Krosno Odrzanskie, Poland). Promoted to first lieutenant in 1925, he was transferred to the Infantry School in October 1928, where he labored as a course adjutant until July 1933. Meanwhile, he was promoted to captain in 1932. From July 1, 1933, to October 1, 1934, Falley commanded a company in the Prussian II Battalion/5th Infantry Regiment (II/5th Infantry) at Stettin. He then spent a year on the battalion staff and, from October 1935 to October 1936, commanded another company in the 5th Infantry. Promoted to major in 1936, he was sent to the War School in Munich as a tactics instructor, and he remained there until Germany mobilized on August 26, 1939. A lieutenant colonel from August 1, 1939, Falley assumed command of the III/238th Infantry Regiment at Stuttgart on mobilization and led it to the Upper Rhine, where it remained during the Phony War period. In January 1940 Wilhelm Falley was sent to the Königsbrück Maneuver Area in the Free State of Saxony (about eighteen miles northeast of Dresden), where he supervised the formation and training of the II/433rd Infantry Regiment. He thus missed both the Polish and French campaigns. He was nevertheless given command of the Prussian 4th Infantry Regiment, which he led on the northern sector of the Russian Front, where he fought at Dünaburg and Demjansk (Demyansk), among other battles. He was awarded the Knight's Cross in late 1941.

Considered an excellent trainer and a competent commander, Falley was promoted to colonel on February 1, 1942, and that summer he was sent back to Germany, where he assumed command of the V Fahnenjunker School for Infantry (V Infantry Officer Training School) at Döberitz on August 1. Shortly thereafter, the school was moved to Posen (now Poznan, Poland). He returned to the Eastern Front and assumed command of the remnants of the 36th Infantry Division near Smolensk on September 12, 1943. An acting commander only, he gave up this unit on September 23 but simultaneously took charge of the 330th Infantry Division near Orscha. The 330th was a *kampfgruppe* (a division reduced by casualties to roughly regimental strength). He assumed command of his own division—the 246th Infantry—on October 5, 1943, and led it on the Vitebsk sector of the Eastern Front until April 20, 1944. (The Red Army destroyed the 246th eight weeks after Falley left.) During this period Falley was wounded but did not give up command of his division. Promoted to major general on December 1, 1943, he was transferred to Normandy, where he assumed command of the 91st Air Landing Division on April 25, 1944. His reputation as a superb trainer of infantry no doubt explains his appointment. He was promoted to lieutenant general on May 1.

Early on the morning of June 6, 1944, Wilhelm Falley was on his way to the 7th Army map exercise at Rennes when he became concerned that the Allied aerial bombardment was too intense and had lasted too long. He decided to return to his division. Within two miles of the chateau that housed his headquarters, Falley heard the sound of an intense firefight. Grabbing a weapon, he rushed into the darkness to investigate and was shot and killed by an American paratrooper. The Battle of Normandy had claimed its first general, and the Allies had not even landed yet.

✦

Like Falley, **Edgar Feuchtinger** was born in the German garrison town of Metz on November 9, 1894. He joined the Imperial Army as a Fahnenjunker when World War I began in August 1914 and was commissioned second lieutenant in the 14th Foot Artillery Regiment in 1915. He served as an artillery officer on the Western Front for the remainder of the war and was selected to remain in the 100,000-man army in 1920. He spent the interwar years in artillery, including the Württemberg 5th Artillery Regiment at Stuttgart (1921–24), the Prussian

2nd Artillery Regiment at Stettin (1924–29), and the Bavarian 7th Artillery Regiment (1929–35). He then became an instructor at the Artillery School at Jüterbog, south of Berlin (1935–37). He was promoted to first lieutenant (1925), captain (late 1929), and major (1935). On more than one occasion in the 1930s, he was attached to the Headquarters of the High Command of the Army (OKH), where he was responsible for the military portion of the Nazi Party's Nuremberg rallies. He quickly became friendly with Adolf Hitler and his cronies. Feuchtinger had a definite talent with ingratiating himself with the powers that be in the Nazi Party (Nationalsozialistische Deutsche Arbeitpartei, or NSDAP), including Martin Bormann. Feuchtinger was given command of the III Battalion of the 26th Artillery Regiment in 1937 and was promoted to lieutenant colonel in 1938. When Germany mobilized on August 26, 1939, he was named commander of the Westphalian 227th Artillery Regiment, which was sent to the Eifel (the German Ardennes). The 227th was a horse-drawn unit made up mainly of Landwehr (older age) personal. It fought in the Netherlands and Belgium in 1940 and was stationed in northeastern France from July 1940 to December 1941. Feuchtinger was promoted to colonel on August 1, 1941.

After Stalin launched his winter offensive of 1941–42, the 227th Artillery Regiment was sent to the northern sector of the Eastern Front. Feuchtinger fought in the Battle of Volchov and the Siege of Leningrad, and he was encircled with his regiment near Lake Ladoga by the 2nd Strike Army in 1942 but was subsequently rescued. Feuchtinger gave up command of the regiment on August 18, 1942, when he was promoted to major general, with a date of rank of August 1. He was sent to France in November, where he was given command of one of the four kampfgruppen stationed outside the French city of Toulon. His forces included elements of the 10th Panzer Division, including the 69th Panzer Grenadier Regiment, the I Battalion/90th Panzer Artillery Regiment, the 90th Tank Destroyer Battalion, and a company of panzer engineers. The German battle groups seized the city but were unable to prevent the French from scuttling their Mediterranean fleet on November 27.

After briefly working with the Führer's secret weapons program, Feuchtinger was named commander of Schnelle Brigade West (a bicycle unit that was also known as the 931st Mobile Brigade) on April 7, 1943, before assuming command of the 21st Panzer Division on May 15, 1943. He received this prize appointment despite the fact that he had absolutely no qualifications for such a post; he owed the promotion solely to his Nazi Party connections. A poor field commander and a conniving one, he used his influence with Hitler to have the best available subordinates sent to his unit. Colonel Hans von Luck, for example, reported to the Headquarters, Panzer Lehr Division, to assume command of the 130th Panzer Regiment. Here he was told that Feuchtinger had learned of his availability and had asked that Luck be assigned to his division. Luck was promptly transferred to the command of the 125th Panzer Grenadier Regiment of 21st Panzer. Feuchtinger managed to build his unit to a strength of 16,297 men by D-Day. It had only 120 tanks on D-Day, however, and eighty of them were of foreign manufacture. Its forty German tanks were mostly obsolete Panzer Mark IVs (PzKw IVs).

Feuchtinger did little to improve the combat readiness of the 21st Panzer Division, although his subordinates did—often by working around him. Colonel von Luck recalled, "Feuchtinger was a live and let live person. He was fond of all the good things in life, for which Paris was a natural attraction. Knowing that he had no . . . knowledge of tank warfare, Feuchtinger had to delegate most things."[3]

The fact that Feuchtinger was married did not alter his behavior. He enjoyed the French nightlife and had to be fetched out of a sleazy Parisian club on the night of June 5–6, 1944, to be informed that Allied paratroopers and gliderborne forces were landing in his area of operations. (To make matters worse, he had not seen fit to tell his staff where he would be, and it took a search detail some time to find him.) He hurried back to Normandy but refused to cooperate with General Erich Marcks, who correctly wanted him to attack toward the British beachheads; instead, Feuchtinger attacked British paratroopers, failed to concentrate his forces, and generally sent many of his men off in the wrong direction. He did little to help the LXXXIV Corps repulse the D-Day invasion. As a result, the counterattack by the 21st Panzer Division's 100th Panzer Regiment was not delivered in anything like the speed Rommel had planned and was not launched until late in the afternoon. Montgomery, meanwhile, had landed two full armored brigades—which were equipped mainly with modern Sherman tanks—and the attack was rather easily repulsed.

Feuchtinger's 192nd Panzer Grenadier Regiment was luckier. Its I Battalion hit a seam between Sword and Juno beaches and penetrated to the coast, which it reached at 8:00 p.m. General Marcks wanted the battalion reinforced, but at 11:00 p.m. a misdirected glider lift for the British 6th Airborne Division landed behind the I Battalion. Feuchtinger, who had joined the I/192nd Panzer Grenadier, immediately jumped to the conclusion that the British were trying to cut him off. He ordered the battalion to abandon its position and to withdraw immediately. The chance to keep the British 2nd Army split was thus forfeited. Colonel Bodo

Zimmermann, Rundstedt's chief of intelligence, accused Feuchtinger of taking to his heels, which seems to be an accurate assessment.

✦

Hermann Oppeln-Bronikowski was born in Berlin on January 2, 1899. He was educated at the Bensberg and Gross-Lichterfelde cadet schools and entered the army as a senior officer cadet in late 1917. He was sent to the Warsaw area of Poland on occupation duty and commissioned in the 10th Ulan Regiment on December 17. Eager to see combat, Oppeln transferred to the Hessian 118th Infantry Regiment on the Western Front in early 1918 and fought at Amiens, Lys, the Somme, and Cambrai, earning both grades of the Iron Cross in the process. After the Armistice, he rejoined his regiment, fought against the Communists in Estonia, and returned with the regiment to its home base of Züllichau, Germany (now Sulechów, Poland). Here he was promoted to captain in 1933.

Oppeln was an excellent horseman and remained in the cavalry branch until 1940. He was a member of the German Olympic equestrian team in 1936 and won a gold medal in dressage—perhaps the most difficult of all riding events. He commanded II/10th Cavalry Regiment (a reconnaissance unit) in Poland and later served on the staff of the general of mobile troops at OKH (1940–41). From 1941 to 1943, he served with Panzer Brigade Eberbach (1941–42), commanded the 35th Panzer Regiment (1942) and the 204th Panzer Regiment (1942–43), and led 11th Panzer Regiment (1943)—all on the Eastern Front. He survived the destruction of his tank by enemy fire on at least three occasions. An incredibly brave officer, Oppeln was also an excellent panzer commander—when he was sober. Known to come in to headquarters drunk at 8:00 a.m., he was not given his own division because he had a drinking problem. Oppeln assumed command of the 100th Panzer Regiment of the 21st Panzer Division in late 1943.

✦

Owing to General Feuchtinger's unauthorized absence and his inability to make a decision as to where to send Oppeln's 100th Panzer Regiment when he did return to headquarters, it was 8:00 a.m. before the tanks started to move—in the wrong direction. Feuchtinger ordered them to attack the British paratroopers east of the Orne. The British and Canadians had already landed on Gold, Juno, and Sword beaches—all west of the Orne. It should have dawned on Feuchtinger that the paratroopers were not the main threat, but apparently it did not.

A little after noon General Marcks contacted Feuchtinger and informed him that the 21st Panzer Division was now subordinate to LXXXIV Corps. He ordered him to leave Battle Group von Luck to deal with the paratroopers east of the Orne. Feuchtinger was to turn the rest of his division around and to head for Caen, the university town against which the Allies were now advancing. This was much more difficult than it would have been a few hours before because the weather had broken and the sky was dominated by hundreds of Allied fighter-bombers, which the Germans called Jabos. Oppeln lost more than 50 of his 120 tanks on the approach march.

Oppeln's regiment had only two battalions: the I, under Captain Wilhelm von Gottberg, and the II, under Major Vierzig. Gottberg had eighty tanks—all of which were of pre-1939 Czech manufacture. Vierzig had forty PzKw IVs, but they were older models and were equipped with obsolete, short-barrel main battle guns, so their range was far too limited.

It was 2:30 p.m. before the 100th Panzer Regiment, which was accompanied by Colonel Joseph Rauch's 192nd Panzer Grenadier Regiment, was in position just north of Caen, facing the British I Corps, which was coming down from the north. Oppeln ordered Captain von Gottberg (with thirty-five tanks) to recapture Periers Ridge, four miles from the coast. Oppeln personally assumed command of the remaining twenty-five or so panzers, which he intended to use to attack the British on the ridge at Bieville. As he prepared to move out, General Marcks appeared and told him that the fate of Germany might well rest on his shoulders. "If you don't push the British back into the sea, we shall have lost the war."[4]

Oppeln was shocked. The fate of Germany depended on a motley collection of sixty foreign-made tanks and a handful of German tanks that had been obsolete for years? He nevertheless struck as quickly as possible.

Oppeln and Gottberg never had a chance. Their obsolete panzers were simply outclassed by the British, who were equipped mainly with American Shermans. (Appendix 4 shows the characteristics of various Allied and German tanks.) Oppeln lost six tanks in fifteen minutes and his own tank was knocked out before he could get close enough to fire a shot. Captain von Gottberg did no better: he lost ten tanks and called off his attack before he even entered range of the British positions. Worse still, the 100th Panzer Regiment was completely shattered. Its morale was broken and was never recovered.

Oppeln now prepared for the British assault on Caen, which did not come that day. The German colonel was completely surprised. Until the day he died, he was convinced that British would have captured Caen if they had attacked it on June 6. I am sure that he knew what he was talking about.

As Oppeln's survivors dug in that evening, he watched small groups of twenty to thirty German soldiers, usually led by an officer, staggering south from the front. The men of the 716th Infantry Division were coming home. "The war is lost," Oppeln said aloud.[5]

◆

Fritz Bayerlein was born in Würzburg, Bavaria, on January 14, 1899, the son of a senior police inspector. He entered the army in 1917 as a Fahnenjunker in the first-class Bavarian 9th Infantry Regiment and in 1918 fought in Flanders, where he was wounded. He remained in the Reichsheer and was commissioned second lieutenant in the 21st Infantry Regiment at Nuremberg in 1922. He remained with this regiment from 1921 to 1933, when he began General Staff training in Berlin (1933–35). He was on the staff of the 15th Infantry Division at Würzberg (1935–37), company commander in the 6th Machine Gun Battalion (1937–38), and Ib of the XV Motorized Corps (1938–39). During the early years of World War II, he served as Ia of the 10th Panzer Division (April 1939–February 1940) and as chief of operations of Guderian's XIX Corps (later Panzer Group Guderian) (February to November 1940) during the French campaign. He continued in this post after the corps was upgraded to 2nd Panzer Group, serving from November 16, 1940, to August 30, 1941, including the early battles of Operation Barbarossa. After a brief furlough, he became the chief of staff of the Afrika Korps on October 5, 1941. He moved up to acting chief of staff of Panzer Army Afrika after General Gause was wounded in the Battle of the Gazala Line (June–August 1942) and temporarily commanded the Afrika Korps in the retreat from Egypt after its commander was captured in the Second Battle of El Alamein (November 1942). Bayerlein was named chief of staff of the 1st Italian-German Panzer Army in March 1943 but was evacuated back to Europe after being wounded in Tunisia in early May 1943. He led the 3rd Panzer Division on the Eastern Front (October 20, 1943–January 5, 1944) before assuming command of the Panzer Lehr Division on January 10, 1944. Meanwhile, he had been promoted to first lieutenant (1927), captain (1934), major (1938), lieutenant colonel (September 1, 1940), colonel (April 1, 1942), major general (March 1, 1943) and lieutenant general (May 1, 1944).

According to author P. A. Spayd, Bayerlein revealed after the war that he had hidden a dangerous secret: his mother, Louise Denkmann, was illegitimate, and his biological grandfather was Jewish. The evidence is difficult to evaluate. One-quarter Jewish or not, it is certain that Bayerlein had a sense of justice and would stand up to the Nazis when he thought it was right to do so. In September 1941, for example, he grabbed a guard who was beating a Russian prisoner, took his whip away from him, and made sure that the "subhuman" received medical attention. During the winter of 1943–44, when he was the commander of the 3rd Panzer Division, he fed Russian refugees in his field kitchens. In the spring of 1944 he protected Archbishop Seridi of Budapest from the Nazis and their allies while the Archbishop was shielding, hiding, and otherwise protecting or trying to protect Hungarian Jews. In October 1944, after Panzer Lehr left for Normandy, Seridi was executed by the security service (Sicherheitsdienst or SD).[6] On another occasion, Bayerlein ordered an SS sergeant to stop abusing some Russian civilians. When the sergeant refused, Bayerlein asked him to go stand by a particular tree. When the SS man asked why, the general replied that he intended to hang him from it in the next five minutes. The SS NCO immediately backed down.

◆

Erich Marcks was an easygoing man who was popular among his men because of his sauve urbanity and serenity. His customary calm was gone by June 6, however, and not because the invasion had come in his zone. Rather, he grew furious because he could not make anybody believe that it had begun. Throughout the day, he was in more or less constant contact with 7th Army, Army Group B, and OB West, demanding that Bayerlein's Panzer Lehr Division and all other available armored units be assigned to him for an immediate counterattack. He was given the 21st Panzer Division shortly after noon; however, it was 3:40 p.m. before OKW (Hitler) released the Panzer Lehr and 12th SS Panzer Divisions to 7th Army.

While his division assembled, Fritz Bayerlein drove to 7th Army Head-quarters, where he met with General Dollmann. To his dismay, Dollmann ordered him to move out for Caen at 5:00 p.m.—in broad daylight! Bayerlein argued that it would be better for the division to arrive one day later (on June 8) than to have it blasted by fighter-bombers, but Dollmann refused to listen. The colonel general even proposed a change in the five preselected march routes, but this time Bayerlein refused to budge. Any deviation at this point would result in chaos, as Dollmann should have known. To make matters worse, the army commander insisted that the division maintain radio silence: "As if radio silence could have stopped the fighter-bombers and reconnaissance planes from spotting us!" Bayerlein snapped later.[7]

It was ninety miles from Nogent-le-Rotrou (seventy-five miles southwest of Paris) to Caen. The Allies spotted the move immediately and pounced on the Panzer Lehr's columns. The ensuing approach march was a nightmare, and nighttime brought no relief because the Allies now knew the location of the columns and illuminated the countryside with dozens of flares. The panzers were relatively safe (Bayerlein lost only five), but the division lost forty loaded fuel trucks, eighty-four half-tracks, prime movers and self-propelled guns, and dozens of other vehicles. The division arrived in the Caen sector in a fragmented and disorganized state. It would not be able to counterattack until June 9. It was joined by the 12th SS Panzer and 21st Panzer divisions—and all three were checked north of Caen.

✦

Wolfgang Pickert was an officer who almost never cooperated with his army counterparts. Born in Posen on February 3, 1897, Pickert joined the army as a war volunteer in the East Prussian 73rd Field Artillery Regiment when Germany began to mobilize for World War I in early August 1914. He saw action at Tannenberg and elsewhere on the Eastern Front before being transferred to the 73rd Field Artillery Regiment of the mediocre 85th Landwehr Division as a battery officer and officer-aspirant at the beginning of 1916. Promoted to second lieutenant of reserves on October 7, 1916, young Pickert was a forward officer on the Eastern Front from December 1916 to August 31, 1917. The next day he became adjutant of the II Battalion and served in Russia, Courland, and the Ukraine. He received an accelerated promotion to first lieutenant on April 3, 1918, and was transferred back to his old regiment, the 73rd Field Artillery, on June 22, 1918. He served on the Western Front, fighting on the Marne, at Verdun, and in the Argonne. He was also wounded at least once during World War I.

After the Great War, Pickert was accepted into the Reichsheer, and he spent the entire 1920–34 period in Königsberg, East Prussia, mainly with the 1st Artillery Regiment, although he did spend two years (1924–26) in subsidiary leadership training with the staff of Wehrkreis I. (Apparently Pickert underwent clandestine General Staff training but, like two-thirds of students, did not successfully complete the course.) He also spent three years (1931–34) as a battery commander. Promoted to captain in early 1931, he was appointed an instructor at the Flak Artillery School on October 1, 1934. Pickert was with the school when it moved from Döberitz (near Berlin) to Wustrow, Rerik (on the Baltic Sea coast in Mecklenburg–West Pomerania), and when it became part of the Luftwaffe on March 9, 1935. Now a member of the air force, Pickert was an adviser to the Inspectorate of Flak Artillery from 1935 to 1937. He was promoted to major in 1936. He commanded a battalion in the 49th Flak Regiment at Mannheim from 1937 to 1938 and became chief of staff of the XIII Air District at Nuremberg on July 1, 1938. He was promoted to lieutenant colonel five months later.

Pickert was named Ia of the important 4th Air Defense Command on October 25, 1939. (This command, which was headquartered at Düsseldorf, was responsible for the air defense of the Ruhr, Germany's most important industrial district.) Promoted to colonel on June 1, 1940, he became chief of staff of Luftwaffe Command Center (another air defense command in the West) on October 1. In 1942, however, his run of good and relatively easy assignments came to an end: he was sent to the Russian Front, where he assumed command of the 9th Flak Division (Motorized) on June 25. His division's task was to provide antiaircraft defense and antitank support for the German 6th Army, which was advancing on Stalingrad.

Pickert did well in his new role—and certainly proved more cooperative with the army's eastern generals than he would with the army generals in Normandy later on. This was at least in part because he was friends with Major General Arthur Schmidt, the chief of staff of 6th Army, and they naturally worked well together. The 9th Flak provided close cover for the German infantrymen in the Stalingrad street fighting and blew away several major bunkers with their deadly 88mm guns, which contributed to Pickert's promotion to major general on October 1. He also provided some excellent advice, informing both Schmidt and Friedrich Paulus, the commander of the 6th Army, that the Luftwaffe could not successfully resupply 6th Army via airlift. As soon as the encirclement began to take shape, Pickert declared that they should "get the hell out of there." After the encirclement was completed, Wolfgang Pickert consistently advocated breaking out to the southwest.

In January 1943, with 6th Army in its death throes, General Pickert handed command of the division over to Colonel Wilhelm Wolff and left the pocket for consultations. He later alleged that he attempted to rejoin his division but was unable to land owing to Soviet fire. Hitler, in the interim, ordered Hans-Valentin Hube, the commander of the XIV Panzer Corps, to fly out of the pocket. The tough, one-armed Hube flatly refused to obey. In the end Hitler had to send a squad of Gestapo agents into Stalingrad; they brought Hube and several of his key men out at gunpoint.

Hube, for one, did not believe Pickert's version of events, verbalized his disbelief rather loudly, and practically called the flak commander a coward. As Göring sputtered, livid with rage, Hube personally pointed out to the Führer that not a single Luftwaffe general remained in Stalingrad when it fell (January 30–February 2, 1943). This blemish on his record probably explains why Pickert was not promoted to lieutenant general until November 1, 1943. In any case

Lieutenant Colonel Richard Haizmann surrendered the remnants of the 9th Flak when Stalingrad fell. The High Command of the Luftwaffe, however, immediately ordered that a new 9th Flak Division (Motorized) be created in the Crimea from the remnants of the original. Wolfgang Pickert was named its commander.

Pickert led the 9th Flak in support of Army Group A during the Kuban campaign, where he was wounded. He also led it in support of the German 17th Army in the Crimean campaign, during which both it and the rest of the 17th Army were largely destroyed when the naval fortress of Sevastopol fell on May 13, 1944. The remnants of the 9th Flak Division had already been evacuated by the German navy and were reassembling in Breslau, Silesia, for another rebuild. On May 18, however, Pickert turned command of the division over to Colonel Wilhelm van Koolwijk and headed west. He had just been named commander of the III Flak Corps on the Western Front.

The III Flak was the former 11th Flak Division (Motorized) and included four flak regiments but without any subordinate divisional headquarters. Field Marshal Rommel demanded that it be concentrated in Normandy, to be used in an antitank role against the Allied invaders. Pickert—backed by Göring—refused to cooperate, however, and scattered the German flak batteries all over the map, protecting bridges, road junctions, and rear-area installations. They were thus in no position to offer the slightest help in the ground defense of Normandy on June 6, whereas they might have played a major role in the defeat of the Great Invasion.

✦

Dietrich Kraiss was born in Stuttgart on November 16, 1889, was educated in cadet schools, and joined the army as a second lieutenant in the 126th Infantry Regiment in 1909. He spent all of World War I with his regiment, fighting on the Western Front in Alsace, the Vosges, Champagne, Flanders, Verdun (1916), the Somme, the Argonne (1917), Flanders again, Picardy (1918), the Lys, Arras, Cambrai, and Ypres, among others. He was wounded on at least one occasion.

Kraiss remained in the Reichsheer (the 100,000 man army) after World War I and spent ten years as a company commander in the 13th Infantry Regiment in Ludwigsburg (1921–31). He then spent three years in the Defense Ministry (1931–34) and was a battalion commander in the Ludwigsburg Infantry Regiment (1931–34) and the 119th Infantry Regiment at Stuttgart (1935–37). He took charge of the 90th Infantry Regiment in Hamburg in October 1937 and led it in Poland (1939) and Holland, Belgium, and France (1940). Placed in Führer Reserve on March 15, 1941, he assumed command of the 168th Infantry

Division on July 8 and fought in the southern sector of the Eastern Front prior to assuming command of the newly formed 352nd Infantry Division in Normandy in November 1943. A holder of the Knight's Cross, General Kraiss was promoted to major general on February 1, 1941, and to lieutenant general on October 1, 1942.

✦

Dietrich Kraiss did an excellent job preparing for D-Day and during the actual battle. In mid-May, Kraiss had been given command of a large coastal zone, including what became the Omaha Beach sector. The unit assigned to the sector belonged to the 77th Infantry Division and was an eastern battalion, attached to the 716th Infantry Division and composed mainly of Poles who could not even speak German. The American commanders knew this and thus they expected limited resistance on Omaha. On May 11, however, Erwin Rommel inspected the area and did not like what he saw. He ordered all of the 77th Infantry's units in the coastal sector replaced by Kraiss's 352nd. During the third week of May, Kraiss replaced the eastern battalion with Colonel Ernst Goth's 916th Grenadier Regiment, which had three times as many men, was better equipped, and consisted of Germans—mainly young veterans of the Eastern Front. The French Resistance informed the Allies of this via the usual method—carrier pigeon. Rommel, meanwhile, had ordered hundreds of men to patrol the coastline with shotguns. Their job was to shoot down carrier pigeons. To defeat this idea, the French sent two carrier pigeons, carrying identical messages, at different times. The odds against the Germans killing both birds were very high—but this time they did. General Bradley did not learn of Kraiss's move until hours after the Americans landed.

Colonel Goth and his men shot several American units to pieces on June 6. Kraiss gave him permission to retreat during the early morning hours of June 7, after he had run low in ammunition and reported that he could no longer hold his forward positions.

Unlike the neighboring 716th Infantry Division, Kraiss's 352nd Infantry was actually more or less intact on June 7. His units had played a significant role in checking the British north of Caen on D-Day and had inflicted severe casualties on the U.S. 1st and 29th Infantry divisions on Omaha Beach. The 352nd continued to fight in the hedgerows. As late as June 24, it had lost relatively few men—5,407—and was at kampfgruppe strength. By July 30 the 7th Army listed it as no longer fit for combat. But it still remained in the line.

✦

Wilhelm Richter was born in Hirschberg, Silesia (now Jelenia Gora, Poland), on September 17, 1892. He joined the army as a Fahnenjunker and was commissioned second lieutenant in the 55th Field Artillery Regiment in 1914, just before the outbreak of World War I. The 55th spent the war fighting in France and Flanders. Richter was selected for the Reichsheer and, after twenty-three years' service, was promoted to lieutenant colonel in 1936. Promotions to colonel (1939), major general (March 1, 1943), and lieutenant general (April 1, 1944) followed. Meanwhile, on April 1, 1939, he assumed command of the 30th Artillery Regiment at Rendsburg, Schleswig-Holstein, near the Danish border. He led his regiment in Poland, Belgium, France, and northern Russia, including in the battles around Lake Il'men. On October 1, 1941, he became commander of the 35th Artillery Command (Arko 35) in the central sector of the Eastern Front. He gave up this command at the end of 1942, attended a four-week division commanders' course, and then spent two months as deputy commander of a Luftwaffe field division. On April 1, 1943, he assumed command of the 716th Infantry Division at Caen, France.

Wilhelm Richter's 716th Infantry Division had ten thousand men with which to defend twenty-one miles of coastline on June 6, 1944. Three of its six infantry battalions (the 439th, 441st, and 642nd) were made up of *Osttruppen* (eastern troops recruited from POW camps). They collapsed immediately, but the German troops put up a spirited resistance and were primarily responsible for denying Montgomery and the British 2nd Army the key city of Caen during the first week of the invasion. The division, however, was crushed. Colonel von Oppeln recalled seeing Richter about 2:30 p.m. on June 6. He "was almost demented with grief," the colonel remembered. "My troops are lost," Richter said through his tears. "My whole division is finished."[8]

Richter was right. By June 11 his division had suffered six thousand casualties, and most of the survivors were rear-area and support personnel. Entire infantry battalions had ceased to exist. Despite the seriousness of the situation in Normandy, the 716th no longer had any combat value and had to be taken out of the line. It was sent to Perpignan on the Mediterranean coast to rebuild but was caught up in the Allied invasion of southern France in mid-August.

✦

Erich Marcks, the son of a prominent history professor and Bismarck scholar at the University of Berlin, was born in Schöneberg (now Berlin-Schöneberg) on June 6, 1891. Marcks studied law and philosophy at Freiberg before joining the 9th Field Artillery Regiment as a Fahnenjunker in 1910. Commissioned second

General of Infantry Erich Marcks, the commander of the LXXXIV Corps in 1944. A bit of a military genius, he performed better than any other German general on D-Day. He was killed by an American fighter-bomber on June 12, 1944.

lieutenant in 1911, he served with his unit in the invasion of Belgium, the Battle of the Marne, in the Aisne sector and in Champagne, and in the Battle of the Somme. Marcks was severely wounded in the face and bore the scars the rest of his life. His nose was particularly disfigured. After his recovery, he was transferred to staff work, and he became a member of the General Staff in 1917. Later he was active in forming Freikorps units to protect the Weimar Republic from unrest—and especially leftists and Communists. He became press chief in the Armed Forces Ministry in 1929 and left the service in 1932 to become press chief for General Kurt von Schleicher's puppet chancellor, Franz von Papen. Later, when Schleicher was chancellor (1932–33), Marcks was his press secretary as well. (Schleicher was replaced by Hitler on January 30, 1933, and was murdered by the Gestapo in 1934. Hitler, OKW, and the Nazis never fully trusted Marcks because of his association with Schleicher.)

Marcks rejoined the service in 1933 as a major and battalion commander in Münster, and, in 1935, became chief of staff of Wehrkreis VIII (later VIII Corps), a post he held when the war broke out in 1939. He became chief of staff of the 18th Army in late October 1939. After the fall of France, he was on detached duty in Berlin, where he authored a plan to invade the Soviet Union. On December 10, 1940, he assumed command of the 101st Jäger Division. He led it into Russia on June 22, 1941, but four days later was seriously wounded. His left leg had to be amputated, and he did not return to active duty until March 25, 1942, as commander of the 337th Infantry Division in France. Later he assumed command of the LXVI Reserve Corps (September 20, 1942), LXXXVII Corps

(October 1, 1942), and LXXXIV Corps (August 1, 1943)—all in the west. He was promoted to general of artillery on October 1, 1942.

Of all of the German generals directly involved with D-Day, only Erich Marcks made no mistakes. As the positions in Normandy solidified, the I SS Panzer Corps took over the German right flank. The LXXXIV Corps defended St.-Lô and the German far left flank. Marcks was badly wounded by an American fighter-bomber just west of St.-Lô on June 12 and bled to death before medical help could arrive.[9]

✦

Bodo Zimmermann was born in Metz on November 26, 1886, and was educated in the cadet school system. He entered the Imperial Army as a *Fähnrich* in the 145th Infantry Regiment in 1906. He became a member of the General Staff, fought in World War I, and was discharged as a major in 1920. Unlike many of his peers, Zimmermann had no desire to resume his military career during Hitler's peacetime expansion and, in fact, did not return to the service until December 1939, when, as a lieutenant colonel, he was appointed to the operations staff of the 1st Army. He became Ia of Army Group D (later OB West) in October 1940 and held this post for the rest of the war, serving under several field marshals: Erwin von Witzleben, Gerd von Rundstedt, Günther von Kluge, Walter Model, Rundstedt again, and Albert Kesselring. He was promoted to colonel (December 1, 1942), major general (December 1, 1944), and lieutenant general (May 1, 1945). He lived in Bonn after the war.[10]

Zimmermann proved to be an excellent chief of operations and recognized that the Normandy landings were, in fact, the Great Invasion far earlier than did Rundstedt, Blumentritt, or OKW. At 7:30 a.m. on the morning of D-Day, when Hitler was seized with indecision as to whether or not to release the panzer divisions to OB West, Zimmermann tried to appeal to the operations staff of the High Command of the Armed Forces to allow the panzers to move forward until a decision was reached. For his troubles, he was chewed out by Major General Baron Horst Treusch von Buttlar-Brandenfels of the OKW operations staff, who told him in no uncertain terms that the tank units belonged to OKW and Zimmermann and his colleagues were to leave them alone. Meanwhile, the Allied tanks and infantry pushed to the south, off the beaches and into hedgerow country.

3

The Battles for the Hedgerows

After the Allied ground forces fought their way off the beaches, they found themselves in the *bocage* or hedgerow country of Normandy. A hedgerow in France was not the same simple bush the average American thinks of when he or she hears the word "hedge." In Normandy it was a rock and earthen embankment, often seven feet high, covered with vegetation, bushes, undergrowth, and even small trees, and they were used to enclose small fields. Very few hedgerows are still in existence in Normandy, but they were everywhere in 1944. On this type of ground, all terrain factors accrue to the defense. Added to that, many of the German defenders were excellent soldiers, toughened by years of fighting, and benefitting from years of experience in defensive combat. They were also well led by outstanding officers, such as Baron Friedrich von der Heydte, Erich Diestel, and Baron Heinrich von Lüttwitz, as well as SS fanatics, led by such men as Werner Ostendorff, Fritz Witt, and Kurt "Panzer" Meyer.

◆

Baron Friedrich von der Heydte was born in Munich on March 30, 1907, the descendant of an old Bavarian family with a strong military tradition. He was educated in a religious school in Munich, became a strong, devout Catholic, and remained so throughout his life. During World War I, he was a page to the royal court of the House of Wittelsbach. In 1925 he joined the Reichswehr as an officer cadet in the 19th Infantry Regiment in Munich but secured a transfer to his family's regiment, the 18th Cavalry, at Bad Cannstatt (near Stuttgart) prior to receiving his commission. In 1927 he was released from active duty to begin studying law and economics at Innsbruck University, from which he received his bachelor's degree. He then continued his studies at the University of Berlin, the Austrian Consular Academy in Vienna, and Gräz University, and he received a stipend from the Carnegie Institute for Peace. He earned his doctorate in 1931. He was deeply involved in Catholic student organizations and took part in several brawls against pro-Nazi student groups, resulting in the Gestapo threatening him with arrest. He could return to Germany in 1934 only by rejoining his old regiment—the Gestapo did not have the authority to incarcerate active-duty personnel. Because of Heydte's strong religious convictions, Hermann Göring later dubbed him "the Rosary Paratrooper"—a nickname that stuck.

Heydte's cavalry squadron was converted into an antitank unit in late 1937. Heydte himself was selected for General Staff training and enrolled in the War Academy in late 1938 but returned to his unit (the 246th Antitank Battalion of the 246th Infantry Division) when Germany mobilized on August 26, 1939. Heydte served on the Saar Front and in France (1940), where he earned the Iron Cross, First Class. After the fall of France, he was named Ib of the 227th Infantry Division. Later that year Baron von der Heydte joined the paratroopers and transferred to the Luftwaffe. After jump school he was named commander of the I Battalion of the 3rd Parachute Regiment, which he led with distinction in the Battle of Crete (May 1941). He was awarded the Knight's Cross and was promoted to major for capturing Canea, the second largest city on the island. Later he was sent to the Russian Front, where he was wounded near Leningrad. In 1942 he was sent to Africa with Hermann-Bernhard Ramcke's Parachute Brigade but fell ill with dysentery and was evacuated back to Europe after the Second Battle of El Alamein.

Heydte was transferred to the 2nd Parachute Division in France in 1943 and later fought in Italy, where he was seriously injured when the reconnaissance airplane in which he was flying crashed. After he recovered, he was sent to France, where he assumed command of the 6th Parachute Regiment.

◆

Heydte led the 6th Parachute in the Battle of Normandy, where it was in combat from D-Day and where it was smashed during the first week of fighting. Heydte's regiment had the misfortune of having to defend the Carentan position, which prevented the U.S. VII Corps on Utah Beach from linking up with the rest of the 21st Army Group. It was gradually pushed back and pounded from all sides until noon on June 11, when the Americans finally gained a foothold in the town and Heydte's exhausted veterans were unable to throw them out.

SS Major General Werner Ostendorff ordered Heydte to hold out until June 12 while he came up with his 17th SS Panzer Grenadier Division, to which the 6th Parachute was now attached. Heydte objected, but Ostendorff insisted. When the parachute colonel returned to Carentan, he found that the Americans had overrun his command post and that the U.S. 101st Airborne Division was closing in on his regiment from behind. Colonel von der Heydte decided to disobey orders and abandon the critical town, in order to avoid encirclement.

Heydte was almost court-martialled for abandoning Carentan, even though his I and II battalions were virtually destroyed and only the III Battalion escaped more or less intact. The 6th Parachute nevertheless remained in the battle and, at various times, was attached to the 17th SS Panzer Grenadier, 2nd SS Panzer, and 352nd Infantry divisions.

✦

Werner Ostendorff was born in Königsberg on August 15, 1903, and, after joining the Freikorps at age fifteen, he helped put down Communist insurrections in his native East Prussia. He joined the East Prussian 1st Infantry Regiment as a private in 1925 and earned a promotion to second lieutenant in 1930. He transferred to the Luftwaffe as a first lieutenant in 1934 and trained as a pilot and aerial observer. He transferred again—this time to the SS—in 1935 and was an instructor (apparently in aerial photo interpretation) until 1938. He then commanded a company in the SS Regiment "Der Führer" and became the commander of the SS-Verfügungstruppe's antiaircraft battalion during the Polish campaign of 1939. In the meantime, he impressed Paul Hausser, who made him the first Ia of the SS Division "Das Reich" (later 2nd SS Panzer) in October 1939. He held this position in the French and Russian campaigns (1940–42) and became chief of staff of the SS Panzer Corps (again under Hausser) in June 1942. This unit was redesignated II SS Panzer Corps in June 1943. He distinguished himself in the Battle of Kharkov in March 1943 and, as a result, was given command of the 17th SS Panzer Grenadier Division "Götz von Berlichingen" in January 1944. Ostendorff, who was one of the few SS officers to refuse to renounce his Christian faith, was promoted to SS captain (1936), SS major (1939), SS lieutenant colonel (1940), SS colonel (1942), SS Oberführer (April 20, 1943), and SS major general (April 20, 1944).

SS General Ostendorff approached Carentan during the night of June 11–12. He led his 17th SS Panzer Grenadier Division in a counterattack on June 12 but was repulsed. On June 13 Ostendorff assembled the 37th SS Panzer Grenadier Regiment, the 17th SS Panzer Battalion, and the 6th Parachute Regiment and launched a major counterattack against the U.S. 501st, 502nd, and 506th Parachute Infantry regiments of the 101st Airborne Divsion, which were defending a mile southwest of Carentan. All three American regiments were seriously under strength, as was the 6th Parachute. In what the Americans dubbed the Battle of Bloody Gulch, Ostendorff pushed them back to the edge of the town. Fortunately for the Americans, Combat Command A (CCA) of the U.S. 2nd Armored Division arrived just in time to throw the Germans back. Both sides suffered heavy losses, but the link between Utah Beach and the rest of the invasion front was now secure.

Ostendorff continued to defend south of Carentan until June 15, when he was seriously wounded. Otto Binge replaced Ostendorff as commander of the 17th SS Panzer Grenadier Division.

◆

Otto Binge was born on May 19, 1895, in Cottbus. He joined the army in August 1914 and was sent to the Eastern Front as an enlisted man in the 26th Foot Artillery Regiment. Later he saw action in Serbia and Macedonia and was commissioned second lieutenant of reserves in 1917. He then came down with malaria and was sent back to Germany. After he recovered, Binge was sent to France in 1918 as a battery officer with the 16th Foot Artillery Regiment. He left the army in 1919 and joined the Freikorps, fighting in Silesia and the Ruhr in "the war after the war."

Binge joined the police in 1922 and served in a number of locations, including Berlin, from 1930 to 1938. When the war broke out, Major of Police Binge was given command of the 22nd Police Battalion. On May 6, 1940, he assumed command of the IV/Artillery Regiment "Police," part of what became the 4th SS Panzer Grenadier Division "Police." He remained with the 4th SS until the fall of 1943 and was acting commander of the division from July 20 to August 25, 1943. Binge then returned to Germany, attended a training class at the Army Artillery School at Jüterbog, and took command of the formation staff of the 17th SS Panzer Grenadier Division until the permanent division commander, Werner Ostendorff, arrived in early January 1944. Binge, meanwhile, assumed command of the 17th SS Artillery Regiment of the division, which he led in Normandy. Promoted to SS colonel on April 20, 1944, Binge was acting commander of the division from June 16 to 18, 1944, after Ostendorff was wounded.

During the rest of June and most of July, the 17th SS Panzer Grenadier was involved in heavy fighting in the bocage country around St.-Lô and Coutances. By early July it was down to a strength of 8,500 men—half of its June 6 total. It nevertheless fought in the Mortain counteroffensive (see below), where its commander, Otto Binge, proved again to be too slow. After Mortain, the army generals broke the division into four kampfgruppen, all of which escaped the Battle of the Falaise Pocket. Binge himself was injured on August 29 during the escape from France and was never given another command.

Otto Baum took command of the 17th SS Division from Binge on June 18 but on July 30 was named commander of the 2nd SS Panzer Division, and Binge became acting divisional commander for the third time. After he was injured in an accident on August 29, he was replaced by Eduard Deisenhofer.

◆

Fritz Witt was born on May 27, 1908, in Hohenlimburg, a suburb of Hagen, a city about eleven miles due south of Dortmund. His father was a textile salesman. Witt followed in his father's footsteps and was a textile salesman from 1925 to 1931. He also became a fervent Nazi, joined the NSDAP in 1931, was a member of the Leibstandarte SS Adolf Hitler (Hitler's bodyguard regiment, or LSSAH) by 1933, and was commissioned SS second lieutenant that fall. In 1934 he was promoted to SS first lieutenant and took command of a company in the SS-Standarte Deutschland, which was part of the SS-Verfügungstruppe (SS-VT) Division. Throughout his career, Witt was known as a sharp dresser and as a commander who truly cared for his men, who idolized him. He took part in the occupations of Austria, the Sudetenland, and Czechoslovakia in 1938 and 1939 and fought in the Polish campaign. Promoted to SS captain shortly thereafter and to SS major in late May 1940, he was given command of the I Battalion/SS Motorized Regiment (formerly Standarte) Deutschland in October 1939. He led it with considerable distinction in the western campaign of 1940. On May 27 his battalion knocked out nine British Matilda tanks using only infantry weapons and hand grenades. He was awarded the Knight's Cross for this feat.

In October 1940 Witt was appointed commander of the III/SS Motorized Regiment "Leibstandarte Adolf Hitler" but was transferred to the command of the I Battalion in late March 1941. He led the battalion in the Balkans campaign, where he seized the critical Klidi Pass in Greece from the British in a three-day battle (April 10–12). Witt took 520 prisoners against a loss of 37 killed and 95 wounded. His brother, Franz, was among the dead. Witt fought on the Eastern Front in 1941, including in the Battle of Kiev; helped clear most of the Crimean peninsula; and fought at Rostov and in the winter battles of 1941–42. The LSSAH was sent back to France to rest and refit in May 1942. An SS lieutenant colonel since November 27, 1941, Witt was named commander of the 1st SS Panzer Grenadier Regiment in August 1942 and was promoted to SS colonel on January 30, 1943. Meanwhile, he took part in the occupation of Vichy France in November 1942 and returned to the Eastern Front in January 1943. He fought in the Third Battle of Kharkov in March. For his part in this victory, Witt was awarded the Oak Leaves and was promoted to SS-Oberführer on July 1.

At the end of July 1943 Witt was named commander of the 12th SS Panzer Division "Hitler Jugend" (Hitler Youth). He was promoted to SS major general on April 20, 1944. He celebrated his thirty-sixth birthday on May 27, 1944. Nine days later, the Allies landed in Normandy.

Beginning June 7 Witt's division was ordered to defend the Carpiquet Airfield sector, north of Caen. Witt had done a magnificent job preparing his division for combat. He also proved to be an extremely capable division commander and held his positions despite constant attacks and British and Canadian aerial and naval superiority. On June 14, however, a British naval barrage barracked his command post. As he was running toward a foxhole, a piece of shrapnel struck him in the head, killing him instantly.[1] Three other SS men were killed in the bombardment, and six members of the staff company were wounded. Ironically, the British shells missed the house that Witt was using as his headquarters. Had he stayed put, he would not have been killed.He is buried in the Champigny-Saint-Andre-de-l'Eure German War Cemetery. He was succeeded as divisional commander by SS Colonel Kurt Meyer.

✦

Kurt "Panzer" Meyer, the son of a factory worker, was born in Jerxheim, Brunswick (now Lower Saxony), on December 23, 1910. His father joined the Imperial Army in 1914 and rose to the rank of sergeant during World War I but

Kurt "Panzer" Meyer, who became commander of the 12th SS Panzer Division when SS General Witt was killed by British naval gunfire. Meyer performed brilliantly but was captured by Belgian partisans before he could get the remnants of his division back to the Siegfried line.

was discharged owing to his wounds, from which he never fully recovered. After completing school, Meyer worked on a factory assembly line and in a charcoal briquette factory. Seeking to avoid a life as a common laborer, he joined the Mecklenburg Police in 1929. He earned his nickname while undergoing training at the Schwerin Police Academy. While attempting to drop a bucket of water on a classmate's head, he slipped and fell from the roof of a two-story building. He broke more than twenty bones on landing. He was expected to die but later regained his full health. His fellow policemen nicknamed him "Panzer" because he was as tough as a tank.

Meyer joined the Nazi Party in 1930 and the SS in 1931. He was commissioned SS-Untersturmführer (SS second lieutenant) in 1932 and joined the LSSAH in 1934. Promoted to first lieutenant in 1936, he was given command of the regiment's antitank company. He directed it in the occupations of Austria, the Sudetenland, and Czechoslovakia, as well as in the conquest of Poland, where he was shot through the shoulder on September 7, 1939. After he recovered, he was named commander of the LSSAH's motorcycle company, which he led in the Low Countries and France (1940). After the fall of Paris, his company was upgraded to a reconnaissance battalion (later the 1st SS Panzer Reconnaissance Battalion), and Meyer was promoted to SS major.

During the Balkans campaign, Meyer stormed the Klissura Pass in Greece. At one point, when the attack stalled, Meyer threw a hand grenade directly behind a group of his own men, to get them moving forward again. The tactic worked; the men surged forward as if they had been shot out of a cannon and overran a surprised Greek machine gun position. The pass fell on April 13, and the Greeks lost six hundred men, against twenty-five SS casualties (two of them killed—none by Meyer). On April 16 Meyer captured another eleven hundred prisoners at Kastoria. He was awarded the Knight's Cross shortly thereafter.

Meyer led his battalion in the early part of the Russian campaign but fell ill and had to be relieved. He returned to active duty in January 1942. He fought against the Soviet winter offensive of 1941–42 and then accompanied the battalion back to northern France, where the LSSAH was rebuilt as the 1st SS Panzer Grenadier Division. Meyer took part in the occupation of Vichy France in November 1942 and in early 1943 returned with the LSSAH to southern Russia, where it took part in the Third Battle of Kharkov. In this battle he earned his Oak Leaves. That summer he was named commander of the 25th SS Panzer Grenadier Regiment of the 12th SS Panzer Division "Hitler Youth" (then forming at Beverloo, Belgium) and was promoted to SS colonel on June 21, 1943.

Spearheaded by Meyer's regiment, the Hitler Youth Division was ordered to rush to Normandy on D-Day and was in action near Caen on June 7, 1944. On the first day, the 25th SS Regiment conducted a skillful ambush and destroyed twenty-eight Canadian tanks, suffering only six casualties itself. A week later the division commander, SS Major General Fritz Witt, was killed by British naval gunfire, and Meyer was appointed his successor. At age thirty-three, Meyer was the youngest division commander in the war.

Meyer was deeply affected by the death of General Witt. He did an excellent job commanding the 12th SS in Normandy and in the ensuing breakout from Falaise, although the division was crushed in the process. During the Normandy campaign and the retreat from France, the strength of the Hitler Youth Division fell from 22,000 to 1,500.

✦

Wilhelm Mohnke, the son of a master carpenter, was born in Lübeck on March 15, 1911. He followed his father into carpentry after dropping out of school. In 1931 Mohnke joined the NSDAP and, a few weeks later, the SS. He spent most of his career in the Leibstandarte Adolf Hitler, commanding the unit (now the 1st SS Panzer Division) during the Battle of the Bulge. Prior to that, he had lost a foot in the Balkans campaign (1941) and commanded the division's panzer battalion in Russia. In Normandy Mohnke commanded the 26th Panzer Grenadier Regiment of the 12th SS Panzer Division. Mohnke was responsible for a number of atrocities, including the murder of Canadian prisoners of war during the Battle of Normandy.

✦

Panzer Group West launched an unsuccessful attempt to throw the Allied invasion back into the sea on June 9, 1944, using the 21st Panzer, 12th SS Panzer, and Panzer Lehr divisions. At 9:17 p.m. that evening, the Allied 2nd Tactical Air Force identified Geyr's headquarters and attacked it with forty rocket-firing Typhoons and seventy-one Mitchell (B-25) medium bombers. They dropped a total of 436 five-hundred-pound bombs in four minutes and killed thirty-two men, including Hugo Burgsthaler and the entire operations staff. SS Captain Wilhelm Beck, the liaison officer between Panzer Group West and the I SS Panzer Corps, was among the dead. (They were buried together in a mass grave, topped by a huge cross.) Geyr's chief of staff, Major General Ritter und Edler Sigismund-Hellmut von Dawans, was also killed. Geyr himself was only slightly wounded but was very shaken. Headquarters, Panzer Group West, had to be withdrawn from the battle, and all thought of counterattacking was forgotten. Field Marshal Rommel had left the headquarters barely an hour before. Ironically, Geyr's last words to Rommel that day were to caution him to be careful, as there were Allied fighter-bombers operating in the area.

◆

Hugo Burgsthaler was an up-and-coming young panzer officer who served as the Ia of the 22nd Panzer Division after it was activated in France in the fall of 1941. In May 1942 the division broke through the Soviet 10th Army on the Kerch Peninsula and played the major role in the destruction of ten Soviet divisions. In 1942, as a major, Burgsthaler assumed command of the II/24th Panzer Regiment, which he led in the Stalingrad campaign. His battalion was one of the few units of the 24th Panzer to escape destruction at Stalingrad. Burgsthaler returned to the 22nd Panzer Division and commanded some of its remnants until it was disbanded on March 4, 1943. Later promoted to lieutenant colonel, he was sent to France as Ia of General Geyr von Schweppenburg's Panzer Group West.

◆

Ritter und Edler Sigismund-Hellmut von Dawans, the chief of staff of Panzer Group West, was born in Erfurt on September 23, 1899. He was educated in cadet schools and entered the service as a Fähnrich in the 110th Infantry Regiment in 1917. He was discharged from the service after World War I ended but managed to enter the Reichsheer as a second lieutenant in 1924. He spent the 1924–30 period in the Baden 14th Infantry Regiment at Konstanz. From 1930 to 1934 he underwent General Staff training in Berlin and with the 5th and 6th Infantry Divisions in Stuttgart and Münster, respectively. After working a year in the Defense Ministry (1934–35), he was assigned to the General Staff of the army (1935–36), and then to troop duty as a company commander with the 111th Infantry Regiment in Baden-Baden. He was Ia of the Wehrkreis I in Königsberg, East Prussia (1937–39), and was on the General Staff of Frontier Sector Command North during the Polish campaign. He was on the General Staff of the 16th Army in late 1939 and was Ia of the 19th Infantry (later Panzer) Division from early 1940 to December 26, 1941. During this period, he saw action in the Netherlands, Belgium, and France, and on the central sector of the Russian Front, including the Battles of Minsk, Smolensk, Nevel, and Moscow. In late December 1941 Dawans became chief of staff of the XIII Corps, also in the Moscow sector. He was chief of staff of the III Panzer Corps from June 1,

1942, to February 13, 1943, and chief of staff of the 4th Army from May 15 to October 15, 1943, when he reported himself sick. He returned to duty as chief of staff of Panzer Group West on December 1, 1943. He was promoted to major (1938), lieutenant colonel (1940), colonel (1942), and major general (February 1, 1944).

✦

British field marshal Bernard Law Montgomery attempted to take Caen via double envelopment on June 9–12. His "left hook" was to be launched by the British 6th Airborne and 51st Highlander Divisions, along with the 6th Armoured Brigade. General of Panzer Troops Adolf Kuntzen, Lieutenant General Erich Diestel, and Colonel Hans von Luck, however, halted the operation before it was launched.

✦

Adolf Kuntzen was born in Magdeburg on July 26, 1889, and joined the 1st Hussars Regiment as an officer cadet in 1909. He fought in World War I, primarily with the 7th Hussars (1914–17). He was transferred to the staff of the XXVI Reserve Corps in early 1917, took an abbreviated General Staff course, and served on the General Staffs of the Military Governor of Metz and the 10th Replacement Division in 1918. Selected for the Reichswehr, he spent the 1920s and early 1930s in General Staff, cavalry, and defense ministry assignments. He was on the staff of the Army Personnel Office until Hitler purged it of anti- and non-Nazis in 1938. Kuntzen was then named commander of the 3rd Light Division. He led this unit in Poland and France and oversaw its conversion into the 8th Panzer Division in the winter of 1939–40. Kuntzen led the LVII Panzer Corps in Russia (1941–42) and took charge of the XXXII Corps Command in 1942. This headquarters was later upgraded to LXXXI Corps.

✦

Hans von Obstfelder was born in Steinbach-Hallenberg, Hessen-Nassau, on September 6, 1886. He entered the service as a Fahnenjunker in the Bavarian 5th Field Artillery Regiment in 1905 and was promoted to colonel on March 1, 1933, a month after Hitler took power. Promotions to major general (1936), lieutenant general (1938), and general of infantry (June 1, 1940) followed. The pro-Nazi Obstfelder commanded the 28th Infantry Division at Breslau (October 6, 1936), in southern Poland (1939), Belgium (1940), and France (1940). On June 1, 1940, he assumed command of the XXIX Corps, which he commanded on occupation duty in northern France and Poland. He led it into southern Russia on June 22, 1941, and fought on the Bug, in the Kiev encirclement, and at

General of Infantry Hans von Obstfelder, who commanded the LXXXVI Corps on the German far right flank during the Normandy campaign. He later commanded the 1st and 19th armies on the Western Front. Despite his competence and his pro-Nazi views, Hitler sacked him on March 26, 1945.

Belgorod. He supported the disintegrating Italian 8th Army on the Don (1942–43) and fought in the Donetz, on the Mius, and in the retreat to the Dnieper.

General von Obstfelder was given command of the LXXXVI Corps in southwestern France on August 25, 1943. It was sent to Normandy in June 1944 and formed the right flank anchor for Army Group B. Obstfelder proved to be an excellent defensive commander, even on the Western Front. He fought in the retreat across France, Belgium, and into the Netherlands and played a creditable role in the defeat of Operation Market Garden.

✦

Erich Diestel was also a highly capable officer. Born in Deutsch Eylau, East Prussia (now Itawa, Poland), on November 8, 1892, he was educated in cadet schools and entered the army as a Fähnrich in the 35th Fusilier Regiment in 1912. Diestel was commissioned in 1913 and went to the field with his regiment. He fought in Lorraine and was seriously wounded on September 19. He returned to the field as a platoon leader in the 270th Reserve Infantry Regiment in late December. Later a battalion adjutant, company commander, machine gun officer, and regimental adjutant, he fought on the Somme, in Galicia, in Russia, and in the Ukraine. He was sent back to the Western Front at the end of the war. Selected for the Reichswehr, Diestel was assigned to the Prussian 5th Infantry Regiment (1920–21) and to the elite 9th Infantry Regiment in Potsdam (1921–33), where he served as a battalion adjutant and company commander. He was an instructor at the War School at Dresden (1935–37), assumed command of the I Battalion/ 68th Infantry Regiment at Brandenburg on October 12, 1937, and led it in the Polish campaign. Later he commanded the 188th Infantry Regiment (1940–42), fighting in Belgium, France, and southern Russia; and the 101st Jäger Division (April 15–September 1, 1942), which he commanded at Rostov, Maikop, and in the Caucasus. He also led the 75th Infantry Division at Voronesh (September 5–13, 1942). He was then transferred to northern France, where he took charge of the newly formed, static 346th Infantry Division on September 20, 1942. He was promoted first lieutenant (1922), captain (1927), major (1934), lieutenant general (1937), colonel (June 1, 1940), major general (August 1, 1942), and lieutenant general exactly one year later.

Diestel commanded the 346th Infantry Division (nonmotorized) in Normandy, Belgium, and the Netherlands. He did an excellent job with a mediocre formation, although it did suffer heavy casualties in the Normandy fight and the retreat across France and was down to kampfgruppe strength by October 16, 1944, when Diestel gave up command and went on leave.

✦

As of June 7 the German defenses east of the Orne were the responsibility of Kuntzen's LXXXI Corps (then part of the 15th Army). His forces included Lieutenant General Erich Diestel's 346th Infantry Division (which was ferried across the Seine during the night of June 6–7), the 711th Infantry Division, the remnants of the 716th Infantry Division, and Battle Group Luck of the 21st Panzer Division. Sensing that the British had planned an offensive and desiring to eliminate the entire Allied airborne bridgehead east of the Orne, if possible, Kuntzen launched a series of spoiling attacks from June 7 to 16. The forces that were supposed to launch Montgomery's left hook against Caen were caught in their assembly areas. Diestel and Luck were particularly aggressive and hand-to-hand fighting was reported in several places. Casualties were heavy on both sides. KG Luck, for example, lost all but eight of the tanks lent to it by the 100th Panzer Regiment. The British, however, were never able to launch the left half of their offensive.

The LXXXI Corps Headquarters was withdrawn from the battle on or about June 21, and responsibility for the German far right flank was taken over by General of Infantry Hans von Obstfelder's LXXXVI Corps, which was called up from southwestern France.

Monty's right hook against Caen was much stronger than his left. On June 11 it scored a significant success when the British 7th Armoured Division attacked through the British 50th Infantry Division and broke through the left flank of the Panzer Lehr Division. Bayerlein's division was in serious trouble because the British 6th Armoured Regiment, supported by Canadian infantry, had pinned the rest of the Lehr down with a series of frontal attacks and he had little to spare for the left flank. On June 12 the British continued to develop their offensive, as they advanced into the void between the loosely joined British and American armies. While the majority of the British 7th Armoured held down Bayerlein's left flank, a strong force (including the 22nd Armoured Brigade, the 1st Infantry Regiment, and the 5th Royal Artillery Regiment) rounded the German flank on the morning of June 13 and threatened Panzer Lehr with envelopment. With his reserves committed, there was little Bayerlein could do but cry for help. Fortunately for him, help was not far off in the form of a platoon of Tiger tanks under SS Lieutenant Michael Wittmann and, behind that, Lieutenant General Baron Heinrich von Lüttwitz's 2nd Panzer Division.

✦

Michael Wittmann, the son of a farmer, was born in the village of Vogelthal in the Upper Palatinate (Oberpfalz) region of Bavaria on April 22, 1914. Although considered by many in the West to be the leading German tank ace of World War II, he actually ranked fourth, behind Kurt Knispel, Otto Carius, and Johannes Bölter.[2] He was, however, the leading tank ace in the SS.

Michael Wittmann did his duty in the Reich Labor Service (Reichsarbeitsdienst or RAD) in early 1934 and joined the army's 19th Infantry Regiment at Freising (near Munich) late that same year. He transferred to the Waffen-SS in October 1936 and was assigned to the Leibstandarte SS Adolf Hitler (then a motorized regiment) in 1937. He took part in the occupation of Austria and the Sudetenland and fought in Poland, France, Greece, and Russia as a crew member and later as a commander of a StuG III. These assault guns, which were mounted on the chassis of a PzKw III, were much more effective than most historians realize. From June 1941 to January 1944, for example, they were credited with destroying twenty thousand Soviet tanks. Wittmann scored his initial victories in Russia with this weapon. He returned to Germany in late 1942 and underwent officer training before being reassigned to the Leibstandarte's panzer regiment as a platoon leader in early 1943. In 1944 he left the 1st SS Panzer Division to assume command of a Tiger company in the 101st SS Heavy Panzer Battalion. Meanwhile, Wittmann, who was known for his infectious laugh, married Hildegard Burmester in Lueneburg, Lower Saxony (about forty miles southeast of Hamburg), on March 1, 1944.

On June 13 Wittmann and four of his tanks were in an ambush position near Villers-Bocage when the advancing British 22nd Armoured Brigade and its supporting infantry decided to take a break in place on the highway, which was flanked by large hedgerows. Wittmann, who was in the lead tank, noticed at once that the British vehicles were too close together and would be unable to maneuver or turn around if he attacked down the highway. He did so immediately. Keeping his frontal armor to the British, he destroyed dozens of half-tracks and trucks with his machine guns while the Allied infantrymen dove out of their vehicles in panic and fled for their lives. Those who did not were shot down. Meanwhile, as the shells from British armored vehicles bounced harmlessly off of his thick frontal armor, Wittmann used his main battle gun—one of the infamous German 88s—to personally destroy six Cromwell tanks, two Shermans, three Stuart (Honey) tanks (an American light/reconnaissance tank), and several half-tracks and trucks. Wittmann single-handedly stopped the advance of the British 7th Armoured Division before his own Tiger was knocked out by a British six-pounder antitank gun. Wittmann and his crew escaped and spent the rest of the day on foot, successfully avoiding capture. For his incredible daring and victory at Villers-Bocage, Wittmann was promoted to SS captain and awarded the Swords to his Knight's Cross with Oak Leaves.

With Michael Wittmann out of the way and on the run, the British were engaged by his other four tanks (three Tigers and a PzKw IV). The Germans destroyed at least fourteen more tanks, bringing the total British tank losses to twenty-five. The British also lost fourteen half-tracks, fourteen Bren carriers, and dozens of trucks to Wittmann and his company. Even so, the British might have been able to rally and resume their advance, but before they could regain their balance, they were pounced on by a new and even more formidable threat: Lieutenant General Baron von Lüttwitz's 2nd Panzer Division.

Baron Heinrich von Lüttwitz was born on the family estate at Krumpach, East Prussia, on December 6, 1896. (Heinrich should not be confused with his first cousin, General of Panzer Troops Baron Smilo von Lüttwitz, who commanded the 26th Panzer Division, XXXXVI Panzer Corps, and 9th Army on the Eastern Front.) Unable to secure his father's permission to enter the service when World War I began, Lüttwitz ran away from home, joined the army as a private, and went to the Western Front at age seventeen. His mother, Klara von Lüttwitz née von Unruh, came from a military family and used her influence to have him brevetted second lieutenant two days before his eighteenth birthday.

Baron Heinrich von Lüttwitz, who did a brilliant job commanding the 2nd Panzer Division in Normandy. Later, as commander of the XXXXVII Panzer Corps, he was much less successful (USAMHI).

Lüttwitz distinguished himself in the trench fighting in France in 1917, during which he was severely wounded. He ended the war commanding a troop of the 1st Ulan Regiment. He was accepted into the Reichsheer as a cavalry officer but was converted to the concept of motorized warfare in 1929 and commanded the 3rd Motorized Battalion in 1936–37. In 1936 he was also leader of the German Olympic equestrian team. Because the team did not win the gold medal, Lüttwitz's career suffered, and he served in backwater posts for several years. (He was not sent to the front in Poland until the campaign was decided, and even then, he was unlucky enough to be severely wounded. He was on garrison duty in Poland during the French campaign of 1940.) Finally, Major General Walter Nehring (future commander of the Afrika Korps and the 1st Panzer Army) rescued Lüttwitz from professional exile and gave him command of the 101st Motorized Infantry Regiment in his own 18th Panzer Division. He was abruptly relieved on orders from Berlin in January 1941—apparently because of his failure in the 1936 Olympics. Nehring strongly protested, as did Guderian and Erich Höpner. This led to Lüttwitz being given command of the 59th Rifle Regiment of the 20th Panzer Division, which he led in Russia with considerable success (1941–42). Lüttwitz was at last out of the professional doghouse. After Stalin's winter offensive of 1941–42 was checked, Lüttwitz commanded the 20th Rifle Brigade (1942), the 13th Panzer Division (1942–43), and the 2nd Panzer Division (which he took command of on February 1, 1944), all on the Eastern Front. He was promoted to lieutenant general on June 1, 1943. After the Soviet winter offensive of 1943–44 was halted, Lüttwitz was ordered to take his division back to France, where he was to rebuild it and train it to meet the Great Invasion.

Although he would later prove to be a mediocre corps commander, Lüttwitz was a masterful divisional commander and turned out to be one of the best training officers in the entire Wehrmacht. In the spring of 1944 he trained each officer and NCO in his division to be able to take command of the unit above him. This proved to be an excellent idea; although the 2nd Panzer lost every major regimental and battalion commander it had during the Battle of Normandy, the Allies never noticed any slackening in its efficiency. It also seems to have received more training in night operations than any other German division in the West. By D-Day the 2nd Panzer was ready. It performed better in Normandy than any other German division, with the sole exception of the 12th SS Panzer Division "Hitler Jugend."

OKW released the 2nd Panzer Division for employment in Normandy on or about June 8. Using radio silence and its considerable skill in conducting night marches, and "going to ground" during the day, the entire 2nd Panzer Division approached the Caen sector undetected. On the evening of June 12, it was ordered to counterattack the British forces turning the Panzer Lehr's flank southwest of Caen.

To the British, Lüttwitz's 2nd Panzer Division seems to appear out of thin air on June 13. It took the 22nd Armoured Brigade in the flank and pushed it, the 7th Armoured Brigade, and their supporting infantry back to near the point where they started, inflicting considerable casualties on them in the process. Montgomery's great envelopment of Caen was checked. (Map 10 shows this battle.)

Meanwhile, a new German division appeared on the battlefield: Heinz Lammerding's 2nd SS Panzer Division "Das Reich."

✦

Heinz Lammerding was born in Dortmund on August 27, 1905, the son of an architect. He received an excellent education, earning the Diplom-Ingenieurs degree, and worked in private industry until 1933, when he joined the army's 6th Engineer Battalion for a brief period of active duty. He joined the SA (Brownshirts) in the early 1930s and became chief of SA engineers in Westphalia in 1934. Later that year he became adjutant and *Referent* (senior civil servant) of the engineer inspectorate of the Eastern SA. He joined the SS in 1935 as an engineer platoon leader with the rank of first lieutenant. By 1937 he was a captain

Map 10. The Battle of Villers-Bocage

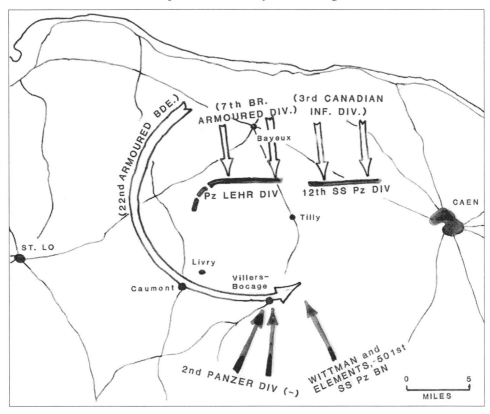

of SS and a company commander, and in October 1939 he was transferred to the "Totenkopf" Division as a major. He became chief of operations of the division on January 1, 1941. Promoted to SS lieutenant colonel in September 1941, he was named commander of the SS Panzer Grenadier Regiment "Totenkopf" in August 1942. Later he was promoted to SS colonel and assigned to the staff of the II SS Panzer Corps (July 1943). He was named commander of the 2nd SS Panzer Division in December 1943 and was simultaneously promoted to Oberführer. His advancement to divisional command was not owing to his military prowess but was attributable mainly to his close personal relationship with the Reichsführer-SS, Heinrich Himmler. Lammerding proved to be a poor to mediocre divisional commander.

Unlike the tightly controlled 2nd Panzer Division, Lammerding's 2nd SS Panzer Division had a great deal of trouble from French partisans during its approach from southern France to Normandy. The SS retaliated, killing 99 men at Tulle and murdering 642 people (including 245 women and 207 children) at Oradour-sur-Glane. Although the evidence is difficult to evaluate, it appears that Lammerding did not order or approve the Oradour Massacre and knew nothing about it for some time. If this is true, it absolves Lammerding of a major war crime, but it also suggests the extent to which he lost control of his unit. He apparently did order the Tulle executions as a reprisal for killings committed by the French Resistance. The 2nd SS Panzer arrived in Normandy in dribs and drabs over a period of five days.

Rommel and the other army generals apparently did not expect much from Lammerding. Instead of employing the division as a unit, they split it into several kampfgruppen and spread them all over the map. Heinz Lammerding led the 2nd SS Panzer Division (in a much reduced form) in Normandy until he was wounded in action on July 26, 1944. He was replaced by SS Lieutenant Colonel Christian Tychsen.

The Oradour Massacre was ordered and personally directed by Adolf Diekmann, the commander of the I Battalion of the 4th SS Panzer Grenadier Regiment "Der Führer." He gave the order after his men found the body of SS Major Helmut Kämpfe, the commander of the III Battalion of the Der Führer Regiment. Kämpfe, who was a pleasant, likeable man, was a good friend of Diekmann's. He had been kidnapped by the French Resistance the day before and handcuffed to a captured German army ambulance, which was then set on fire. Kämpfe and the wounded German soldiers inside burned to death.

When Sylvester Stadler, the commander of the 4th SS Panzer Grenadier, learned about the massacre, he brought court-martial charges against Diekmann. Lammerding did not block the proceedings. The court-martial never took place because Diekmann (who was only twenty-nine) was killed in action in Normandy on June 29. Some of his colleagues believed that the distraught Diekmann committed suicide by deliberately exposing himself to enemy fire, but this cannot be proved.

Meanwhile, the Americans, led by the aggressive Gen. J. Lawton "Lightning Joe" Collins, drove across the Cotentin and toward the strategic objective of the campaign: the port of Cherbourg.

4

Cherbourg

After securing the beachheads, the strategic objective of the Allied landings was Cherbourg. The Allies needed a good natural port to supply their drive to Paris and beyond, once they broke out of bocage country. Lieutenant General Karl-Wilhelm von Schlieben was charged with the task of denying them this prize.

✦

Karl-Wilhelm von Schlieben was born in Eisenach, Thuringia, on October 30, 1894. His father, Major Wilhelm von Schlieben, was killed in action on November 14, 1914, while commanding the 83rd Reserve Infantry Regiment. Young Karl (who was 6 foot 4½) joined the Imperial Army as a Fahnenjunker when World War I broke out and was commissioned shortly thereafter in the elite 3rd Foot Grenadier Regiment. He joined the 3rd Foot in the field on September 13, 1914, and took part in the drive across Belgium toward the Marne, but was so badly wounded on September 26 that he could not return to full duty until the spring of 1916. Initially a company officer (1914–16), he became a battalion adjutant in the 3rd Guards later that year. He was seriously wounded on the Somme Front on November 29, 1916, but resumed his adjutant duties when he returned to the front in January 1917. After another stay in the hospital (January–April 1917)—this time owing to illness—Schlieben joined the LX Corps Staff as an orderly officer. He was selected for the Reichsheer and from 1920 to 1924 was adjutant of the II Battalion, "Infantry Regiment von 9" in Potsdam. In 1924 he transferred to the cavalry and was with the Prussian 7th Cavalry Regiment at Breslau from 1924 to 1929. After that, he spent five years (1929–34) as a squadron leader in the 12th Cavalry Regiment in Dresden. He then served as adjutant of Cavalry Command Stettin (1934–35), as adjutant of the 1st Cavalry Brigade (1935–36), and on the staff of Higher Cavalry Command 1. He was adjutant of Wehrkreis XIII (XIII Corps) when World War II started (1937–40).

At the end of the French campaign (June 1940), Schlieben made the rather belated transfer from the horse to the motorized branch when he was named commander of the elite 1st Rifle Regiment of the 1st Panzer Division. On August 15 his regiment was divided, and he became commander of the 108th Rifle Regiment of the 14th Panzer Division, which had not yet been formed. After seeing this unit through its birthing phases at the Königsbrück Troop Maneuver Area in Saxony, Schlieben led the regiment in the conquests of Yugoslavia and in the invasion of the Soviet Union, where it fought at Kholm, on the Don, at Rostov, in the retreat across the Mius, and in the Second Battle of Kharkov. On July 20, 1942, Schlieben was promoted to the command of the 4th Panzer Grenadier Brigade of the 4th Panzer Division, which he led in the Orel sector (1942–43). In February and March 1943 Schlieben served as acting commander of the 208th Infantry Division (also on the central sector of the Eastern Front), and on April 1, 1943, he reached the high point of his military career when he was named commander of the 18th Panzer Division. Schlieben directed the depleted 18th Panzer at Orel, Kursk, Bryansk, Orscha, and Vitebsk before it was withdrawn to Lithuania to reorganize. During the heavy fighting on the central sector, the 18th Panzer Division was, at one point, surrounded. Schlieben asked for permission to break out, and when this was not forthcoming, he acted on his own initiative and broke out anyway. Acts of this nature had cost more than one German general his career or even his head. Schlieben was not among these unfortunates, but he does seem to have earned the censure of Führer Headquarters.

On December 12, 1943, the 18th Panzer Division was converted into the mobile 18th Artillery Division. Schlieben was not retained as its commander, nor was he given another tank division. Instead, he was transferred to the Cotentin Peninsula of France, where he was given command of the static 709th Infantry Division—a definite demotion. He nevertheless was promoted to lieutenant general on May 1, 1944. Earlier he had been promoted to first lieutenant (1925), captain of cavalry (1929), major (1935), lieutenant colonel (1938), colonel (August 1, 1941), and major general (May 1, 1943).

On June 6 Schlieben assembled an ad hoc battle group and attempted to recapture Ste.-Mere-Eglise, which had been captured by elements of the U.S. 82nd Airborne Division. He failed, largely because of American fighter-bombers, the toughness of their paratroopers, and the fact that the U.S. 4th Infantry Division quickly secured the Utah Beach area and linked up with the paratroopers. The fact that Schlieben had gone to Rennes for the famous map exercise and did not reach his own headquarters until shortly after noon did not help the German situation. Schlieben then fell back to positions north and east of Carentan to contain the U.S. VII Corps and defend the Cherbourg Landfront.

He was placed in charge of the 77th Infantry, 243rd Infantry, 709th Infantry, and 91st Air Landing divisions—the last two of which were only remnants. He was also given a battle group from the 265th Infantry Division and the 100th Panzer Replacement Battalion, and his headquarters was redesignated Group von Schlieben.

Cherbourg was the peacetime home of the French Atlantic Fleet, and its port was the strategic objective of the D-Day landings. Even so, because of their need to secure and link their bridgeheads and to ferry new divisions from England to France, the Americans could not launch their offensive against Cherbourg until June 11. They were commanded by Lt. Gen. J. Lawton Collins's VII Corps and included the U.S. 90th, 9th, 4th, and 79th Infantry divisions. All were fully motorized and at more or less full strength. On the southern edge of the American advance, Gen. Omar Bradley (the commander of the U.S. 1st Army) committed Maj. Gen. Troy H. Middleton's VIII Corps, which included the U.S. 82nd and 101st airborne divisions.

Utah Beach during the buildup phase, June 9, 1944. The failure of the Luftwaffe's 3rd Air Fleet to interfere with the Allied landings and subsequent buildup or to protect German ground forces from Allied fighter-bombers was cited by Field Marshal Rommel as the major reason for the defeat of the Wehrmacht in Normandy (USNA).

The defeat of Schlieben's largely static units was entirely predictable. It took them a week, but at 5:05 a.m. on June 18 the American spearheads captured the tiny port of Barneville and looked down on the waters of the Atlantic. Cherbourg was cut off from Army Group B.

Heinz Hellmich was born in Karlsruhe on June 9, 1890, and joined the 136th Infantry Regiment as a Fahnenjunker in 1908. He went to war with the machine gun company of his regiment and was severely wounded on the Eastern Front (then in East Prussia) on September 13, 1914. After he recovered, he rejoined the 136th as a company commander on January 27, 1915. He was captured by the Russians in September 1915 and spent more than two years in the czar's POW camps before he escaped and made his way back to German lines at the end of 1917. He rejoined his regiment on February 26, 1918, but was soon selected for General Staff training, which he finished in late 1918. During the Reichswehr era, he alternated between infantry and General Staff assignments. He was considered a rising star in the Wehrmacht and held a number of important General Staff posts—including a tour of duty as a branch chief in the Air Ministry. Clearly earmarked for greater things, Hellmich was named commander of the elite Berlin-Brandenburg 23rd Infantry Division while only a colonel—a rare sign of official favor in 1940. (He was promoted to major general on September 1, 1941.) He led the division skillfully on the Eastern Front, but his health and his nerves collapsed during the Russian winter offensive and he had to be relieved of his command, ruining a most promising career. (Three of his regimental commanders also collapsed.) Hellmich returned to duty in Prague on April 1, 1942, as commander of Special Administrative Divisional Staff 141 (which later became the 141st Replacement Division)—a definite and serious demotion. Later he was inspector of Osttruppen, but he was not given another combat unit until early 1944, when he assumed command of the 243rd Infantry Division.

Hellmich led the 243rd Infantry Division in Normandy, doing an excellent job with very limited resources against overwhelming forces, until June 16, when he was killed by a 20mm shell from an Allied fighter-bomber.

Rudolf Stegmann was born in Nikolaiken, East Prussia (now Mikolajki, Poland), on August 6, 1894. He entered the service as a Fahnenjunker in the 141st Infantry Regiment in late 1912 and was commissioned second lieutenant on May 20, 1914. He went to war with his regiment, which fought at Gunbinneu and Tannenberg on the Eastern Front and in France (1915–18). He remained in the Reichswehr and was a major when Hitler took power in 1933. An infantry or motorized infantry officer throughout his career, he was commander of the II/14th Rifle Regiment in Poland (1938–39), commander of the 14th Rifle Regiment in France and Russia (late 1939–February 5, 1942), and commander of the 2nd Panzer Grenadier Brigade and 36th Panzer Grenadier (later Infantry) Division on the Eastern Front (1942–44). He was seriously wounded in the successful defensive battle around Bobruisk on January 10, 1944, and did not return to active duty until May 1, 1944, when he assumed command of the 77th Infantry Division in the St.-Malo–St.-Brieuc sector of Brittany. He had been promoted to major general on August 1, 1943.

Stegmann's 77th Infantry Division was an understrength, nonmotorized division made up mainly of *Volksdeutsche* (ethnic Germans from the East), Poles, and Tatars from the Volga region, whose loyalty to the Third Reich was questionable at best. It was initially positioned to cover Omaha and Utah beaches, but Rommel—who suspected that the Allies might land in this sector—inspected the area on May 11 and did not like what he saw. He moved the unreliable 77th to southern Brittany and replaced it with the 352nd Infantry Division, which consisted largely of German veterans from the Eastern Front.

The 77th was alerted on D-Day but was not engaged. It was ordered to join Group von Schlieben west of Ste.-Mere-Eglise on June 7. Lacking transport, it marched to the front and first engaged the Americans on June 10, defending the hedgerow country on both sides of the Merderet River and preventing much stronger elements of the U.S. VII Corps from outflanking the critical position of Montebourg, a major road junction on the highway to Cherbourg. Meanwhile, however, Lt. Gen. J. Lawton Collins's VII Corps broke through Group von Schlieben south of the 77th and reached the coast near Barneville on the morning of June 18, cutting off Group von Schlieben in the northern part of the Cotentin Peninsula.

General Stegmann had held up the advance of the much stronger U.S. 90th Infantry Division, proving that he could achieve excellent results from a very mixed team. On June 18 Field Marshal Rommel authorized the 77th Infantry Division to break out to the south, but Hitler promptly countermanded the order. Stegmann broke out anyway. He had, in fact, been secretly preparing the breakout since June 16, even though General Pemsel, the chief of staff of 7th Army, had denied Stegmann permission to make the attempt.

Eastern troops (former Soviet or Polish soldiers serving with the German army) captured on D-Day. Most of these men—who were not loyal to the Third Reich—were happy to be out of the war. They did not know that many of them would be returned to Russia after the surrender. Most were later murdered by the Communists (USNA)

Stegmann planned for the 77th Infantry to break out in five different columns. Some elements, however, where too heavily engaged with the Americans to make the attempt. One column, which included the division's artillery regiment and most of its transport, was destroyed by an American artillery regiment. Some of the other columns were scattered, but the division overran part of the U.S. 47th Infantry Regiment and took 250 prisoners. Some 1,500 badly needed infantrymen reached German lines on June 20. General Stegmann was not among them, however. He was killed on June 18, near the village of Bricquebec, when his car was spotted by an American fighter-bomber, which dived almost to ground level and opened up on it at close range. The general's body was riddled with 20mm shells, one of which struck him in the head.

Had he lived, Stegmann would likely have been court-martialled for disobeying the Führer's orders. Dead, he was posthumously promoted to lieutenant general. Nazi Germany and its conquered territories were indeed strange and lethal places to be in the last year of Hitler's reign.

◆

Rudolf Bacherer was born on June 19, 1895, in Pforzheim, Baden. He married his hometown sweetheart, Melanie Hausch, who reportedly gave him three daughters. Bacherer joined the army when World War I began as a member of the 22nd (3rd Baden) Dragoons Regiment and earned a commission. He was discharged in 1919 but returned to active duty as a first lieutenant in the 18th Cavalry Regiment at Bad Cannstadt in 1935. Promoted to captain two years later, he was part of the 156th Reconnaissance Battalion during the Polish campaign, fought against the British in Belgium in 1940, and was involved in the drive on Moscow. Bacherer, who was promoted to major of reserves in December 1941, commanded the battalion from 1941 to June 1942, when he became commander of the 234th Infantry Regiment in the same division (the 56th Infantry). He was, however, severely wounded on October 6 and did not return to his post until January 4, 1943. He was promoted to colonel of reserves on July 10, 1943, and led the 234th until October 1943, when he fell ill and returned to Germany. He assumed command of the 1026th Grenadier Regiment in early December 1943, and the 1049th Grenadier Regiment of the 77th Infantry Division on February 6, 1944.

Bacherer assumed command of the 77th Infantry Division when General Stegmann was killed on June 18. He broke through American lines and led the remnants of the division to safety on June 20.

On June 19, less than twenty-two hours after cutting Group von Schlieben off from the rest of the German army, the American advance on Cherbourg resumed. Lightning Joe had struck again. He reached the outer defenses of Cherbourg on June 21.

Schlieben knew that his situation was hopeless; however, it was essential to the German war effort that the port of Cherbourg be rendered useless to the enemy. Fortunately for the Third Reich, Field Marshal von Rundstedt reached this conclusion on June 9. That night, without bothering to consult Berlin, he ordered that the destruction of the harbor and its facilities begin "at once." By June 22 the demolitions program was in an advanced state of completion.[1]

The task of destroying the harbor fell to Rear Admiral Walter Hennecke, the naval commander of Normandy; Major General Robert Sattler, the city commandant; and Naval Captain Witt, the harbor commander.

Walter Hennecke was born in Bethelm, Hanover, on May 23, 1898. He entered the navy as a war volunteer in 1915 and received his commission as an ensign in 1917. He spent most of his career on line ships and in ship artillery school units. From 1925 to 1927 he commanded the Artillery School Ship *Delphia*, and from May to October 1941 he commanded the obsolete battleship *Schleswig-Holstein*. In 1940 he was earmarked to command Training Formation 2 during Operation Sea Lion, the invasion of Great Britain. He spent most of World War II, however, commanding the Ship Artillery School. He became commander, Sea Formations, Normandy, on May 6, 1943, and was promoted to rear admiral on March 1, 1944.

✦

Hennecke, Sattler, and Witt carried out one of the best-planned and best-executed feats of destruction in military history, and they continued wreaking havoc until the very end. At 7:00 p.m. on June 25, for example, the American infantry was within a hundred yards of Schlieben's command bunker when Captain Witt's demolitions teams blew up what was left of the harbor with thirty-five tons of dynamite. U.S. colonel Alvin G. Viney, the engineer charged with the task of rehabilitating the harbor after Cherbourg was liberated, reported, "The demolition of the port of Cherbourg is a masterful job, beyond a doubt the most complete, intensive, and best-planned demolition in history." The U.S. Army's official history recorded that "the whole port was as nearly a wreck as demolitions could make it." It would be three weeks before the Allies got the slightest use out of the place.[2] Hitler was so pleased with Admiral Hennecke's work that he awarded him the Knight's Cross, even though he was in captivity.

Schlieben held out until 1:30 p.m. on June 26. He then surrendered his command bunker only. Some 842 Germans, including Admiral Hennecke, poured out of the underground facility and marched off into captivity. Hitler was furious at Schlieben and later denounced him as "a disgrace to his uniform and the lowest form of a German general!"[3]

✦

Robert Sattler, the city commandant of Cherbourg, was born in Königshütte, Upper Silesia (now Chorzow, Poland), on December 6, 1891. He joined the Imperial Army in 1911 and was commissioned second lieutenant in the 63rd Infantry Regiment in 1913. He was part of the 12th Infantry Division, which fought in France and (briefly) on the Russian Front. Retained in the Reichswehr, he was a major in 1935. Promoted to lieutenant colonel in 1937, he was on the staff of the 24th Infantry Regiment in 1938 and was named commander of the 176th when it was mobilized at Intersburg, East Prussia, on August 26, 1939. Sattler led the 176th in Poland, Belgium, and France and commanded it on occupation duty in Brittany from July 1940 to January 1941. Sent back to East Prussia, the regiment took part in the invasion of the Soviet Union on June 22, 1941. It was part of Army Group North and fought at Riga, Reval, in the sweep through the Baltic States and at Volchov, south of Leningrad. Sattler, meanwhile, either fell ill or was wounded (probably the former). He gave up command of the 176th on April 1, 1942, and did not return to active duty for eight more months. In January 1943 he became an acceptance/inspection officer for the Replacement Army and was stationed in Wehrkreis IX (Kassel). A colonel since

April 1, 1940, he was promoted to major general on October 1, 1943. This was a late promotion and was ultimately his last. After Russia, he never held another field command. He was unemployed from December 1, 1943, until the spring of 1944.

Sattler was commandant of Cherbourg from April 1944 until June 27, 1944, when he, along with four hundred of his men, surrendered to the Americans.

✦

Cherbourg cost the American VII Corps 22,000 men, including 2,811 killed. The U.S. VIII Corps also suffered casualties—perhaps as many as 3,000. Group von Schlieben, on the other hand, was wiped out. Losses were estimated as 47,070 killed, wounded, or captured, including 826 officers and six generals. By July 1 Eisenhower had 929,000 men ashore in Normandy, and was adding two to three divisions per week. Rommel had about a third that many. He did, however, have the advantage of terrain. As long as he could hold out in hedgerow country, Germany had a chance to hold Fortress Europe.

A German soldier, killed in the street fighting in Cherbourg.
He is clutching a live grenade in his right hand (USNA).

5

Attrition

By the third week of June the thin German line in Normandy consisted (east to west) of Hans von Obstfelder's LXXXVI Corps (on the German right flank); the I SS Panzer Corps (Sepp Dietrich), defending the critical city of Caen; the German center, the so-called Caumont Gap, which was defended by Baron Hans von Funck's weak XXXXVII Panzer Corps; II Parachute Corps (General of Paratroops Eugen Meindl), holding the St.-Lô sector; and Dietrich von Choltitz's LXXXIV Corps, holding the 7th Army's left flank. Field Marshal Rommel already considered Group von Schlieben in Cherbourg a write-off. (Table 5.1 shows the German Order of Battle as of June 21.)

From June 6 on, the Allies launched small-scale and medium-scale attacks every day. Montgomery's next major offensive, however, began west of Caen on June 25. Code-named Operation Epsom, it involved a major secondary attack west of the small Odon River by the British XXX Corps, the purpose of which was to force the Germans to commit their reserves. The main attack was to be delivered in the adjacent sector east of the Odon June 26 by the British VIII and I Corps. The objective of the operation was the vital Hill 112, southwest of Caen. If he could capture and hold this position, Monty realized, Rommel would have to abandon Caen. Both the XXX Corps and VIII/I Corps blows would fall in the zone of General of Waffen-SS Sepp Dietrich's I SS Panzer Corps. Just as Montgomery hoped, Hitler's former bodyguard mishandled the battle.

◆

Josef "Sepp" Dietrich was born in Hawangen, Swabia (Bavaria), on May 28, 1892, the son of a master meatpacker. He dropped out of school at age fourteen and became an agricultural driver. Later he was an apprentice in the hotel trade. He joined the Royal Bavarian Army in 1911 and was discharged soon after, but he was recalled to active duty when World War I broke out. He served in the artillery and was wounded by shrapnel in the lower leg and by a lance thrust above his left

Table 5-1. THE ORDER OF BATTLE, ARMY GROUP B
JUNE 21, 1944

Panzer Group West (1)	British 2nd Army
LXXXVI Corps	Orne River Sector
716th Infantry Division	
346th Infantry Division	
7th Mortar Brigade	
KG Luck	
I SS Panzer Corps	Caen Sector
21st Panzer Division	
12th SS Panzer Division	
Panzer Lehr Division	
7th Army	
XXXXVII Panzer Corps	Caumont Gap
2nd Panzer Division	
17th SS Panzer Recon Battalion	U.S. 1st Army
Elements, 2nd SS Panzer Division	
II Parachute Corps	St.-Lô Sector
3rd Parachute Division	
Elements, 353rd Infantry Division	
Remnants, 30th Mobile Brigade	
KG, 352nd Infantry Division	
LXXXIV Corps	West Coast
17th SS Panzer Grenadier Division (2)	
6th Parachute Regiment	
Elements, 353rd Infantry Division	
KG, 265th Infantry Division	
KG, 77th Infantry Division	
KG, 91st Air Landing Division	
KG, 243rd Infantry Division	

Notes:
(1) Reactivated on June 29
(2) With KG, 275th Infantry Division, 635th Ost Battalion, and 7th Army Assault Battalion
    attached, but with its reconnaissance battalion detached to XXXXVII Panzer Corps
KG = Kampfgruppe (a battle group or a division at regimental or battle group strength.
Sources: Friedrich Hayn, *Die Invasion von Cotentin bis Falaise* (1954), pp. 69–71; Tessin, various volumes.

SS Colonel General Sepp Dietrich, the commander of the I SS Panzer Corps and 5th Panzer Army during the Normandy campaign. He later commanded the 6th Panzer (later SS Panzer) Army during the Battle of the Bulge and on the Eastern Front. He lacked any qualifications for these positions and was indeed a poor to mediocre commander (USNA)

eye. He fought on the Western Front throughout the war, was wounded a third time, and ended up in one of Germany's few tank units. At one point, he rescued a bottle of schnapps from a burning panzer while under enemy fire. After the war, he fought with the Freikorps and joined the Bavarian *Landespolizei* (provincial police) and the Nazi Party. He went on leave and paid his own way to Annasberg, where he fought against the Polish military for free. Dietrich took part in the Beer Hall Putsch of 1923 on the side of the Nazis, which accounts for his sudden dismissal from the police. He worked at various jobs in Munich from 1924 to 1929 and, in the meantime, joined the SS. He became Hitler's bodyguard and one of the Führer's favorites at this time. He was selected to be a member of the Reichstag in 1930 and an *SS-Gruppenführer* (major general) in 1931. In March 1933 Dietrich organized the Leibstandarte SS Adolf Hitler unit. It eventually grew from 117 men into the 1st SS Panzer Division, with a strength of 21,000 men. Dietrich commanded it for ten years, fighting in Poland (1939), the West (1940), and Russia (1941–43). In late 1941 he flatly told Hitler that he had been wrong to fire Field Marshal Gerd von Rundstedt as commander in chief of Army Group South. As a result, Hitler named Rundstedt commander in chief of OB West in March 1942. (Rundstedt later described Dietrich as "decent but stupid.") In July 1943 Dietrich became the commander of the I SS Panzer Corps.

Sepp Dietrich was a poor to mediocre tactical commander who had a marked tendency to commit his reserves prematurely and at the wrong places. He was not qualified for corps or higher command either by inclination or education, of which he had little. These weaknesses, however, were partially offset and sometimes neutralized by a good, hardheaded Bavarian common sense and an undeniable talent for choosing talented subordinates, on whom he rightly relied a great deal.

✦

On June 25 the British XXX Corps attack was met by the much-reduced Panzer Lehr Division, which checked it at Fontenay Ridge with bitter hand-to-hand fighting. Just as Montgomery hoped, Dietrich committed his reserves to this sector. When Montgomery's main blow fell on the 12th SS Panzer Engineer Battalion of the 12th SS Panzer Division at 7:00 a.m. on June 26, there was nothing left to support it. The entire 12th SS Panzer Engineer was overrun or surrounded, as was much of the 26th SS Panzer Grenadier Regiment. Fortunately, the engineer commander, SS Major Siegfried Müller, turned his headquarters into a strongpoint and significantly delayed the British before he managed to escape with his last seven men. Other members of Kurt Meyer's Hitler Youth Division, which the English and Scots had bypassed, refused to surrender and became snipers in the British rear. At the front, the attitude was the same: self-sacrifice in the face of overwhelming odds. Even the divisional commander fought on the front line, personally firing an antitank gun.

Only the fanatical resistance of the teenage SS warriors slowed the Allied advance and gave the German generals time to salvage the situation. The bravery of these young men was worthy of a better cause.

For once, General Dollmann, the commander of the 7th Army, reacted quickly and correctly. He committed his reserves to the threatened sector. These included three battalions of the 2nd SS Panzer Division, a battle group from the 21st Panzer Division, the entire 7th Mortar Brigade, and most of the 8th Mortar Brigade. Dietrich, meanwhile, was able to recall part of his reserves in the form of the Tigers of the 101st Heavy Panzer Battalion.

German resistance was fierce, and losses on both sides were heavy, but the Allies could afford them; the Germans could not. By June 27 the 12th SS Panzer Division was down to a strength of fifty-six operational tanks—25 percent of its authorized strength. Panzer Lehr Division had fifty-three operational tanks on June 26. Three weeks before, this total stood at 190. And still the British 11th Armoured Division pushed on toward Hill 112. Late on June 28, however,

A staged photograph of a German sniper in Normandy, complete with a pair of stick grenades at his elbow (Bundesarchiv).

Rommel was ready to play his trump card: the II SS Panzer Corps, which consisted of the 9th SS Panzer Division "Hohenstauffen" and SS Oberführer Heinz Harmel's 10th SS Panzer Division "Frundsberg" (see Map 11). The II SS Panzer, which had just been transferred from the Eastern Front, was commanded by General of Waffen-SS Paul Hausser.

✦

Paul Hausser, perhaps the single greatest influence of the military development of the Waffen-SS, was born in Brandenburg on October 7, 1880, the son of Major Kurt Hausser, a Prussian officer. He was educated in the cadet school at Köslin, Pomerania, and at Gross Lichterfelde (located in Berlin-Lichterfelde), from which he graduated in 1899. Günther von Kluge was one of his classmates. Hausser was assigned to the 155th (7th West Prussian) Infantry Regiment at Posen and served eight years of regimental duty. He attended the War Academy in Berlin (1908–11), became a member of the General Staff in 1912, and held

Map 11. The Epsom Offensive

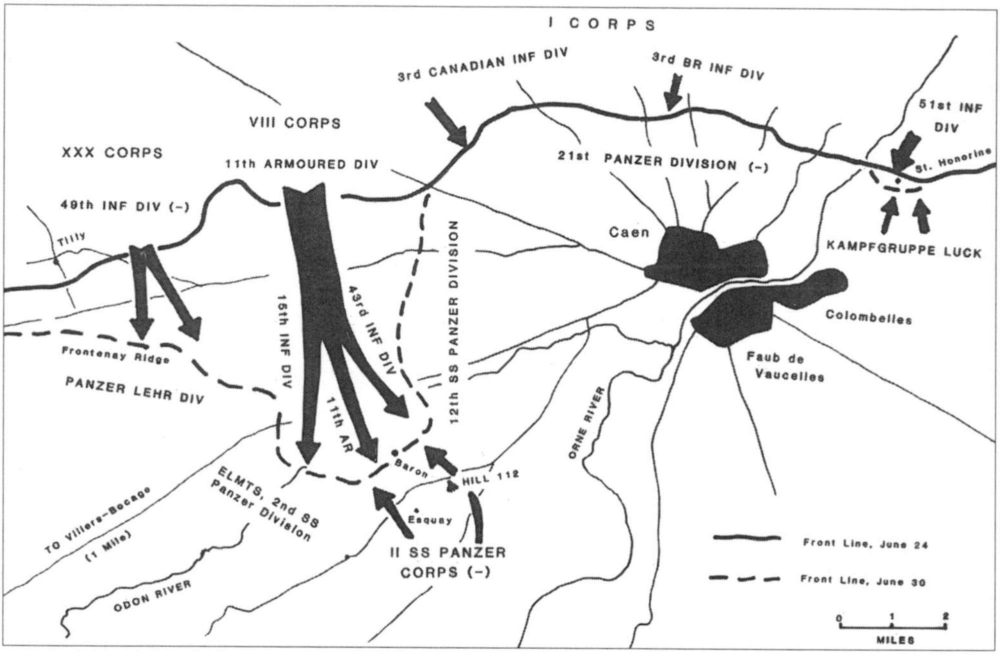

several General Staff positions during World War I, including Ia of the 109th Infantry Division (October 1916–January 1918), serving in Courland and Romania. He reportedly served with the Freikorps against the Poles after the war. Hausser married Elisabeth Gerard in 1912. They had one child, a daughter, born in late December 1913. He joined the Reichsheer in 1920 and held several positions of responsibility, including Ia of Wehrkreis II (1919–20), Ia of the 2nd Infantry Division (1920–22) (both in Stettin), company commander in the Prussian 5th Infantry Regiment (also in Stettin) (1922–23), commander of the III Battalion/4th Infantry Regiment at Deutsch Krone and Schneidemühl (1923–25), chief of staff of Wehrkreis II at Stettin (1925–27), commander of the Saxon 10th Infantry Regiment at Dresden (1927–30), and Infantry Commander IV and deputy commander of the 4th Infantry Division at Magdeburg. He retired from the Reichsheer as a major general in 1932, with an honorary promotion to lieutenant general.

An early Nazi by political conviction, he joined the SS as chief training officer for the SS-VT, the embryo of the Waffen-SS, in 1934 as an SS colonel. He was later promoted to *SS-Oberführer* (1935), SS major general (1936), SS lieutenant general (1939), general of Waffen-SS (October 1, 1941), and SS colonel general

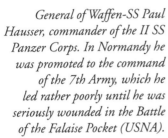

General of Waffen-SS Paul Hausser, commander of the II SS Panzer Corps. In Normandy he was promoted to the command of the 7th Army, which he led rather poorly until he was seriously wounded in the Battle of the Falaise Pocket (USNA).

(August 1, 1944). He soon became responsible for the military training of all SS troops except Theodor Eicke's "Death's Head" concentration camp guards. He was SS liaison officer to the army's ad hoc Panzer Division "Kempf" during the Polish campaign of 1939. In late 1939 Hausser was named commander of the SS-VT Division, which he led in France in 1940. This unit later became the 2nd SS Panzer Division "Das Reich," and Hausser led it until October 14, 1941, when he was badly wounded on the Eastern Front and lost his right eye. After he returned to active duty in late May 1942, he was named commander of the SS Panzer Corps (later II SS Panzer Corps), which he led on the Eastern Front in 1943–44, with uneven results.

Hausser renounced his Protestant religion in 1940 and declared himself "*Gottgläubig*" (a believer in God). This was the Nazis's "politically correct" version of a Christian—one who did not live his religion and who rarely (if ever) went to church.

Paul Hausser arrived in the Hill 112 area during the night of June 28–29, and by morning most of his corps' combat units were ready to counterattack Montgomery's British 2nd Army. Hausser, however, was an eastern general. Unfamiliar with how to deal with an enemy's complete aerial dominance, he did not maintain radio discipline, he assembled his strike forces too close together, and he did not properly camouflage them. As a result, Montgomery and his officers were able to identify Hausser's location. On June 29 the II SS Panzer Corps was blasted with massive aerial, artillery, and naval artillery bombardments. By the time Hausser and his men regained their balance, Hill 112 had fallen. Meanwhile, Erwin Rommel lost yet another senior commander.

Friedrich Dollmann's performance as commander of the 7th Army left much to be desired in 1944, especially on June 6, 1944, when his order to move the Panzer Lehr in daylight led to the division being decimated by Allied fighter-bombers long before it made contact with Allied ground forces. Although he was an early and fervent supporter of national socialism within the military, he later became deeply troubled by the Nazis' actions and had ceased to support them by 1944. Hitler wanted Rommel to relieve him of his command but the field marshal—who felt a sense of loyalty to Dollmann—refused to do so. On June 29, 1944, Hitler decided to sack Dollmann without Rommel's cooperation. The general, however, died of a heart attack at his command post at Le Mans, France, later that same day. Hitler had already issued orders relieving him of his command, but they had not yet reached him.

Rommel wanted to replace Dollmann with General of Infantry Kurt von der Chevallerie, a competent officer who was commanding the 1st Army in south-western France.[1] Hitler, however, had other ideas. Despite Hausser's varied performance as a corps commander in Russia and his failure at Hill 112, Adolf Hitler promoted him to the command of the 7th Army in Normandy. His performance did not improve. Still, his appointment as commander of the 7th Army did have one important, positive benefit for the German army in the West: it resulted in Wilhelm Bittrich being promoted to commander of the II SS Panzer Corps.

✦

Wilhelm Bittrich, the son of a German trade representative, was born on February 26, 1894, in Wernigerode-am-Harz. He joined the 19th Reserve Jäger Battalion when World War I broke out but transferred to the air service in the fall of 1914. Here he was wounded twice and ended the conflict as a second lieutenant and a fighter pilot. He was a member of the Freikorps von Hülsen in the early 1920s and fought against the Poles in the Eastern Marchlands. He joined the Reichsheer as a pilot in 1923 and trained German aviators in Russia in the 1920s. Later he was a civilian employee of the Luftwaffe, working as an instructor pilot, and was involved in training aviators at the secret German air base in Russia. He joined the Nazi Party in 1932 and entered the SS in July 1933. A member of the SS-VT, Bittrich was soon given command of a battalion (I/SS "Germania" Regiment) because of his solid and varied military background and was an SS Oberführer commanding the SS-Regiment Deutschland in late 1940. Later he was promoted to SS major general (October 19, 1941) and SS lieutenant general (May 1, 1943). He took charge of the 2nd SS Panzer Division after Paul Hausser was wounded in late 1941 but had to give it up after he fell ill in early January 1942. In May 1942 Bittrich assumed command of the 8th SS Cavalry Division "Florian Geyer," which he led against partisans in the Balkans until December. On February 15, 1943, he assumed command of the 9th SS Panzer Division "Hohenstaufen," which was just being formed. Bittrich assumed command of the II SS Panzer Corps when Hausser was elevated to the command of the 7th Army on June 29, 1944. He was temporarily succeeded as commander of the 9th SS Panzer Division by SS Colonel Thomas Müller, who had previously commanded the 20th SS Panzer Grenadier Regiment.

◆

Headquarters, Panzer Group West, was reactivated on June 29 and assumed command of the vital (right) flank of the German defenses in Normandy. Rommel assigned the less important left flank to Hausser's 7th Army. (If the left flank collapsed, the Third Reich would lose part of the 7th Army and much of France. If the right flank collapsed, Germany would lose France, Paris, most of Army Group B, and quite possibly the entire war. This is why Rommel concentrated his panzer divisions on the right throughout his tenure as commander in chief of Army Group B.)[2] His first orders to Geyr were to counterattack and recapture Hill 112. Geyr naturally delegated this task to Bittrich, with his two relatively fresh SS panzer divisions.

On June 30, his first full day as a corps commander, Bittrich scored a major success when he recaptured Hill 112 from the British 29th Armoured Brigade; meanwhile, a few miles to the west, Panzer Lehr beat back attacks from the British 49th and 50th Infantry and 2nd Armoured divisions.

Throughout this battle, a major gap existed in German lines west of Hill 112. Rommel was aware of this gap (called the Caumont Gap) but could not do anything about it. On June 30, however, the introduction of the II SS Panzer Corps into the German line of battle made a kampfgruppe from the 2nd SS Panzer Division available. Geyr was also able to pull the nearly exhausted Panzer

Lehr out of the line. Rommel sent both units to the Caumont Gap. He placed them under the command of General of Panzer Troops Baron Hans von Funck's XXXXVII Panzer Corps.

✦

Sylvester Stadler was born in Steiermark, Austria, on December 30, 1910. In his late teens he attended a technical school and became an electrician. At the age of twenty-three, he joined the Austrian SS, which sent him to Nazi Germany for further training. He attended the SS Junkerschule (Officers' Training School) at Bad Tölz and earned his commission. In 1939 he fought in Poland with Panzer Division "Kempf," a mixed ad hoc force of army and SS men, for which Stadler commanded the signals company. In 1940 he was a company commander in the "Der Führer" SS Motorized Infantry Regiment during the campaign in the West and in the early weeks of Operation Barbarossa, the invasion of the Soviet Union. He was named commander of the II Battalion/"Deutschland" SS Motorized Infantry Regiment in September 1941.[3] Stadler was wounded shortly thereafter and, because he was unfit for field duty, was used as an instructor at the Bad Tölz and Brunswick SS war schools. In March 1942 he returned to Russia as a company commander. Shortly thereafter, he assumed command of the II Battalion of the "Der Führer" Regiment. In this position he distinguished himself in the Second Battle of Kharkov (May 1942) and earned the Knights' Cross. In June 1943 he was given command of "Der Führer" and led it in the Battle of Kursk and in the Mius River battles.

Thomas Müller commanded the 9th SS Panzer Division "Hohenstaufen" until July 10, when Stadler arrived as the new permanent divisional commander. Stadler earned a reputation as a good divisional commander in the hedgerow fighting on the Caen sector of the Normandy Front. He was wounded in action on July 10 but returned to duty five days later. He was again wounded on July 31—more seriously, this time—and did not resume his command until after the fall of France.

Stadler's chief of operations with the 9th SS Panzer Division was Walter Harzer.

✦

The son of a building inspector, **Walter Harzer** was born in Stuttgart on September 29, 1912. He studied construction engineering at a higher technical school but joined the Nazi Party in 1930 and the SS in late 1931. After briefly serving in the army, he attended the SS Junker School at Bad Tölz and was commissioned in the SS in 1936. He commanded a company in Poland, was an instructor at Brunswick from late 1939 to 1941, and led an SS infantry battalion on the Eastern Front from June 1941 to May 1942. After undergoing an abbreviated General Staff training program, Harzer became Ib of the 9th SS Panzer Division "Hohenstaufen" in February 1943. He became divisional Ia in April 1944.

Harzer performed well in Normandy and became commander of the remnants of the division in September 1944. (Stadler was still in the hospital with wounds; temporary divisional commander SS Colonel Friedrich-Wilhelm Bock was with the rest of the division, which had already moved back to Siegen in Germany.) Harzer was later to distinguish himself in the Battle of Arnhem.

Heinz Harmel was born in Metz on June 29, 1906, the son of a doctor. While working as a civil servant, he joined the Nazi Party in 1926 and became an SS man in 1935. By early 1937 he was an SS second lieutenant and platoon leader, and in early 1941 he was on the staff of the II Battalion, "Der Führer" SS Motorized Regiment. He rose rapidly during the campaigns in the East and, in October 1942, was commander of the SS "Deutschland" Motorized Regiment. On May 1, 1944, Harmel was given command of the 10th SS Panzer Division "Frundsberg" and was promoted to SS-Oberführer eighteen days later.

Like most of the leaders in the II SS Panzer Corps, Harmel did well in the Battle of Hill 112 and in the ensuing fighting in the bocage country. Another officer who distinguished himself in Normandy was Fritz Krämer, Sepp Dietrich's Ia, who did much to make up for the deficiencies of his commander.

Fritz Krämer was born in Stettin, Pomerania, on December 12, 1900, and joined the army just after the end of World War I. He was discharged about 1920 and joined the Prussian police, where he served until 1934, when he reentered the army as a first lieutenant. He attended the War Academy almost immediately, graduated in 1936, and became a company commander in the 55th Infantry Regiment (1936–39). He served on the staff of the 13th Motorized Infantry Division in Poland and France (1939–40) and became its Ia on October 11, 1940, the same day the division became the 13th Panzer Division. He served in this post until August 1, 1943, when he was attached to the SS as an Oberführer. In the meantime he earned the Knight's Cross and promotions to lieutenant colonel (1942) and colonel (January 1, 1943). He served as chief of staff of the I SS Panzer Corps under Sepp Dietrich (1943–44). Krämer permanently transferred to the

SS in 1944 and was promoted to *Brigadeführer und Generalmajor der Waffen-SS* on August 1, 1944.

One of the few really capable General Staff officers in the SS, Fritz Krämer did a brilliant job in Normandy. He became acting commander of the I SS Panzer Corps on August 9, the day Sepp Dietrich moved up to the command of the 5th Panzer Army. He held the post until August 16, when General of Waffen-SS Georg Keppler arrived to take permanent command of the corps. Krämer returned to his job as chief of staff of the I SS Panzer Corps.

✦

Georg Keppler, the son of an army colonel, was born in Mainz on May 7, 1884. He followed in his father's footsteps and joined the army as a Fahnenjunker in 1913. Commissioned in the 73rd Fusilier Regiment in June 1914, he was wounded in action at St.-Quentin, France, on August 29. Following his recovery, he served on the staffs of the 39th Infantry Brigade and the 19th Reserve Division and was wounded twice more. Not selected for the Reichsheer, he joined the State Police in Hanover in 1920. Later he transferred to Thuringia and Jena. Keppler joined the NSDAP in 1930 and rejoined the army in briefly in 1935, before transferring to the SS-VT as an SS major in the fall of 1935. He commanded a battalion in the Deutschland Regiment before becoming the first commander of the "Der Führer" Regiment in Vienna in 1938. After leading it in the western campaign of 1940 and in the early stages of the Russian campaign, Keppler became acting commander of the "Totenkopf" SS Division on July 15, 1941. When the division's permanent commander recovered from his wounds and returned, Keppler was named temporary commander the "Nord" SS Division, but he soon fell ill with a brain tumor. He was not able to return to duty until the spring of 1942, when he assumed command of the 2nd SS Panzer Grenadier Division "Das Reich," which was rebuilding in France. Keppler's tumor flared up again, and he was hospitalized or on medical leave from February until the end of August 1943. When he returned to active duty, Keppler was named commander of the Waffen-SS District Bohemia and Moravia. From April to August 1944 he was commander of Waffen-SS in Hungary. Meanwhile, he was promoted to SS lieutenant general (April 1, 1942) and general of Waffen-SS (June 21, 1944).

Keppler temporarily replaced Sepp Dietrich as commander of the I SS Panzer Corps in France from August 16 to October 24, 1944, and fought in the Battle of the Falaise Pocket and at Mons. He led the corps out of France; then he was replaced by General of Waffen-SS Hermann Priess, who led it for the rest of the war.

✦

Field Marshal von Rundstedt, the OB West, pretty much allowed Rommel to conduct the defense of Normandy on his own and also backed Rommel's sound military ideas against Hitler on every occasion. By the beginning of July, however, the floodgates were creaking on the Western Front, and it was obvious to every senior commander that the Allies would eventually crack the thin German line in Normandy and break out to the south, overrunning France in the process. Rundstedt had a telephone conversation with Hitler's lackey, Field Marshal Wilhelm Keitel, the commander in chief of OKW.

"What can we do, what can we do?" Keitel moaned.

"Make peace, you fools! What else can you do?" Rundstedt snapped, just before he slammed the telephone down in Keitel's ear. The OKW chief immediately informed the Führer of Rundstedt's defeatist attitude. The old marshal was retired again on July 2, 1944. As he left, Gerd von Rundstedt thanked God that he would not have to preside over the coming military disaster.[4] He was succeeded by Günther von Kluge. (Map 12 shows the Normandy Front on July 1, the day before he took charge.)

✦

Map 12. The Normandy Front, July 1, 1944

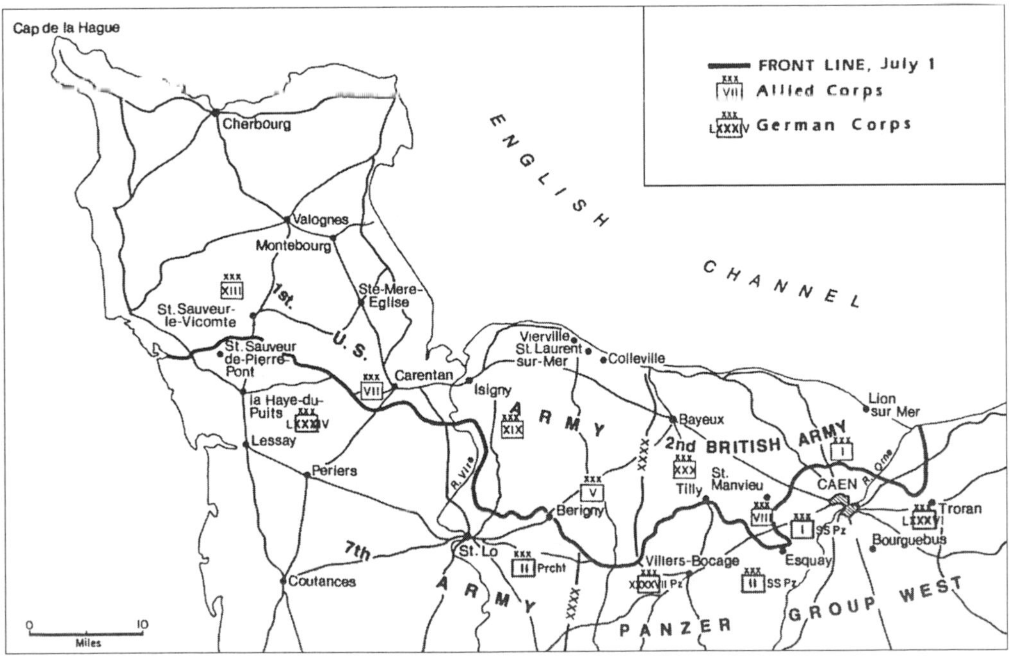

Günther "Hans" von Kluge was born in Posen, Prussia, on October 30, 1882. He attended the cadet schools, joined the Imperial Army as a Fähnrich in 1900 and was commissioned in the 46th Field Artillery Regiment at Wolfenbüttel in 1901. He spent several years as adjutant of the II Battalion before being sent to the War Academy to undergo General Staff training in 1908. He was promoted to first lieutenant in 1910 and, after graduating in 1911, was attached to the Greater General Staff until 1914, when he was sent to war as adjutant of the XXI Corps (1914–15). He later led a battalion on the Western Front (November 1915–April 1916) before returning to General Staff assignments with the 89th and 236th Infantry Divisions. He fought at Artois and in Flanders and was seriously wounded at Verdun in October 1918. After the war, he served on the staff of the army's Peace Commission (1919–21), on the staff of the 3rd Infantry Division in Berlin (1921–23), on the staff of the Training Department in the Defense Ministry (1923–26), as commander of the V Battalion/3rd Artillery Regiment at Sagan (now Zagan, Poland) (1926–28), and as chief of operations of the 1st Cavalry Division at Frankfurt/Oder (1928–30). In 1930 he succeeded Baron Werner von Fritsch as commander of the 2nd Artillery Regiment, and the following year he became Artillery Commander III (*Artillerieführer III*) and deputy commander of the 3rd Infantry Division. In February 1933 he was promoted to major general and was named inspector of signal troops. The next year he was promoted to lieutenant general and became commander of the VI Military District (*Wehrkreis VI*) and the 6th Infantry Division in Münster. He was promoted to general of artillery in 1936.

Kluge disliked the Nazis and their methods and was appalled by their treatment of the Jews. He was firmly on the side of Baron von Fritsch, the commander in chief of the army, during the Blomberg-Fritsch crisis of early 1938, but for once he had miscalculated politically. Fritsch was dismissed as commander in chief of the army on false charges of homosexuality, and Kluge narrowly escaped forced retirement after the dictator replaced Fritsch with Walter von Brauchitsch on February 4. Kluge nevertheless became commander of Army Group 6 in November 1938. His new command was headquartered in Hanover and controlled Wehrkreise IX, X, and XI in northern Germany. In August 1939, just before the war began, Army Group 6 became 4th Army.

Kluge was not Hitler's first choice for this post, but, for once, the Nazi leader allowed himself to be overruled by his military experts, although he made it clear to Kluge that he was on probation. To Hitler's surprise, Kluge led his army very well in Poland, before he was severely injured in an airplane crash near the end of the campaign. Hitler promoted him to colonel general effective October 1, 1939.

General von Kluge was shocked and horrified in late 1939, when he learned that Reinhard Heydrich and his security groups were murdering Jewish civilians in Poland. Unlike Johannes Blaskowitz, who ruined his career by protesting, Kluge remained discreetly silent, although he inched closer to joining the anti-Hitler conspiracy. He would vacillate on this issue for several more years but was eventually deterred by the Führer's power, his immense popularity, and the loyalty oath he (and all of the German officers) had sworn to Adolf Hitler. He also relished the glory, promotions, decorations, and monetary rewards bestowed on him by the Führer.

After Kluge returned to the command of the 4th Army, he led it in the western (French) campaign of 1940, during which he demonstrated surprising daring and innovation. Hitler, who was by now convinced that his previous misgivings about Kluge had been misplaced, promoted him to field marshal on July 19, 1940.

The following year Kluge led 4th Army in Operation Barbarossa. (He was one of the few German generals to favor the invasion.) Here he proved a much better commander of infantry than of armor, which earned him the censure of both Hermann Hoth, the commander of the 3rd Panzer Army, and Heinz Guderian, commander of the 2nd Panzer Army. When the German army stalled before Moscow, Kluge was given command of Army Group Center on December 18, 1941, replacing Fedor von Bock. Here he demonstrated a talent for surviving politically, escaping blame for disasters, extracting revenge, and finding scapegoats. Colonel Seaton later wrote, "If scapegoats were needed, von Kluge could find them; if heads must fall, von Kluge took good care to see that his would not be among them."[5] Among others, he fired Colonel General Adolf Strauss, the commander of the 9th Army; Colonel General Erich Höpner, the commander of the 4th Panzer Army; and General of Mountain Troops Ludwig Kübler, who had succeeded him as commander of the 4th Army. Most notably, he secured the dismissal of his old enemy, Colonel General Heinz Guderian, the father of the blitzkrieg, who commanded the 2nd Panzer Army in Russia and who was relieved on December 25, 1941. (Kluge and Guderian hated each other, and Guderian had once challenged Kluge to a duel, before cooler heads intervened.) In justice to Kluge, however, it must be noted that he was usually able to obtain Führer approval for the necessary withdrawals in the winter of 1941–42, even if Hitler gave permission only with the greatest reluctance.

Largely thanks to General Model, the commander of the 9th Army, Kluge managed to stabilize the German line in early 1942. Later that year he conducted a brilliant deception campaign and convinced the Soviets (including Stalin) that the German main offensive that summer would be directed at Moscow. It was, in fact, aimed at the Volga, Stalingrad, and the Caucasus oil fields. Hitler was obviously pleased with Kluge's performance because he sent him a check for 250,000 Reichsmarks that October.

During the winter of 1942–43, Army Group Center fought several severe defensive battles. It lost Velikiye Luki and its seven thousand–man garrison but generally managed to hold its positions.

In the upper echelons of the army, Kluge was nicknamed *"Der kluge Hans"*—which means "Clever Hans," a play on words with his name and his ability to be on both sides of an issue. No better example of this character flaw can be found than his attitude toward Operation Citadelle, the Kursk offensive of 1943. Kluge arrived at Führer Headquarters in May 1943, firmly in favor of delaying the offensive. Then he learned that Hitler had already decided to postpone the attack. When he met with Hitler later that day, he spoke out strongly *against* delaying the offensive, so that he would avoid any future blame if the offensive failed—which it did. To further insulate himself from blame, he assigned the task of launching the northern pincer (Army Group Center's portion of the offensive) to Colonel General Model and had as little to do with the offensive himself as was possible. After the attack began on July 5, 1943, Kluge was one of the first to call for a suspension of the offensive.

His attitude toward the anti-Hitler conspiracy was similar. He gave non-committal encouragement to the conspirators but would never commit himself 100 percent to their cause. This was typical of the man. His chief of operations, the extremely capable Colonel Henning von Treschow, was at first hopeful that he could enlist Kluge in the plot but eventually became disillusioned. In March 1943, with Kluge's cooperation, Treschow managed to lure Hitler to the headquarters of Army Group Center for the purposes of assassinating him. However, when Kluge learned that Treschow intended for a group of officers to shoot Hitler at lunch, the field marshal forbade it, on the grounds that it would be dishonorable for officers to murder their supreme commander in this way. Treschow and his confederates went ahead without Der kluge Hans by placing a bomb aboard Hitler's airplane, but it failed to explode. Treschow was fortunate that one of his aides was able to recover the bomb before the Nazis discovered it.[6] General von Treschow committed suicide by blowing himself up with hand grenades on July 21, 1944, the day after the conspiracy failed.

After the failure of the Kursk offensive, Kluge faced massive attacks from the Red Army. Despite his vacillating character, Günther von Kluge did possess a considerable amount of professional skill. He was able to slow down the surging Soviets but not to stop them. Kluge gradually retreated to the Hagen line, along the Dnieper, on August 17. Three days later OKH took five divisions from him and sent them to Army Group South. Kluge protested, stating that he could not guarantee that he would be able to hold the line without these divisions, but Manstein's situation in the south was even more desperate than Kluge's. The transfer of units went forward, and the Soviets broke through the Hagen line on August 29, just as Kluge had predicted. As of September 7, Kluge had only 108 tanks and 191 assault guns left. Bryansk fell on September 17, and Smolensk and Roslavl were lost a week later. Kluge continued to retreat toward the Panther line in Belorussia. The following month he lost Gomel and Nevel but was generally able to check the Soviets everywhere.

Kluge led Army Group Center until October 28, 1943, when his car (which was trying to avoid a Soviet fighter) skidded on some ice, and he was seriously injured in the ensuing crash. He did not return to active duty for eight months. Earmarked for a command on the Western Front, he spent several days at the Führer's headquarters in Berchtesgaden, during which he acquired an overly optimistic view of the situation in Normandy. On July 2, 1944, he succeeded Gerd von Rundstedt as OB West. He immediately clashed with Erwin Rommel, the commander of Army Group B, who saw the situation as it was. The argument became so violent that Kluge ordered everyone to leave the room except himself and the field marshal. Even after Kluge adopted Rommel's views, the friction between the two remained.

Rommel conducted a brilliant defensive campaign in Normandy in 1944. Seeing the handwriting on the wall and realizing that Hitler was a criminal who was dragging Germany down to defeat, he joined the anti-Hitler conspiracy. Despite being outnumbered roughly 3 to 1, Rommel nevertheless kept the Allies in check until July 17, when he was critically wounded by an Allied fighter-bomber. Initially, he was not expected to live. After he regained consciousness and partially recovered, he returned home to Germany. One of the great captains of world military history, he never exercised command again.

Field Marshal Hans von Kluge did not interfere with Rommel's conduct of operations in Normandy. When Rommel was wounded, however, Kluge assumed the post of commander in chief of Army Group B himself because he was afraid Hitler might appoint SS Colonel General Paul Hausser to the vacancy. Kluge knew Hausser from their days as cadets at Gross Lichterfeldt and had little respect for his abilities—a correct view, as subsequent events proved.

Kluge was an on-again, off-again anti-Hitler conspirator. However, there were other, more principled men in the Paris area who had less difficulty making up their minds about Hitler and the Nazis. Among them was Carl-Heinrich von Stülpnagel, the military governor of France.

Carl-Heinrich von Stülpnagel, the son of Lieutenant General Hermann von Stülpnagel (1839–1912), was born in Berlin on January 2, 1886. He entered the service as a Fahnenjunker in the 115th Infantry Regiment in 1904, was commissioned in January 1906, and was promoted to first lieutenant in 1913 and to captain in 1915. He was regimental adjutant when World War I began and fought in Luxemburg, in the Ardennes, and on the Marne and the Somme. In March 1915 he became a General Staff officer and was assigned to the IV Reserve Corps. He later fought in Serbia, in Macedonia, and on the Western Front, and he ended the war as chief of operations of the 18th Infantry Division. He joined the Freikorps in "the war after the war" and helped put down Communist revolts in the Ruhr and Silesia. He joined the Reichswehr and was on the General Staff of the VI Infantry Command (1922–24), was a company commander in the

General of Infantry Carl-Heinrich von Stülpnagel, the military governor of France. He was hanged on August 30, 1944, for his part in the conspiracy to assassinate Adolf Hitler and overthrow the Nazi regime.

Prussian 3rd Infantry Regiment at Deutsch-Eylau (1924–26), and served in the army organization branch in the Defense Ministry (1926–27). Clearly a Prussian general in training, Stülpnagel became Ia of the 6th Infantry Division at Münster, Westphalia (1927), and commander of the II/5th Infantry Regiment at Stettin (1929); was on the Army General Staff in Berlin (1931); and commanded the 30th Infantry Division in Lübeck (1936–1938). Returning to Berlin, he became chief of the operations staff of OKH in 1939. His promotions had come regularly: major (1925), lieutenant colonel (1930), colonel (1932), major general (1935), lieutenant general (1937), and general of infantry (1939). On May 5, 1940, he took the next step on the professional ladder when he assumed command of the II Corps during the French campaign. It soon became obvious, however, that Stülpnagel could not effectively lead a corps. He was replaced after three weeks and was appointed to the Franco-German Armistice Commission.

OKH and the Army General Staff saw Stülpnagel's poor performance as a corps commander in France as an aberration. He was therefore named commander of the 17th Army on February 15, 1941, and led it on the Russian Front. His performance again was poor, and he was relieved of his command by Field Marshal von Brauchitsch, the commander in chief of the Army, on November 25, 1941—a move that effectively ruined his career. Thanks to Franz Halder, the chief of the General Staff, he was named military governor of France on February 13, 1942, but he was in a dead-end job.[7]

◆

Stülpnagel had detested Hitler and the Nazis since the 1930s. As a military commander, he did perhaps the best planning of his career in Paris, where he was the leader of the anti-Hitler conspiracy in the West.

Shortly after noon on July 20, 1944, Colonel Claus von Stauffenberg placed a bomb under Hitler's map table and left the room. It exploded a few minutes later. Unlike the case in Berlin—or anywhere else— Stülpnagel and his confederates actually succeeded in seizing control of the city. He arrested the Gestapo, the general SS, the SD, and other senior Nazi officials. By late afternoon, twelve hundred Nazis were under lock and key, and some of Stülpnagel's security men were actually piling up sandbags in the courtyard of the École Militaire, where the executions were going to take place. Unfortunately, the coup in Berlin was collapsing. Hitler, it turned out, was not dead—only wounded. At 6:15 p.m., Stülpnagel received a call from Field Marshal von Kluge's headquarters, asking him and his chief of staff, Luftwaffe Lieutenant Colonel Caesar von Hofacker,

A pregnant moment in the history of World War II: Adolf Hitler shakes hands with an officer while Colonel Count Claus von Stauffenberg (left) looks on. Stauffenberg has a bomb in his briefcase. This photo was probably taken on July 17, 1944, and is believed to be the last photograph of the colonel ever taken. Three days later, Stauffenberg detonated the bomb under Hitler's map table but failed to kill the Führer. This sealed the fate of Erwin Rommel, Günther von Kluge, and several other generals of the Western Front. Field Marshal Wilhelm Keitel, the commander in chief of the High Command of the Armed Forces, is on the right (USNA).

to come to La-Roche-Guyon for an important conference, which was to begin at 8:00 p.m.

The field marshal arrived back from a trip to the front at 6:00 p.m. After making several telephone calls, Kluge determined that Hitler was still alive. He was in a good mood when he met with General von Stülpnagel and listened patiently to Hofacker's passionate appeal for him to break with the Führer and assume leadership of the anti-Nazi movement in the West. Kluge then happily informed the military governor that the coup had failed and invited the four officers from Paris to join him for dinner. (Stülpnagel had brought his aide, Hofacker and Dr. Max Horst [General Hans Speidel's brother-in-law and a member of Stülpnagel's staff]). Also present were General Blumentritt, the chief of staff of OB West, and General Speidel, the chief of staff of Army Group B. Speidel later recalled that the candlelight-and-wine affair—which was taking place less than sixty miles from the Normandy Front—was like dining in the house of the dead. Only the cheerful Kluge spoke.

Before the meal was over, Stülpnagel asked to speak with Kluge alone. They adjourned to an adjoining room, where he shattered Kluge's good mood. He told the marshal that the entire SS/SD apparatus in Paris was under lock and key. Dinner resumed, but in total silence.

After dinner, about 11:00 p.m., Kluge relieved Stülpnagel of his duties as military governor of France and, as he walked him to his car, advised him to get into civilian clothes and disappear. Stülpnagel, however, said that he could not leave his fellow conspirators in the lurch; he was returning to Paris instead.

"If only the swine were dead!" Kluge snapped.

Hofacker seized the moment to make another appeal to Kluge's patriotism, but the OB West would have none of it.[8]

Meanwhile, Hofacker's cousin, Colonel Count von Stauffenberg, called from Berlin and declared that the coup had failed and that his executioners were literally beating on his door. He was shot shortly thereafter.

At 1:37 a.m. on July 21, Admiral Krancke, the commander of Naval Group West, signaled Stülpnagel that he knew what was happening in Paris and would march on the city with a thousand marines if the military governor did not release the SS and SD men immediately. When he received his dispatch at 2:00 a.m., General von Stülpnagel dissolved the revolt.

Meanwhile, almost as soon as his guests left la-Roche-Guyon, Kluge sent a message to Hitler, calling the conspirators of July 20 "ruthless murderers" and assuring the Führer of his own "unchangeable loyalty."[9]

Günther von Kluge tried to cover up his previous sympathy for and weak support of the conspiracy, but it was too late. The Gestapo arrested Colonel von Hofacker on July 26. Since his own guilt was easily proved, Hofacker averred that he alone was responsible for the revolt in Paris; he broke under prolonged and brutal torture by the Gestapo, however, and eventually implicated both Kluge and Rommel.[10] Within the next few days, several of Kluge's former officers in Russia went over to the Soviets or committed suicide.

From this point on Kluge was walking a tightrope. "After July 20," author John Keegan wrote, the field marshal was forced "to play the super-loyalist for the sake of self-preservation."[11] Kluge did not fail to notice that Hitler's dispatches became more and more pointed and insulting. For Kluge, there was now more at stake than winning or losing the battle—his own life was in the balance. He dared not fail or disappoint the Führer again. He had to try to carry out his orders, no matter how irrational or out of touch with reality they seemed. This is the attitude that characterized every move he made during the decisive days of late July and August 1944 and indeed that shaped the entire German battle plan as disaster finally overtook the defenders of Fortress Europe.

Meanwhile, Carl-Heinrich von Stülpnagel was summoned to Berlin on July 21 to explain why he had arrested more than a thousand Nazi officials the day before. He drank heavily that night and had loud, irrational conversations with himself. The next day he set out by car for Germany. Near Verdun, where he had distinguished himself as a junior officer in World War I, he got out of the car and ordered his driver and his aide to continue without him. He wanted to visit the battlefields of his youth, he said, and told them to meet him in the next village. They were concerned about partisans, but the general insisted. After they left, he ripped off his Nazi era decorations, waded into the Meuse Canal, and shot himself. He destroyed both of his eyes but did not kill himself. His aide and driver heard the shot and, assuming he had been ambushed by partisans, pulled his unconscious body out of the canal and carried him to a hospital. Here, in delirium and with Gestapo agents by the side of his bed, he called out Rommel's name several times and implicated the field marshal in the conspiracy. After he regained consciousness, however, he implicated no one else—not even Kluge— except people who were already known to be guilty or who were already dead.

General of Infantry Carl-Heinrich von Stülpnagel was expelled from the army by the so-called Court of Honor and was hanged by piano wire at the Berlin-Plötzensee prison on August 30, 1944.

Back in Normandy, the Americans muscled their way into the important crossroads town of St.-Lô, and Montgomery finally took Caen—six weeks behind schedule.

6

St.-Lô

On the German left flank, the numerically superior U.S. 1st Army pounded Hausser's 7th Army for days on end. Its object was the crossroads town of St.-Lô, defended by the II Parachute Corps, which included the 3rd Parachute Division and the 352nd Infantry Division, with the 12th Assault Gun Brigade in support. (Why the 12th was called a brigade is a bit of a mystery. Like all of the German assault gun brigades, it had the strength of a battalion. An assault gun brigade was rarely commanded by anyone over the rank of major.)

The task of defending St.-Lô fell primarily to three men: Richard Schimpf, the commander of the 3rd Parachute Division; Eugen Meindl, the commander of the II Parachute Corps; and Dietrich Kraiss, the commander of the 352nd Infantry Division.

✦

Richard Schimpf was born on May 16, 1897, in Eggenfelden, Lower Bavaria. He joined the army as a cadet in 1915 and was commissioned a year later into the Bavarian 9th Infantry Regiment of the Bavarian 4th Infantry Division and fought on the Somme, in Flanders, and in northern France. He became a platoon leader, company commander, and battalion adjutant and was wounded at least once. He joined the Reichsheer and spent five years as a platoon leader in the 21st Infantry Regiment at Nuremberg (1920–25) before being promoted to first lieutenant (1925), undergoing flight training, secret General Staff training, and photographic officer training until 1929, when he officially retired. In reality Schimpf worked at the Scientific Research and Testing Institute at the secret German aviation base at Lipezk in the Soviet Union. Returning to Germany in 1930, he enrolled in the Berlin Technical University and graduated with an advanced engineering degree while simultaneously working at the Army Weapons Office. He transferred to the Luftwaffe on February 1, 1935—five weeks before it was legalized. He initially commanded a reconnaissance squadron and the Münster Air Base. He also served in the Reichs Aviation Ministry (RLM). He was promoted rapidly in the Luftwaffe: major (1935), lieutenant colonel (1937), colonel (October 1, 1939), major general (March 18, 1943), and lieutenant general (August 1, 1943)—five promotions in less than nine years.

In early 1940 Schimpf became Ia to the Luftwaffe general attached to Army Group A in the West. He became chief of staff of 4th Air Fleet in November 1940 and, from February 1941 to September 1942, was chief of staff of several Luftwaffe territorial commands in the East, including Kiev and Kharkov. On September 27, 1942, he was given command of the 21st Luftwaffe Field Division, which he led on the northern sector of the Eastern Front for more than a year. He was in Führer Reserve from October 1943 to February 1944. The records do not indicate whether he was wounded or ill. In any case he was given command of the 3rd Parachute Division on February 17, 1944.[1]

Schimpf led the 3rd Parachute Division in Normandy with great effectiveness, despite heavy odds against it, and repelled several major American attacks. He was seriously wounded on August 20, during the Falaise breakout. His men carried him off the field on a repaired armored personnel carrier.

✦

Eugen Meindl was born on July 16, 1892, in Donaueschingen, Baden. His father was a forestry official for the prince of Fürstenberg. After school, Meindl joined the 67th (2nd Lower Alsace) Field Artillery Regiment in Hagenau as a Fahnenjunker in 1912. He was commissioned second lieutenant on February 17, 1914. A fine athlete, he competed in the 1914 Olympics in track and field. He was also an excellent skier, mountain climber, and horseman. For relaxation, he did wood carvings and painted. During World War I, he was a platoon and battery commander and a regimental adjutant on the Western Front. He also served as adjutant of the 52nd Artillery Command and as a balloon observer; he was shot down three times.

Meindl was retained in the Reichsheer, serving as a battery officer in the 13th Artillery Regiment in Magdeburg (1919–20) and the 5th Artillery Regiment in Ulm (1920–24). He underwent secret General Staff training from 1924 to 1927. He returned to the 5th Artillery as a staff officer (1927–28), commanded a squadron in the 5th Transport Battalion (1928–29), returned to the staff of the 5th Artillery (1929–30), and served as regimental adjutant (1930–33). He had, in the meantime, been promoted to first lieutenant (1917) and captain (1924). He became a major in 1934.

Meindl was an instructor at the Artillery School at Jüterbog from 1933 to October 15, 1935, when he became commander of the I Battalion of his old regiment, the 5th Artillery. Promoted to lieutenant colonel in 1936, he held this appointment until 1938, when he assumed command of the 112th Mountain Artillery Regiment in Austria. (This was the former 5th Light Artillery Regiment of the Austrian army, which was incorporated into the Wehrmacht earlier that year.) He was promoted to colonel on April 1, 1939.

Part of the 3rd Mountain Division, Meindl led his regiment in Poland and Norway, where he made a parachute jump at Narvik, even though he had no parachute training. Apparently he liked jumping out of airplanes, however. Later that year, on November 1, he transferred to the Luftwaffe and became commanding officer of the 1st Parachute Assault Regiment, which he led at Crete, where he was seriously wounded by a bullet in the chest. During the winter of 1941–42, Meindl created the first Luftwaffe field division, which was initially called Group Meindl. Eventually it became the 21st Luftwaffe Field Division. On October 1, 1942, he was named commander of the XIII Air Corps, the headquarters responsible for creating and organizing most of the twenty-two Luftwaffe field divisions. Later it was redesignated I Luftwaffe Field Corps, and it operated on the northern sector of the Eastern Front. Meindl, meanwhile, was promoted to major general (January 1, 1941) and lieutenant general (February 1, 1943). He became inspector of Luftwaffe field units on July 21, 1943, and, on November 5, 1943, was given command of the II Parachute Corps, which was then in Italy. He was promoted to general of parachute troops on April 1, 1944.

◆

Throughout World War II, Meindl was noted for both his competence and his arrogance. He led his II Parachute Corps in the Normandy campaign, where it formed the right flank of the 7th Army (LXXXIV Corps formed the left) and was responsible for defending St.-Lô. He and his corps fought brilliantly and tenaciously against overwhelming odds and took maximum advantage of the excellent defensive terrain; Meindl prevented the Americans from capturing St.-Lô for more than five weeks with three burned-out divisions: the 266th Infantry, the 352nd Infantry, and the 3rd Parachute. (The 17th SS Panzer Grenadier Division had to be withdrawn from the battle in June, and the 266th was placed under the operational control of General Kraiss and the 352nd Infantry Division.) He also controlled the much-reduced 6th Parachute Regiment.

U.S. general Collins redeployed the victors of Cherbourg to the south and, on July 4, America's Independence Day, unleashed a major offensive against the II Parachute Corps. Collins controlled the U.S. 4th, 9th, and 83rd infantry divisions and the 3rd Armored Division (as of July 7) but, because of the swampy terrain, could employ only the 83rd initially. It lost fourteen hundred men on the first day. The slaughter was so bad that Colonel von der Heydte returned captured U.S. medical personnel to the Americans to take care of their wounded.

The U.S. VII Corps continued attacking for four days. They gained less than two and a half miles and were forced to halt on July 7.

Undetered, General Bradley committed the U.S. XIX (Maj. Gen. Charles H. Corlett) and V Corps (Maj. Gen. Leonard T. Gerow).[2] The XIX controlled the 29th, 30th, and 35th Infantry divisions while Gerow commanded the U.S. 1st Infantry, 2nd Infantry, and 2nd Armored divisions. Meindl and Schimpf again put up a fierce resistance, but the Americans began to close in on the city on July 11. That evening, Meindl requested reinforcements or permission to abandon the city. SS General Hausser, who had no reinforcements to send him, denied him permission to abandon St.-Lô and repeated Hitler's orders that the crossroads be held at all costs.

Meindl and Schimpf continued to fight tenaciously, but by nightfall on July 11, the 3rd Parachute was down to 35 percent of its preinvasion strength. The Germans continued to take a heavy toll on their attackers until July 16, when the Americans captured Hill 112, just three thousand yards north of St.-Lô, from the 352nd Infantry Division. The next day Paul Hausser reversed himself and told his chief of staff, Max Pemsel, to ask Army Group B's permission to abandon the city. Field Marshal Rommel was absent (and, in fact, would never return), and Colonel Hans Tempelhoff, his chief of operations, knew that to forward the request to OB West and OKW would almost certainly result in Hitler's rejecting it. Tempelhoff instructed Pemsel to take whatever actions 7th Army felt necessary; it was simply to report later that it had been broken through in several places and that it was lucky to reestablish a line of resistance to the rear.

Meindl abandoned the important road junction on July 19. The Americans had captured a field of ruins and were still not out of bocage country, which extended several miles south of St.-Lô. They had lost forty thousand men.[3]

Eugen Meindl also took part in the Falaise breakout, during which he was wounded and most of the II Parachute Corps was lost.[4]

◆

Gerhard Grassmann was born in Neisse, Upper Silesia, on October 20, 1893. He joined the army as an artillery Fahnenjunker in 1912 but, for some reason, was discharged two months later—perhaps owing to an injury during training. In any case he went to law school (1912–14) but enlisted as a war volunteer in 1914. Commissioned in the 16th Field Artillery Regiment in 1915, he spent the entire

First World War with his regiment and fought at Tannenberg (1914); elsewhere on the Eastern Front (1914–16); in France, including the Battle of Verdun (1916); Russia again (1916–17); and France again (1917–18). He commanded a battery and ended the war as a battalion adjutant. He joined the Reichswehr and spent virtually his entire career in the artillery, including seventeen years with the East Prussian 1st Artillery Regiment at Königsberg (1921–38). He was a lieutenant colonel and an instructor at the Artillery School at Jüterbog when World War II began. Later he was promoted to colonel (September 1, 1940) and major general (March 1, 1943). He was on the artillery staff of Army Group C (1939–40), commanded the 26th Artillery Regiment (1940–42) on the Eastern Front, and commanded the 122nd Artillery Command (Arko 122), also in Russia (1942). He briefly commanded the 333rd Infantry Division on the Eastern Front (December 10, 1942–March 22, 1943). He was attached to the staff of the General of Artillery at OKH and was not given another field command until September, when he took over Harko 311 (the 311th Higher Artillery Command), which was supporting 1st Panzer Army on the Eastern Front. Grassmann assumed command of Harko 309 on January 16, 1944.

Initially, Major General Gerhard Grassmann's 309th Higher Artillery Command supported 16th Army on the Eastern Front but was transferred to France in the early summer and was given the task of supporting 7th Army in Normandy. Here its batteries became masters of camouflage and inflicted heavy casualties on the Americans but also suffered heavy losses, mainly because of the Jabos. It developed the technique of concentrating all of its fire at a predetermined time—sometimes five minutes per hour—so that it could give maximum fire support to German troops and so that the enemy could not identify the location of most of its guns. Lack of ammunition was frequently a consideration in these bombardments.

A similar situation existed on the German right flank, where the floodgates were also creaking. Here the struggle centered around the ancient university town of Caen, which had already been reduced to rubble.

7

Caen

While the Americans closed in on St.-Lô, Montgomery continued to hammer Panzer Group West's defenses around Caen with his British 1st and Canadian 2nd armies. One of the defending units was the 16th Luftwaffe Field Division, which was commanded by Major General Karl Sievers.

Karl Sievers was born in Lehrbach, Hesse, on January 2, 1892. He joined the army as an officer cadet in 1912 and was commissioned into the 161st Infantry Regiment in 1913. He fought on the Western Front in World War I, served in the Reichsheer, assumed command of the III Battalion/119th Infantry Regiment at Stuttgart in late 1938, and led it in the Saarpfalz (Saar-Palatinate) against the French. Promoted to colonel in 1940, major general on October 1, 1943, and lieutenant general on October 1, 1944, he became commander of the 168th Infantry Regiment on November 1, 1939, and led it in France (1940), on occupation duty in the Netherlands (1941–42), and in action on the southern sector of the Russian Front (June 1942–March 1943), where he fought at Belgorod, Kursk, and Voronesch, among other places. He commanded the War School at Metz (1943), before returning to the Eastern Front as acting commander of the depleted 321st Infantry Division in central Russia (August 22–September 23, 1943), fighting in the Bryansk and Rogatschev sectors.[1]

Meanwhile, Hitler declared Hermann Göring's experimental plan to create air force infantry divisions—called Luftwaffe field divisions—a failure. On November 1, 1943, he turned these units over to the army. The Army Personnel Office (HPA) promptly replaced several air force divisional commanders with army commanders. On November 5 Karl Sievers assumed command of the 16. Feld-Division (L), the new designation of the former 16th Luftwaffe Field Division. He replaced Luftwaffe colonel Otto von Lachemair.

The 16th Luftwaffe Field Division had been formed in the Gross-Born Troop Maneuver Area on December 1, 1942, and was sent to the Amsterdam area in

January 1943 to replace an army division that was on its way to the Eastern Front. The divisional headquarters was transferred to Amstelveen (three miles south of Amsterdam) in April and remained there for more than a year, directing occupation forces in the Ijmuiden-Haarlem-Leiden-Scheveningen area.

In late June the 16th Field was sent to Normandy and on July 2 replaced the Panzer Lehr Division on the front line of Army Group B. The next day the British launched a major offensive on Caen and immediately overran the 16th, which fled in all directions. It lost 75 percent of its men within hours. General Sievers was reported as nearly demented with grief, wandering the battlefield, trying in vain to organize a remnant of his division. The men of 16th (or what was left of them) were collected and attached to the 21st Panzer Division. Eventually they withdrew from the line and consolidated with the 158th Reserve Division to form the 16th Infantry Division, which continued to serve on the Western Front until the end of the war. The 16th Field Division, meanwhile, was officially dissolved on August 4, 1944.

Although he was given another division, Sievers was held partially responsible for the disaster at Caen.

◆

Hans-Ulrich von Luck und Witten was a charming, highly cultured, sophisticated, aristocratic gentleman of the Old World who had a wonderful talent for making friends. Along with his professionalism, courage, and competence, these attributes made him a great success, both on and off the battlefield.

The son of a naval officer, he was born in Flensburg on July 15, 1911.[2] Luck graduated from the Monastery School in Flensburg in 1929 (where he received a classical education) and successfully applied for acceptance into the Reichsheer as a Fahnenjunker in the cavalry. Initially, he was assigned to a cavalry regiment in Silesia but was soon involuntarily transferred to the 1st Motorized Battalion in Königsburg, East Prussia (now Kaliningrad, Russia). Luck was greatly disappointed, but the transfer turned out to be beneficial to his career. Each of Germany's seven Wehrkreis had a motorized battalion, and they soon formed the nucleus of the Panzerwaffe (armored branch).

In 1931–32 Luck attended the Officers' Training Course at the War School in Dresden. Here he met and became a staunch admirer of Major Erwin Rommel, one of the instructors at the school, and a man whom he was destined to meet again.

Luck graduated, was commissioned in 1932, and was assigned to the 2nd Motorized Battalion at Kolberg (now Kolobrzeg, Poland), on the Baltic Sea coast of Pomerania. Four years later he was transferred to the 8th Panzer Reconnaissance Battalion at Potsdam in 1936, as a platoon leader in the motorcycle company. In 1938 he was posted again, this time to the 7th Panzer Reconnaissance Regiment of the 2nd Light Division at Bad Kissingen, in northern Bavaria. He served with this unit during the Polish campaign.

That winter, the 2nd Light was converted in the 7th Panzer Division and was placed under Rommel's command. The reconnaissance regiment was reduced to a single battalion (the 37th). Along with most of the rest of the German army, the 7th Panzer Division attacked the French and Belgian armies on May 10, 1940. Luck (who was now a captain) took charge of the battalion when his commanding officer was killed in action on May 28. After the French signed the armistice, Luck accepted the surrender of Bordeaux. After training in the Paris area for the invasion of England, the 7th Panzer Division was sent back to the Bordeaux area while the plans for the invasion were quietly shelved. Meanwhile, Major von Paar superceded Luck as battalion commander.

In early February 1941 Rommel departed for Africa and was replaced by Major General Baron Hans von Funck, an officer who never fully earned Luck's confidence. (Unlike the dashing Rommel, who led from the front, Funck was more traditional and directed the division from his headquarters in the rear.) Funck named Luck his adjutant, even though the young captain wanted to remain with his unit. Luck served General von Funck during the first operations of the Russian campaign, including the battles of Minsk and Vitebsk. In the final stages of clearing the Vitebsk pocket, however, Major von Paar was killed in action. Funck immediately ordered Luck to replace him as battalion commander, much to the delight of the young officer. He left for the front that same evening.

Captain von Luck led the 37th Panzer Reconnaissance Battalion in the final stages of the clearing of the Vitebsk Pocket, in the Smolensk encirclement, in the battles of the Dnieper crossings, in the Battle of Yyazma, and in the drive on Moscow. In North Africa, meanwhile, Rommel selected Luck to command the 3rd Panzer Reconnaissance Battalion of the 21st Panzer Division. Funck objected, however, and began a battle of influence between the two generals in which Luck was the prize. Funck managed to block the captain's transfer for some time, and Luck narrowly escaped death in the winter campaign of 1941–42. In mid-January 1942 Rommel had enough of the political maneuvering and threatened Funck with personal consequences if he persisted in retaining Luck. Realizing that Rommel had considerably more political influence with the Nazis than he, Funck relented, and Luck and his driver were soon on their way to

Berlin. Once there, however, Luck was informed that he would have to go on leave, whether he wanted to or not. He spent most of the time in Paris and finally, in early April, arrived in Libya, where he was given command of the 3rd Panzer Reconnaissance Battalion of the 21st Panzer Division. He had, in the meantime, been promoted to major.

Luck's first battle with the Afrika Korps was almost his last. On May 27 a piece of shrapnel caught him in the upper right thigh and knocked him to the ground. Fortunately for Luck, the shell fragment missed both his manhood and a major artery by a narrow margin. A scout car took the nearly unconscious commander to an aid station, but five days elapsed before he received proper medical attention. By then, Luck's wound had become infected. After an operation, he was evacuated back to Italy by hospital ship. He was impatient to return to the front, but it was September before the medical staff in Germany deemed that he was again fit for combat. Like many young men of his generation, Luck was quite dissatisfied while he was on wounded leave. He was glad when he returned to North Africa and the front. His unit was stationed far to the south, at the Siwa Oasis.

Montgomery launched his long awaited El Alamein offensive on October 23. Rommel checked attack after attack, but by November 2 the exhausted Panzer Army Afrika was in remnants and on the verge of collapse. That day the supply units and bakery platoon of the 3rd Recon evacuated the Siwa Oasis. The combat units fell back the next day.

Luck's task now was to identify and report or defeat any attempt to outflank Rommel's retreating army from the south. He would have been captured when Tunis fell in May 1943, but Rommel's successor, Colonel General Jürgen von Armin, sent him on a mission to Führer Headquarters. Major General Rudolf Schmundt, the pro-Hitler chief of the Army Personnel Office, decided to keep Luck in Führer Reserve for an entire year.[3] Horrified at the thought and wanting another command, Luck visited Schmundt and talked himself into a six-month assignment as an instructor at the Panzer Reconnaissance Commanders' School in Paris, which would last from August 1943 to March 1944, followed by a new combat command.

Meanwhile, Luck enjoyed a two-months' furlough in his friend's penthouse. One night at a party he met Dagmar, the attractive and sophisticated daughter of the owner of Europe's largest tree nursery. The fact that she was eleven years his junior and officially classified as one-eighth Jewish did not deter Luck in the slightest.[4] They were soon lovers, and she joined him in Paris after he reported to the panzer reconnaissance school. In August 1943, two weeks after Hans von Luck left Berlin, the penthouse he was using was destroyed by an incendiary bomb.

Luck completed his tour of duty at the reconnaissance commanders' school at the end of April, and he happily reported to Fritz Bayerlein, the commander of the newly formed and exceptionally well-equipped Panzer Lehr Division. Bayerlein (an old friend from Africa) had earmarked Luck to be the new commander of the elite (130th) Panzer Lehr Regiment, but when Luck arrived, Bayerlein had some bad news for him. Major General Edgar Feuchtinger, the politically well-connected commander of the newly reconstituted 21st Panzer Division (fifteen thousand men), had learned of Luck's availability and had used his influence at Führer Headquarters to have Luck transferred to his unit.[5] When he reported to the 21st Panzer, Feuchtinger named him commander of the 125th Panzer Grenadier Regiment, which was stationed northwest of Caen in Normandy. The mission of the division was to counterattack against the D-Day invasion—if it came in Normandy—and to throw the Allies back into the sea.

✦

Luck's regiment had only two battalions (I, equipped with Schützenpanzerwagen [SPW] armored half-tracks, and II, which rode in trucks) but was reinforced with two batteries of self-propelled assault guns. The 125th was in action from the very beginning of the D-Day invasion, as we have seen, although its counterattack was badly mishandled by General Feuchtinger. By June 9 Luck's command, which was now designated Kampfgruppe (KG) Luck, included his own regiment, the 21st Panzer Reconnaissance Battalion, a company of the battered 22nd Panzer Regiment, three batteries of the 200th Assault Gun Battalion, and a company of the 220th Antitank Battalion, which was equipped with 88mm guns. Operating more or less independently of his division, Luck's task was to contain the British airborne bridgehead east of the Orne. The battle group clung to its positions in the Norman hedgerows and cornfields and was in action every day, as the British forces (the British 6th Airborne and 51st Highland Infantry Divisions and an assortment of attached units) doggedly probed, pushed, and tried to expand their positions to the south and southeast, because the Normandy bridgehead had inadequate depth. June and July were very hot, and the mosquitoes and lack of relief made the conditions even more miserable.

By the middle of July Luck's battle group had received considerable reinforcements and included his own regiment, all five companies of the 200th Assault Gun Battalion, the 503rd Heavy Panzer Battalion (equipped with superior Tiger tanks), a battalion of the 16th Luftwaffe Field Division, three sections of 88mm antitank guns, and a detachment of rocket launchers. KG Luck was backed by the 155th Panzer Artillery Regiment and strong elements of Dietrich's II SS Panzer Corps. Unknown to the Germans, however, Montgomery was secretly reinforcing the bridgehead at night and on a massive scale. By July 17 he had the 7th, 11th, and Guards Armored divisions east of the Orne, along with five armored brigades.

Meanwhile, on July 14, at the urging of Dietrich and Feuchtinger—both of whom assured him that no major British offensives were expected for ten days—Luck went on a three-day furlough to Paris, where he spent his birthday with Dagmar, who was now his fiancée. (Dietrich knew of her Jewish blood but had nevertheless asked Führer Headquarters to give them permission to marry. When the request was denied, Dietrich promised Luck to make a personal appeal to Hitler the next time he was at Berchtesgaden. Unfortunately, he had not been able to do so, owing to the invasion.)

When Luck returned to his command post shortly after 9:00 a.m. on July 18, he found his staff very tense and nervous. The Allies had carpet-bombed the Kampfgruppe's front lines and followed this with a creeping artillery barrage from hundreds of guns. The aerial and artillery bombardment had lasted about four hours and now the staff was unable to contact any of the frontline units. Later Luck learned that twenty-five hundred Anglo-American bombers, a thousand field guns, and massive amounts of heavy naval artillery had been employed in the bombardment.

Luck immediately suspended (and later relieved) his second in command, who had become paralyzed during the crisis and had done nothing. He then personally set out on the main road to Caen. When he arrived at what was left of the village of Cagny, he found that his I Battalion had been smashed and that twenty-five to thirty British tanks had already crossed the main Caen road and were heading south, with dozens of others behind them, driving from north to south. Luck also found a Luftwaffe battery of 88mm guns, all of which were aimed at the sky. He quickly ordered the young captain in charge to open up on the Allied flank, in order to halt the British advance. To his amazement, the captain calmly replied that he had orders to shoot down enemy airplanes; fighting tanks was the army's job.

Luck immediately drew his pistol, aimed it at his face, and declared, "Either you are a dead man or you can earn yourself a medal!"

Realizing that Luck was serious, the air force captain opted for the medal.[6] Moments later his men were blasting the British tanks, which were defenseless against the heavy flak guns. Fortunately for the Germans, the confused British did not react quickly and launch a ground attack against the battery, which was extremely vulnerable to enemy infantry.

Gradually the truth of the situation became clear. The Allies had blasted a huge gap in the German front line east of Caen and were pouring through it with their armor. Luck found that the Tiger battalion and a nearby PzKw IV battalion had been knocked out, but Major Becker had two intact batteries of assault guns ready for action. Luck committed them to the right of Cagny, to prevent the British from flanking the village to the north. He also reinforced the Luftwaffe battery with a platoon from his staff company, fighting as infantry. Soon at least forty British tanks were burning in the cornfields, most of them knocked out by the 88s. With the remnants of his own regiment and the surviving panzer reconnaissance troops, he formed a thin line on the eastern edge of the British armored corridor.

Luck's line held on July 18 and all day on July 19. With only four hundred infantrymen, his position was definitely still vulnerable, but the Allies did not launch any major attacks against his front. Finally, about 5:00 p.m., the vanguards of the depleted 12th SS Panzer Division "Hitler Youth" arrived to relieve KG Luck. By this time the main British offensive (dubbed Operation Goodwood) had been halted. It had gained less than five miles. Shortly thereafter, Luck was awarded the Knight's Cross for his part in this victory.

Luck's battle group was relieved during the night of July 19–20, an operation made more difficult by a terrible rainstorm. The Allied Jabos were grounded the next day by the weather. In the German rear Luck and his staff rebuilt the I Battalion, which had been almost wiped out by the Allied bombers. Luckily for him, the division had just received a well-trained battalion of replacements from Germany, complete with brand new SPW armored personnel carriers. The task of rebuilding the I Battalion was completed quickly.

That was fortunate for Major von Luck. After less than a week's rest, the kampfgruppe rejoined the 21st Panzer Division, which was shifted to the sector south of Villers Bocage, to block the important Highway 175, which ran from Bayeux on the coast to Falaise.

◆

The Allies rained blow after blow against the German line throughout the summer of 1944. Finally, on July 25, the Americans broke through on the German left flank. On August 17 two Canadian divisions and the 1st Polish Armored Division broke through the 21st Panzer Division, trapping Kampfgruppe Rauch

Three German panzers hiding in the hay. Because of the Allied "Jabos," the Germans became masters of camouflage (USNA).

(100th Panzer Regiment, 192nd Panzer Grenadier Regiment, and the 21st Reconnaissance Battalion, all under Colonel Joseph Rauch) in the Falaise Pocket. KG Luck was lucky: it had been on the division's right flank and thus escaped encirclement. Rauch managed to break out but lost many of his men and all eight of the division's remaining tanks in the process. On August 21 Feuchtinger handed command of the operational units of the division over to Luck and took Rauch's shattered units back across the Seine, where they were to be rebuilt. Luck had the unenviable task of trying to delay Montgomery's advance and then escaping across the river with his battle group. This he did on August 29 in an amphibious Volkswagen car. It was a harrowing adventure because of Allied fighter-bomber attacks and because no one knew if the VW would actually float or not. (It did.) Most of his men escaped on pontoon ferries and by constructing mini-ferries made from doors of local houses and empty fuel cans. Luck then had to march in a wide circle to the north and west, trying to avoid being trapped by Patton's rampaging army in the process. This he managed to do by a narrow margin, arriving at his assigned positions west of Strasbourg on September 9. By now his average company was down to a strength of fifty men.

8

The Americans Break Out

Owing to the Allies' mounting casualties and limited territorial gains, Lt. Gen. Omar Bradley, the commander of the U.S. 1st Army, concluded that the Normandy stalemate could not be broken by conventional means. He therefore decided to use strategic (heavy) bombers in a tactical role. Once the bombers had broken the German line, he would commit his armor.

Bradley's plan (dubbed Operation Cobra) called for 2,500 airplanes to attack a 7,000-yard wide by 2,500-yard deep rectangular target area due south of the Périers-St.-Lô Highway. In two and a half hours they would deposit almost 5,000 tons of high explosives, napalm, white phosphorous, and 100-pound and 260-pound fragmentation bombs in a six-square-mile area. All of this excludes the machine guns of hundreds of fighters and fighter-bombers. The aerial attack would be followed by an artillery bombardment of more than 1,000 guns (including nine battalions of heavy artillery), which would fire 125,000 rounds in support of the breakout.

The breakout forces themselves would be commanded by Gen. J. Lawton Collins's U.S. VII Corps, whose frontage had been reduced to four and a half miles to achieve maximum concentration. Initially, Collins's infantry (the U.S. 4th, 29th, and 30th infantry divisions) would secure the flanks of the breakthrough; then Collins would commit his armor: the U.S. 2nd and 3rd armored divisions and the motorized 1st Infantry Division. They would pour through a three-mile gap, drive fifteen miles to the southwest, and capture the city of Coutances, which would cut off Choltitz's entire LXXXIV Corps and rip the German left flank wide open. To prevent Choltitz from launching counterattacks against Collins or escaping, he was to be pinned down by attacks from Middleton's U.S. VIII Corps, which controlled the U.S. 8th, 79th, 83rd, and 90th infantry divisions and the 4th and 6th armored divisions. According to American estimates, they would outnumber the Germans 5 to 1, even before the aerial bombardment began.

The final American objective was the city of Avranches, at the base of the Cotentin Peninsula. If they could capture Avranches, they would be in a position to overrun France. The offensive was scheduled to begin on July 24.

113

Once the breakthrough was achieved, Headquarters, U.S. 3rd Army, would be activated, under the command of Lt. Gen. George S. Patton. It would assume command of the American right flank (including the breakout forces) and would control the U.S. VIII, XII, XV, and XX corps. The U.S. 12th Army Group, under Bradley's personal command, would be activated the same day (August 1), to direct the U.S. 3rd and 1st armies. Lt. Gen. Courtney Hodges would succeed Bradley as commander of the 1st Army, which would control the V, VII, and XIX Corps. Simultaneously, the British 21st Army Group would be activated under Montgomery. It would control the British 2nd Army (Sir Miles Dempsey) and the Canadian 1st Army (Lt. Gen. Henry D. G. Crerar). Montgomery would remain overall Allied ground commander until September 1, when Dwight D. Eisenhower's Supreme Headquarters, Allied Expeditionary Force (SHAEF), would become operational in France.

The offensive would strike the German 7th Army on Kluge's left. It included LXXXIV Corps on its left (coastal) flank and weak II Parachute Corps on the right. Left to right, the LXXXIV controlled the remnants of the 243rd Infantry Division on the coast; the 91st Air Landing Division (with the remnants of the 77th Infantry Division and an exhausted battle group from the 265th Infantry Division attached); much of the still battleworthy 2nd SS Panzer Division, which controlled the 6th Parachute Regiment as well; the remnants of the 17th SS Panzer Grenadier Division; Gustav Wilke's 5th Parachute Division, which was down to a single regiment; and the Panzer Lehr Division, which had recently been inserted into the line. Choltitz's only reserve was the depleted 353rd Infantry Division, which was resting a few miles south of Périers.

On Choltitz's right flank lay Meindl's II Parachute Corps, which had only two divisions: Kraiss's 352nd Infantry on the left, holding positions south of St.-Lô and still firing occasional mortar and/or artillery bombardments into the city; and Schimpf's 3rd Parachute Division, with a regiment of the 5th Parachute Division attached, on the right.

Kraiss's division had been in action since D-Day and was down to a strength of 650 combat troops. Meindl and Hausser, the 7th Army commander, reinforced it with battle groups from the 266th, 275th, 343rd, and 353rd infantry divisions, so it would be capable of holding its positions against moderately strong American attacks.

Meindl had no reserves worth mentioning. Hausser had only a battle group from the 2nd SS Panzer Division (two panzer and two panzer grenadier companies) and elements of Hans Schmidt's 275th Infantry Division, which was just arriving from Brittany. It controlled three weak infantry regiments but only one battle group (KG Heinz) had arrived. It was posted just behind the Panzer Lehr Division.

Field Marshal von Kluge was dissatisfied with 7th Army's dispositions. Several days before Cobra began, he recommended to SS General Hausser that he replaced the mobile Panzer Lehr Division in the front line with the 275th Infantry Division and that he replace the 2nd SS Panzer with the 353rd Infantry. Hausser and Kluge, however, had been cadets together at Gross Lichterfelde more than thirty years before and were not friends. Hausser ignored Kluge's suggestions. As a result, when Cobra struck, he would have two mediocre marching infantry divisions in reserve, instead of two highly mobile and highly respected panzer divisions.

The target of the offensive was Fritz Bayerlein's Panzer Lehr Division, which lay on the extreme right flank of Choltitz's LXXXIV Corps. It also lay entirely within the rectangle Bradley planned to bomb out of existence. The division had been in more or less constant action since D-Day and controlled twenty-two hundred combat effectives from its own battalions, plus 450 combat troops from the depleted Kampfgruppe Heinz (275th Infantry Division). It also controlled the 15th Parachute Regiment (on loan from General Wilke's 5th Parachute Division, most of which was with LXXXIV Corps on the German left flank) and a few elements from the 2nd SS Panzer Division, giving Bayerlein a total of five thousand men, of which thirty-two hundred were combat effectives (excluding medical personnel, supply and support troops, etc.). His division alone had had fifteen thousand men—including more than seven thousand combat troops—on June 5. When the Battle of Normandy began, Panzer Lehr had more than two hundred tanks and armored fighting vehicles. On June 23 only forty-five of these were still operational.

Operation Cobra failed on the first attempt owing to the weather. Because of thick, overcast clouds and poor visibility, British air chief marshal Trafford Leigh-Mallory ordered the operation postponed, but his orders did not reach every unit, several of which were already airborne. They dropped their bombs all over the map, but they mainly landed on the Panzer Lehr and U.S. 30th Infantry divisions, killing twenty-five Americans and wounding 131 others. Among the dead was Lt. Gen. Leslie J. McNair, who had recently succeeded George Patton as commander of the U.S. 1st Army Group in England. (This force was a deception unit, located opposite the Pas de Calais. It did not control any real combat divisions.) One of the unsung heroes of the American war effort, McNair worked under U.S. Army chief of staff Gen. George Marshall as chief of Army ground forces. He had been extremely instrumental in building the U.S. Army from a force slightly smaller than the Portuguese army in 1939 into a global force of several million men. In Normandy to observe Cobra, McNair was hurled a considerable distance by the bombs. His headless body was found beside a dirt road and could be identified only because one of his shoulder epaulets had three stars on it. He was secretly buried that night and replaced by Lt. Gen. John L. DeWitt. To continue deceiving the Germans, news of his death was not released for some time. Today, his grave is in the American cemetery on the escarpment overlooking Omaha Beach.

The American generals were afraid that the abortion of July 24 would tip off the Germans as to what was afoot. Remarkably, it did not. Only General von Choltitz drew the correct conclusions, but his dispatch to 7th Army Headquarters drew a one-word response: "Nonsense."[1] Hausser believed that the bombing attack was a feint: the real Allied offensive would come in the Caen sector. Kluge, for once, agreed with Hausser, and even Fritz Bayerlein was completely convinced that the Caen sector would be the real Allied target. He was in for an education.[2] Beginning at 11:00 a.m. on the morning of July 25, his division was pulverized by a bomber stream a hundred miles long. Once again, some of the bombs fell short, killing or wounding another six hundred American troops. But that was nothing compared to what they did to Panzer Lehr, the attached 15th Parachute Regiment and the adjacent 13th Parachute Regiment. More than twenty-five hundred heavy and medium bombers dropped more than sixty thousand bombs into a 3.5-by-1.5-mile rectangle. That amounted to twelve bombs for every German soldier in the rectangle.

As soon as the American air armada appeared, Bayerlein's antiaircraft artillery unit, the 311th Army Panzer Flak Battalion, opened up on it. Within minutes half of the battalion's guns were knocked out and the rest—whose officers and men realized that to continue firing meant certain death—fell silent as their crews "went to ground." This saved some but certainly not all of them. Panzer Lehr lost at least a thousand of its thirty-two hundred combat effectives killed or critically wounded, and most of the rest were less seriously wounded or dazed. Tanks flew into the air like toys, artillery batteries literally disintegrated under the impact of the bombs, entire companies were buried alive, and three battalion command posts simply disappeared. Bayerlein reported at least 70 percent casualties. The headquarters of the elite 901st Panzer Grenadier Regiment vanished in flames, never to be seen again, and the regiment was virtually annihilated. The 15th Parachute Regiment also ceased to exist as an organized combat force. General Bayerlein himself survived only because he happened to be visiting a regimental command post that was housed in an old Norman chateau with walls that were ten feet thick. Bayerlein recalled, "The planes kept coming over, as if on a conveyor belt. . . . I had no communication with anybody, even by radio. By noon nothing was visible but dust and smoke. My front lines looked like the face of the moon. . . . All my forward tanks were knocked out, and the roads were practically impassable."[3]

Shortly after the war, Bayerlein wrote, "Again and again the bomb carpets rolled toward us. . . . Quick glimpses outside showed the whole area shrouded in a pall of dust, with fountains of earth spewing high in the air. . . . It was afternoon before I was able to get out of the chateau and ride back on my motorcycle to Division H.Q. (I had long since learned to prefer a motorcycle to a car, having had six cars shot up during the invasion battle and several drivers killed.) We were repeatedly troubled by fighter-bombers on the way back."[4]

After the aerial bombardment, the American artillery poured 125,000 shells into the chaos. That amounted to twenty-five shells per German soldier who had been alive in the rectangle *before* the bombing. Not all of the artillery, however, fired on Panzer Lehr. Some of it fired over Bayerlein's division and into the zone of Kampfgruppe Heinz, which was the only battalion or regimental-sized unit still intact in the Panzer Lehr Division's area of operations. The battle group was also pounded by bombers and Jabos. Lieutenant General Hans Schmidt commanded KG Heinz.

✦

Hans Schmidt was a big man known for his imperturbability. Born in Bayreuth, Upper Franconia, on March 14, 1895, he entered the army as an officer cadet in the Bavarian 7th Infantry Regiment in August 1914. Schmidt fought on the Western Front in World War I and remained in the army. A major when Hitler came to power, he commanded III/41st Infantry Regiment at Amberg in the Upper Palatinate (1935–38), the 46th Replacement Training Regiment in Bayreuth (1938–40), and the 245th Infantry Regiment (1940–43) in France and on the Eastern Front, where he fought at Kiev, Kharkov, Kursk, and Voronesch, among other battles. As a colonel, he assumed command of the 68th Infantry Division near Voronesch in early 1943. Promoted rapidly to major general (April 1, 1943) and lieutenant general (October 1, 1943), Schmidt was an excellent divisional commander, but he could not prevent his unit from being smashed in the Battles of Kiev and Zhitomir. Named commander of the 275th Infantry Division in Brittany on December 10, 1943, he took the motorized third of his new unit to Normandy as Kampfgruppe Heinz.

✦

After the Allied bombers destroyed the Panzer Lehr Division on July 25 and had banked for home, Hans Schmidt led his kampfgruppe in an immediate counterattack against the Allied spearheads, in hopes of deceiving the American generals into thinking that they had not done as much damage as they in fact had done. The attempts of Schmidt and others almost succeeded. Eisenhower and Bradley were convinced that Operation Cobra had failed, and Eisenhower—pacing up and down—swore that he would never again use strategic bombers in a tactical role. Only General Collins suspected the truth. The following morning, he committed his armored reserve.

It was the turning point of the Battle of Normandy. The Americans swept away the remnants of the Panzer Lehr Division and Kampfgruppe Heinz. Bayerlein was forced to escape by foot across country. Walking alone down a road, he was picked up by a German motorized patrol. Hans Schmidt was also lucky

U.S. Lt. Gen. J. Lawton "Lightning Joe" Collins, the commander of the U.S. VII Corps, which captured Cherbourg and spearheaded the Operation Cobra breakout. He later received a fourth star and became chief of staff (commander) of the U.S. Army (USNA).

enough to escape with his life. He was sent back to the German frontier with orders to rebuild the 275th Infantry Division.

On the German left flank, Generals von Choltitz and Hausser acted quickly. Choltitz committed half of his reserve—about half of the 353rd Infantry Division—to the battle.

The 353rd had been sent to reinforce the German left flank in Normandy in early July 1944. Commanded by Lieutenant General Paul Mahlmann, the 353rd formed part of the LXXXIV Corps and fought effectively in the hedgerows. The 353rd was almost constantly in action for several weeks; by the third week of July it had been so badly battered and reduced by casualties that it had lost most of its combat value. Accordingly, it was pulled out of the line to rest. On July 25 it was the only division in LXXXIV Corps reserve.

◆

Paul Mahlmann was born in Gispersieben, a suburb of Erfurt, Thüringia, on December 10, 1892. He was educated in cadet schools and entered the service as a second lieutenant in the 98th Infantry Regiment in 1914. He fought on the Western Front in World War I, served in the Reichsheer (mainly in infantry assignments), and assumed command of the Württemberger 181st Infantry Regiment at Siegen on mobilization on August 26, 1939. He led this regiment in the Saar (1939), in France (1940), and on the central sector of the Russian Front (1941–42), where he fought in the Battle of Moscow and against the Soviet winter offensive of 1941–42, among others. He was acting commander of the 137th Infantry Division from February to May 1942 (also in central Russia) and, after a brief tour of staff duty in Germany, assumed command of the 147th Reserve Division (December 25, 1942–July 31, 1943). He also commanded the 39th Infantry Division in the retreat to the Dnieper (1943) before becoming the initial commander of the 353rd Infantry Division, which was formed in Brittany on November 20, 1943. Mahlmann was promoted to lieutenant colonel (1936), colonel (1939), major general (January 1, 1943), and lieutenant general (June 1, 1944). He led the 353rd until February 15, 1945, except for a few weeks in July and August 1944, when he was apparently recovering from wounds. Mahlmann was noted for his cool detachment in all situations.

◆

When the U.S. armor broke out on July 26, Mahlmann attacked their right flank and attempted to seal off the breakthrough. He failed, but at least this fine leader's 353rd Infantry managed to escape the disaster that overtook most of the rest of Choltitz's LXXXIV Corps. Meanwhile, a regiment of the 275th Infantry

Division was coming up from Brittany. Hausser threw it into an immediate counterattack against Collins's left, in order to seal off the gap from that direction and convince the American generals that Operation Cobra had failed. Neither Choltitz's effort nor Hausser's had the slightest impact on the battle. The regiment from the 275th fell victim to American fighter-bombers near Canisy, which blew it apart. Collins continued to roll south and southwest while the U.S. 30th Infantry and Combat Command A of the U.S. 2nd Armored Division turned southeast, into the rear of Kraiss's 352nd Infantry Division.

That same day, July 26, Lieutenant Colonel Günther von Kluge appeared at Bayerlein's headquarters with an order from his father, directing Bayerlein to hold his positions. With great bitterness, the general replied that every man in the division was his position. "Everyone! My grenadiers and my engineers and my tank crews—they're all holding their ground. Not a single man is leaving his post . . . for they are dead. Dead! Do you understand? You may report to the Field Marshal that the Panzer Lehr Division is annihilated."[5]

For some reason, Kluge was slow to react to the American breakthrough. He spent July 27 inspecting Panzer Group West (the Caen sector). That night, he signaled Bayerlein and promised to send him an SS panzer battalion of sixty tanks. When it arrived, it had five panzers, not sixty, bringing Bayerlein's total tank strength to fourteen runners.

CCA of the U.S. 2nd Armored Division continued its advance into the rear of the German 352nd Infantry Division and pushed within a mile of General Kraiss's command post. Kraiss and his staff escaped only because the Americans did not know they were there. Another German general was on the run.

The U.S. 3rd Armored Division's CCB and the U.S. 1st Infantry Division continued pushing down the excellent road to Coutances, meeting only scattered opposition. The encirclement of Choltitz's LXXXIV Corps was taking shape.

✦

Dietrich von Choltitz was born on November 9, 1894, in Wiese-Gräflich near Neustadt, Oppeln District, Upper Silesia. He was the son of an estate manager, Hans von Choltitz, who became a colonel and commander of the 10th Ulan Regiment during World War I. Dietrich enrolled in the Dresden Cadet School in 1907 and later served part-time as a page at the Saxon Royal House. In 1914 he joined the 107th (8th Saxon) Infantry Regiment in Leipzig as a Fähnrich. He remained with this West Saxon unit throughout the war, fighting in the Battle of the Marne, Flanders, the Somme (1916 and 1918), and St.-Quentin, among others. In the process he served as a company commander, battalion adjutant, machine gun platoon leader, and adjutant of the regiment's replacement battalion after he was wounded in 1918. In late 1917 he was awarded the Royal Saxon Military Order of St.-Heinrichs—the Saxon equivalent of the *Pour le Mérite*. Commissioned second lieutenant on October 1, 1915, he was selected for the Reichsheer but was not advanced to first lieutenant until 1924—typically slow promotions for a small army.

Choltitz spent the Weimar era in infantry and mounted infantry units. He was a squadron leader in the 12th Mounted Infantry Regiment (1929–34) and a company commander of the 26th Infantry Regiment (1934–37). In 1929, the year he was promoted to captain, he married Huberta von Garnier, the daughter of General of Infantry Otto von Garnier, a holder of the *Pour le Merité*. In 1935 he was promoted to major. He assumed command of the III/16th Infantry Regiment (later an air landing battalion), which he led in the air assault against Rotterdam in 1940. He assumed command of the 16th Air Landing Regiment on September 10, 1940. When the Russian campaign began, Choltitz and his regiment were assigned to guard the Ploesti oil fields in Romania against a possible Soviet attack. Later he led the 16th across the Dnieper and in the Crimea and played a major role in the successful attack on Sevastopol in the summer of 1942. When the battle began, Choltitz had four thousand men; only 347 were still standing at the end. Choltitz was among them, although he had been wounded in the arm.[6]

After the fall of the Red naval fortress, the 16th Regiment was sent to Crete, but Choltitz was named acting commander of the 260th Infantry Division (August 27–October 12, 1942), which he led in the street fighting in northwest Stalingrad. At the end of this tour, he was transferred to the Panzer School at Wünsdorf (near Berlin) to undergo tank training. He was then attached to the 100th Panzer Brigade in Paris for further training. Finally, he returned to Russia and on December 7 became deputy commander of the XVII Corps (later Army Detachment Hollidt), which he led in the Donetz fighting, on the Mius, and at Stalino and Kharkov. During this retreat, he reportedly destroyed the city of Kovel in forty minutes. "Since Sevastopol, it has been my fate to cover the retreat of our armies and destroy the cities behind them," Choltitz observed.[7]

Choltitz was promoted to lieutenant colonel (1938), colonel (April 1, 1941), major general (September 1, 1942), and lieutenant general (March 1, 1943). On March 5, 1943, he was named commander of the 11th Panzer Division.

Choltitz led the 11th Panzer until October 1, 1943, when he was named acting commander of the XXXXVII Panzer Corps. He fell sick and was in Führer Reserve from November 15, 1943, to March 1, 1944, when he became acting commander of the LXXVI Panzer Corps in Italy, where he fought at Anzio. He was unemployed from April 16, 1944, when he was sent to France to serve as a commanding general (or acting commanding general) of whatever division or corps the OB West assigned to him.

✦

On June 12, 1944, Choltitz was ordered to travel immediately to St.-Lô, Normandy, where General Marcks had just been killed by an American fighter-bomber. He arrived on June 15 and took over command of the LXXXIV Corps from General of Artillery Wilhelm Fahrmbacher, who had been acting as corps commander until Choltitz arrived. Between then and July 25, Choltitz repulsed several major American attacks. After July 25, as Operation Cobra developed, he faced frontal attacks from the U.S. VIII Corps and the tanks of the U.S. VII Corps in its right flank and rear. He scraped together every reserve he could—which did not amount to much. He nevertheless threw the 353rd Infantry Division (a kampfgruppe) and a battle group of the 2nd SS Panzer Division against the American flank. The Americans, however, turned back these weak forces with relative ease.

Although Choltitz had performed flawlessly, Field Marshal von Kluge needed scapegoats to blame for the successful Allied breakout from hedgerow country, so he relieved the general of his command on July 30. As if to send Kluge a message, Hitler and OKH promoted Choltitz to general of infantry on August 1.

Meanwhile, back at the front, another German general fell—this one of SS. Heinz Lammerding, the commander of the 2nd SS Panzer Division "Das Reich," was seriously wounded on July 26. His medical staff managed to evacuate him to the rear area of 7th Army before the jaws of the American trap completely closed around LXXXIV Corps, and he returned to command on October 23. In the interim, SS Lieutenant Colonel Christian Tychsen took over his command.

✦

Christian Tychsen, the son of a master carpenter, was born on December 3, 1910, in Flensburg, Schleswig-Holstein. He joined the SS in December 1931 and transferred to the SS-VT in 1934. Commissioned on January 30, 1937, he was promoted to SS first lieutenant in 1938, SS captain in 1939, and SS major in 1942. He became a platoon leader in 1936 and commanded a reconnaissance (later motorcycle) company from 1938 to 1942. He took part in the Polish and French campaigns and was seriously wounded on the Russian Front on February 12, 1942; his face was badly scarred in the process. Tychsen returned to the division in October 1942 and was named commander of the II Battalion,

2nd SS Panzer Regiment, on the Eastern Front. Here he won both the Knight's Cross and the Oak Leaves in 1943, but his route to further advancement was blocked by his regimental commander, SS Lieutenant Colonel Baron Hans-Albin von Reitzenstein. The two men did not like each other. When Reitzenstein was foolish and brutal enough to rape an attractive and popular female Ukrainian kitchen helper, Tychsen made sure that senior SS authorities learned of the incident. According to Nazi logic, this crime was more serious than murder because it violated the Nuremberg racial laws, which forbade Aryans from having sexual intercourse with *Untermenschen* (subhumans), such as Jews and Slavs. Had Reitzenstein simply shot the girl, it is virtually certain that he would not have been punished. Thanks to Tychsen, however, an investigation was launched, which led to Reitzenstein's suicide on November 30, 1943. The senior battalion commander, Tychsen, succeeded him that same day.

What were Tychsen's motivations when he turned in Reitzenstein? Were they Nazi/SS idealism, the desire for personal gain, or a combination of the two? This very question divided the Old Comrades Association of the 2nd SS Panzer Division into Tychsen and Reitzenstein factions years after the war. They never reached a definitive conclusion. In any case Tychsen was promoted to SS lieutenant colonel on January 30, 1944. He continued to command the 2nd SS Panzer Regiment with some skill until Heinz Lammerding was wounded in action on July 26. He then became divisional commander—in a rapidly deteriorating situation.

As the U.S. VIII Corps and elements of the VII closed in on the LXXXIV Corps, Tychsen and his driver, SS Corporal Lemke, climbed into a Kubelwagen (the German equivalent of a jeep) and went on a reconnaissance on July 28, seeking a way out of the encirclement. They ran into an American ambush near Gavray instead and were killed by members of the U.S. 2nd Armored Division. Some reports state that Tychsen was still alive when the Americans reached the Kubelwagen and that he was captured but his wounds were so severe he died shortly thereafter, without regaining consciousness.[8]

✦

Otto Baum, the son of a merchant, was born in Stettin bei Hechingen-Hohenzollern, Swabia (southwestern Germany), on November 15, 1911. After attending an agricultural school in Stuttgart, he matriculated in 1934 and promptly joined the SS. He attended the first class of the SS Junker School at Braunschweig (Brunswick) in 1935 and was commissioned in the SS Germania Regiment in 1936. He became a company commander in the Leibstandarte Adolf

Hitler in 1938 and fought in Poland and France. He eventually transferred to the 3rd Totenkopf ("Death's Head") Infantry Regiment, rose to the command of the III Battalion in 1941, and was awarded the Knight's Cross during the Battle of Demyansk on the Eastern Front. In March 1943 Baum was promoted to SS lieutenant colonel and was commander the 5th Panzer Grenadier Regiment of the 3rd SS Panzer Division "Totenkopf," fighting on the Eastern Front. He was wounded for the third time on August 21, 1943. After he recovered, Baum (now a full colonel of Waffen-SS) was transferred to the West and briefly commanded the 17th SS Panzer Grenadier Division after Werner Ostendorff was wounded in the early stages of the invasion.

After the death of Christian Tychsen, SS Colonel Baum, still acting commander of the 17th SS Panzer Grenadier Division, became the acting commander of the 2nd SS Panzer Division as well. (Three days later, SS Colonel Otto Binge assumed command of the 17th SS Panzer Grenadier.) Baum led the SS troops in the subsequent breakout and was generally successful.

✦

Meanwhile, SS General Hausser ordered the corps to escape to the southwest and to rally at Roncey, about four miles southwest of Coutances. Choltitz protested immediately because this order would strip the German western flank, allow the Americans to advance down the coastal road with little opposition, and cause a huge pileup of vehicles at Roncey, but Hausser refused to rescind the order.

When Kluge learned of the order, he was so angry that he almost became violent. He ordered Hausser to rescind the order, but it was too late: both the command posts of the 7th Army and LXXXIV Corps were behind American lines. Hausser and Choltitz had to make their way through U.S. units on foot to regain their freedom of action. At one point, an American aimed at the SS general, who had to throw himself into a muddy ditch to keep from being killed.

Choltitz was right to oppose Hausser's plan. On July 29 a huge German traffic jam developed along the road to Roncey, with German motorized and horse-drawn vehicles stacked up for two miles—three abreast in places. The American Jabos appeared and had a field day. They attacked virtually nonstop for six hours, destroying hundreds of vehicles, including a hundred tanks and assault guns and 250 motorized vehicles. The slaughter soon became known as "the Roncey Massacre."

Wilke's 5th Parachute Division was down to one rifle regiment when the Americans cut off LXXXIV Corps at the end of July 1944. Wilke, however, managed to lead the regiment through American lines and escape. Later he led it out of the Falaise encirclement as well. He had proved himself to be an excellent commander with a talent for extricating his units from the most difficult situations.

✦

Gustav Wilke was born in Deutsch-Eylau, East Prussia (now Ilawa, Poland), on March 6, 1898. He joined the 4th Grenadier Regiment as an officer cadet in late 1916 and fought in World War I, serving as a company officer in Russia and Belgium (1914–17), Russia again (July–November 1917), and France (late 1917–18). Discharged in January 1920, he reentered the army in February 1925 as a second lieutenant in the Prussian 2nd Infantry Regiment at Allenstein (now Olsztyn, Poland). Except for a year's detached duty with the 1st Artillery Regiment at Königsberg, he remained with the 2nd Infantry until 1935, when, as a captain, he switched over to the Luftwaffe, successively commanding a pilot training company at Perleberg (1935–37), a bomber squadron at Giebelstadt (1937–38), and a flight training company and then a battalion in the 23rd Flight Training Regiment at Magdeburg (1938–39). He then commanded a group in Air Landing Wing Hagenow/Lippstadt (late 1939–1940) and was a group (battalion) commander in the 1st Glider Wing at Griefswald (1940–41). He was assigned to work with Messerschmitt in 1941 to develop large gliders. In May 1942 he commanded a Luftwaffe field regiment on the Eastern Front, and from September 30, 1942, to June 30, 1943, he commanded the 1st Luftwaffe Field Division from its creation at Königsberg to the battles of Lake Ilman and Novgorod on the Eastern Front. On December 9, 1943, he became acting commander of the 2nd Parachute Division when General Ramcke fell ill. He held this post until March 31, 1944, fighting in the battles of Kirovograd, Uman, Kiev, Korsun, and Kishinev on the southern sector of the Eastern Front.

Wilke was initially posted to Brittany but was named commander of the new 5th Parachute Division on April 1, 1944, and was promoted to lieutenant general on May 1. Earlier he had been promoted to second lieutenant (early 1918), first lieutenant (1927), captain (1934), major (1937), lieutenant colonel (November 1, 1939), colonel (1942), and major general (March 1, 1942).[9]

✦

On July 28 Kluge placed the 2nd and 116th Panzer divisions under the command of General von Funck's XXXXVII Panzer Corps and ordered it to move west, to rescue the LXXXIV Corps. Owing to the state of the heavily bombed road network and the ubiquitous fighter-bombers, however, it took days, not hours, to reach the threatened sector. By the time the divisions arrived, it was all over for LXXXIV Corps. Of its thirty thousand men, only ten thousand escaped. The other twenty thousand surrendered by the end of July. By August 2 the U.S. Army reported that it had counted 66 tanks and assault guns, 204 vehicles, and 11 guns destroyed, and 56 tanks/assault guns and 55 motorized vehicles captured or simply abandoned.

While Patton bounced into Brittany with the U.S. VIII Corps and elements of the U.S. XV Corps rounded the German left flank, the U.S. XX Corps and elements of the XV conducted pinning attacks against the 7th Army in Normandy. On August 2, 1944, they scored a significant victory and did not even know it. Lieutenant General Dietrich Kraiss, whose 352nd Infantry Division had inflicted such heavy casualties on the Americans at Omaha Beach on June 6, was struck down by U.S. artillery fire south of St.-Lô. He died on August 6 and was posthumously awarded the Oak Leaves to the Knight's Cross.

9

Counterattack

In early August 1944 Adolf Hitler came up with a plan to snatch victory from the jaws of defeat. He would concentrate the remaining German armor on Army Group B's far left (western) flank and counterattack due west, to Mortain and the sea. In one fell swoop he would thus restore the German front in Normandy and cut off Patton's U.S. 3rd Army, which would then be forced to surrender.

Like most of the Führer's plans in 1944, this one was totally unrealistic. In view of Allied aerial superiority, it exceeded German capabilities by a wide margin. Responsibility for the execution of this flight of strategic fantasy was given to the senior panzer commander available: General Hans von Funck. Funck was an officer who did not like Hitler, and Hitler did not like him either.

◆

Baron Hans Emil Richard von Funck's family originated in East Prussia and were Junker landowners by 1542. Hans von Funck was born at the family estate near Aachen, North Rhine–Westphalia, on December 23, 1891, and grew to be a tall, well-built youth. He was educated at the usual schools in nearby Elbing. His mother died in 1902, and his father passed away in 1914.

It was being orphaned at the age of twenty-three that prompted Funck to volunteer for the Army. He was urged on by his brother, who was already a Leutnant at the outbreak of hostilities on August 3, 1914.[1] On October 11 the younger Funck took the field as a Fahnenjunker and platoon leader in the 2nd Dragoon Regiment, serving on the Eastern Front. He was wounded in action on December 24 and was in the hospital until February. He returned to the field in early May and was promoted to second lieutenant on June 15, 1915. He later served as regimental ordnance (orderly) officer; commander of the machine gun platoon; regimental food, supply, and signals officer; squadron leader; and machine gun squadron leader.[2]

The end of the war in November 1918 had little real effect on the status of units serving in the East, despite the Brest-Litovsk Treaty of earlier that year. White

General of Panzer Troops Hans von Funck, commander of the 7th Panzer Division on the Eastern Front and the XXXXVII Panzer Corps in Normandy. Although Funck was an extremely effective commander, Hitler disliked him and sent him into involuntary unemployment in September 1944 (USAMHI).

Russians, Poles, renegade Soviet bandits, Ukrainian dissidents, and various kinds of deserters all concentrated along the German border, and the 2nd Dragoons was one of the few highly mobile forces available to oppose encroachments. Hans von Funck was seriously wounded in one of these skirmishes on May 21, 1919, and remained in the hospital of the Iron Division until September. The young baron was then sent back to Germany, where he was accepted into the Reichswehr in 1920. He was assigned to the Prussian 6th Cavalry Regiment at Pasewalk, Mecklenburg–West Pomerania.

In 1924 Funck was sent to the Senior Leadership and Tactics at the Stettin War College. After graduation, Lieutenant von Funck was assigned a desk in the Motor Transport Branch of the Reichswehrministerium (Reichs Defense Ministry), where he remained for a year. He then returned to the 6th Cavalry (1927–28), then went back to the Defense Ministry (1928–32), where he headed the motorized arms carrier desk in the inspectorate for motorized troops. He commanded the I Squadron of the 11th Cavalry Regiment near Berlin, where he headed the experimental mechanized units attached to the regiment. On July 1, 1933, he became adjutant to General of Artillery Baron Werner von Fritsch, the newly appointed *Chef der Heeresleitung* (commander in chief of the army). Promotions to major and lieutenant colonel followed in 1934 and 1936. He was sent to Spain as German military attaché to Francisco Franco later that year.

The Blomberg-Fritsch crisis took place in late January 1938. Blomberg was dismissed as defense minister for marrying a former prostitute, and Fritsch was relieved of his command on trumped-up charges of homosexuality. Colonel von Funck's position was also effectively destroyed. He had made an enemy in the arrogant Colonel Walter Warlimont, who was now, as a close associate of Alfred Jodl, the chief of operations of OKW.[3] Funck was stripped of any real power and was eventually packed off to Lisbon as German military attaché.

World War II began on September 1, 1939. Colonel von Funck at once wrote to the HPA for a field assignment; luckily at that time, Heinz Guderian (whom Funck had befriended at Stettin in 1924) was begging for officers to staff the four light divisions that had proved so ineffective in Poland and were being converted into the 6th, 7th, 8th, and 9th Panzer divisions. Funck was hoping for an assignment with one of these new tank divisions. On September 30, however—to his surprise and delight—he was ordered to take command of the veteran 5th Panzer Regiment of the 3rd Panzer Division at Wünsdorf. He led it with great success in the invasion of France. That fall, he was named acting commander of the 3rd Panzer Brigade, which was used to form the cadre of the 5th Light Division. Funck assumed command of this unit on November 1.

Baron von Funck was promoted to major general on January 1, 1941, and was simultaneously earmarked to command the Afrika Korps and sent on a fact-finding mission to North Africa. His negative report to Hitler on the situation in Libya resulted in his appointment being aborted; instead, the new command went to Erwin Rommel. Funck was given Rommel's old division, the 7th Panzer, as sort of a consolation prize.

Funck led the "Ghost Division" from February 1940 until August 16, 1943, when he collapsed owing to exhaustion and wounds during the Battle of Kharkov. It was late November before he secured a clean bill of health from the Medical Board to resume active duty. At that time, he was again ordered to the Eastern Front. On December 4, 1943, General of Infantry Johannes Friessner, the commander of XXIII Corps, had gone on a long-delayed rest leave, and Funck (who had been promoted to lieutenant general on September 1, 1942) was asked to substitute for him. Friessner resumed command on December 20, and Funck returned to Wünsdorf for the dismal Christmas season. On February 15 he was attached to the staff of Lieutenant General Nikolaus von Vormann's XXXXVII

Panzer Corps, which was attempting to break open the Korsun (Cherkassy) Pocket. On March 1 Funck became general of panzer troops and succeeded Vormann as commander of the XXXXVII Panzer Corps. Vormann (who was also promoted) subsequently took over the 9th Army in central Russia.[4] On May 12, 1944, orders arrived from Berlin for the officers of the corps headquarters to fly immediately to France, as a sort of intermediate headquarters for the several panzer divisions was being rebuilt there.

✦

On June 6, 1944, the Allied landings were a success, in part because of the total confusion among the senior German commanders. Geyr quickly moved his panzer group's command post to Chateau-le-Caine, near Thury-Harcourt on the Caen River, so as to better coordinate his forces. He simultaneously ordered Funck to bring his headquarters forward—in hopes that Funck could take over a couple of divisions. The move was hampered—as was everything else—by a cloud of Allied fighter-bombers, which hit anything that moved. Colonel Georg von der Marwitz, Ia of Panzer Group West, reached Vimont with Geyr's operations staff on June 7, but the general himself did not get there until June 8.

On June 9, guided by radio direction finders, the Allied air forces carpet-bombed Geyr's headquarters, wounding the general himself and slaughtering his operations staff. Although Geyr was able to continue on duty, the command apparatus for the panzer group was shattered. Funck immediately put his own staff at Geyr's disposal; XXXXVII Panzer Corps was activated—at a newer, safer headquarters in a concrete reinforced cellar on the outskirts of St. Martin des Besaces. From June 15, Funck was responsible for the Caumont Gap. On July 2 General von Geyr was summarily relieved of his command over what was left of Panzer Group West by a Führer Order, and General der Panzertruppen Hans Eberbach arrived from the southern sector of the Russian Front to take over the command. Though doubtless Eberbach was a very senior general, it was a personal affront to Funck, who had been deliberately passed over. Both men, however, acted together in a friendly and efficient manner.

During July, the situation grew worse as the Allied forces pushed farther and farther into the country. Under Eberbach, Funck's corps headquarters commanded two infantry divisions and the 116th Panzer Division (Lieutenant General Count Gerhard von Schwerin). Kluge had replaced Gerd von Rundstedt as commander in chief, OB West on July 2 and on July 17 Erwin Rommel was severely wounded by a fighter-bomber attack on his staff car and was sent home more dead than alive.

Losses among the men mounted steadily: the equipment suffered even worse, and thanks to the Allied air supremacy, little if any replacement matériel could be brought up. Even food and fuel were in short supply. (Fortunately for Germany, Normandy was an agricultural region, or the situation would have been even worse.) Despite all of this, the Supreme Command—Hitler—expected nothing less than miracles from its field commanders: ground was to be held no matter what and counterattacks were to be launched whether they were possible or not. Thus, on August 2, orders from SS Colonel General Paul Hausser, commander of the 7th Army, reached Funck: the Führer had demanded an attack beginning on August 8 by every available panzer unit against the Allied forces at Mortain and Avranches. XXXXVII Panzer HQ would coordinate the blow.

The plan was ambitious in the extreme. Break through the right flank of the U.S. 1st Army, capture Mortain and Avranches, and cut off the U.S. 3rd Army, which would soon be out of supplies and would be effectively destroyed. Hitler wanted to wait until August 8 so that more American divisions would advance south of Avranches and would thus be destroyed when Funck reached the west coast of the Cotentin.

"My God!" the baron shouted at Colonel Walter Reinhardt, his chief of staff. "What are they thinking of? August 8th—five days? The Jabos will smash every vehicle we possess! We can't group up because of those airborne devils and if we don't group, we can't attack!"

"General Hausser agrees," Reinhardt replied, offering another piece of paper. "He advocates an immediate attack with everything we can scrape together—at dawn tomorrow, the 3rd."[5]

OKW, however, refused that suggestion; Hitler wanted the time to mass every piece of offensive equipment available—to be ready by August 10. By then, he observed, even larger numbers of American forces would have gone through the gap in the German lines and would thus be cut off by the counterattack.

General von Funck appealed to Hausser, who then contacted Kluge. Perhaps the attack could be scheduled for August 6, at dawn? No, OKW retorted angrily. The attack must be postponed until August 8, not a day earlier. Meanwhile, collect every tank, gun, assault gun, armored car—everything and anything. Hausser relayed this to Funck, who at once agreed with him that such a concentration would attract every Allied attack plane in the area. Then Kluge sent a final order: attack at once—by 2200 hours (10:00 p.m.) of August 6—with everything you can lay your hands on! (Map 13 shows this attack and the American reaction.)

Map 13. The Battle of Mortain, August 6–7, 1944

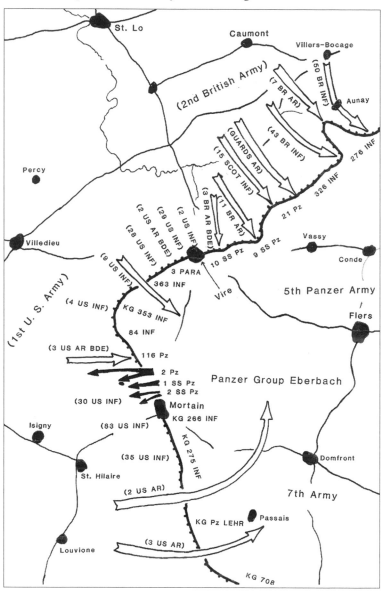

This was what the baron wanted. Orders were despatched to the units involved: Lieutenant General Baron Heinrich von Lüttwitz's 2nd Panzer, Count von Schwerin's 116th Panzer, the few remnants of Fritz Bayerlein's Panzer Lehr Division, SS Major General Theodor Wisch's 1st SS Panzer Division "Leibstandarte

Adolf Hitler," Lammerding's 2nd SS Panzer Division "Das Reich" (now under SS Colonel Baum), and the hastily brought up battle group of the 17th SS Panzer Grenadier Division "Götz von Berlichingen" under SS Colonel Eduard Diesenhofer.

At 10:00 p.m., the right-wing forces lunged forward and, under the cover of darkness (and later heavy overcast), made excellent progress. On the left, however, Schwerin was out of touch with his scattered units and only a mixed battle group of motorcycles, half-track infantry, and three tanks got under way.

"Where is Wisch?" Schwerin's operations' officer, Major Holtermann, telephoned Reinhardt. "He is supposed to be here to back us up!"

Some time later, Reinhardt found out what had happened to the tanks of the Leibstandarte: traveling along a two-mile stretch of sunken road, the column was halted by the purely fortuitous crash of an Allied night fighter on the lead tank—the whole cursing parade had to laboriously back up over a mile to take another road.

"Von Schwerin has utterly fouled us up!" Funck growled at Hausser over the phone sometime later. "My right wing will be held up until after dawn!"

Still the baron and the *Oberstgruppenführer* were relatively well satisfied with the pace of the advance. Dove, Mesnil-Dove, Mesnil-Adelée all fell, and Avranches was less than ten miles distant. When Leibstandarte and the 116th got under way, St.-Barthélmy was overrun before the tanks ran into units of an American armored division on the main Avranches road and a hard but indecisive battle began.

Supported by the survivors of the 17th SS, Otto Baum's "Das Reich" Division smashed the U.S. 30th Infantry Division at Mortain. By 9:00 a.m. on August 7, however, the heavy mists lifted and the sun shone out of a clear sky—which was soon full of Allied warplanes. The attack was effectively stalled and German losses mounted under continual aerial assaults. Despite Hitler's promise that the attack would be supported by three hundred combat aircraft, not a single German airplane managed to reach the Avranches Front.

By nightfall of August 7, Funck was advocating a withdrawal to his starting line. His unit commanders had all reported in—with most pessimistic statements. The 116th was still engaged to the west of Gathemo; the 2nd Panzer had just lost Mesnil-Adelée, which it had captured only that morning; "Leibstandarte" was under powerful assault about five miles east of Juvigny, and though Baum's panzers of the "Das Reich" were still fighting in Mortain, his flanks were being decimated. Diesenhofer's battle group had been driven out of Barenton by a U.S.

heavy weapons battalion. In all, Funck had lost 70 of the 120 operational tanks with which he had begun the battle.

On August 8 General Hans Eberbach was ordered to give over command of his 5th Panzer Army (formerly Panzer Group West) to Sepp Dietrich and take command of a nebulous force to be designated Panzer Group Eberbach.[6] This headquarters was inserted between XXXXVII Panzer Corps and 7th Army and was ordered to renew the attack on August 9. Eberbach protested this unnecessary lengthening of the chain of command, but to no avail.

Funck was also displeased—not so much at being under Eberbach, whom he respected, but at the obvious slap at him for his failure to succeed in his attack—an attack no other general could have carried out any more successfully. He also recommended that Count Gerd von Schwerin, the commander of the 116th Panzer, be relieved of his command. SS General Hausser considered the matter but put it on the back burner for the time being. Meanwhile, circumstances were playing havoc with the XXXXVII's staff. Colonel Reinhardt was transferred to the command of one of the 116th Panzer Division's panzer grenadier regiments, and Colonel von der Marwitz—from Russia—had been brought in to succeed him as corps chief of staff (August 8). Patton had rounded the German left flank, Montgomery continued to pound the right, and the situation continued to deteriorate (Map 14).

✦

Count Gerhard "Gerd" von Schwerin was born in Hanover on June 23, 1899. He attended cadet schools and joined the army as a senior officer cadet on August 10, 1914. Assigned to the elite 2nd Foot Guards Regiment, he was commissioned in 1915 and spent World War I on the Western Front. He was not selected for the Reichswehr and was discharged from the service in 1920. Throughout his career, however, he showed a remarkable ability to make friends in and exert influence on the High Command. He was allowed to join the Reichswehr as a second lieutenant in the Prussian 1st Infantry Regiment at Königsberg in the summer of 1922. When World War II began, he was a lieutenant colonel on the staff of OKH. At the end of the Polish campaign, he was given command of the I Battalion of the elite Grossdeutschland Infantry Regiment—a prized assignment. He led it in the conquest of France, including the decisive Battle of Sedan. He finally gave up command of the I/GD on January 16, 1941, to assume command of the 200th Special Purposes Regiment in Libya.[7]

In North Africa the aristocratic Count von Schwerin was not able to get along with the commoner, Lieutenant General Erwin Rommel, the commander of the Afrika Korps. Rommel sacked Schwerin, his divisional commander, General

Map 14. The Normandy Sector, August 7–11, 1944

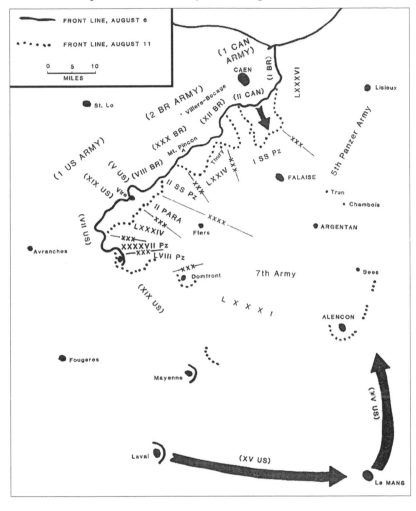

Johannes Streich of the 5th Light, and several others. Fortunately for these men, Franz Halder, the chief of the General Staff, disliked Rommel intensely, so men sacked by Rommel (including Schwerin and Streich) were often given second chances. Streich was given command of the 16th Motorized Infantry Division but was again found lacking. He was relieved by General Guderian during the Russian campaign of 1941 and was finished as a field commander.[8] Schwerin, however, was unemployed for several months, but on July 20, 1941, was named commander of the 76th Motorized Infantry Regiment of the 20th Motorized Division, on the northern sector of the Russian Front.

U.S. Lt. Gen. George Patton (right) exchanging insincerities with British field marshal Sir Bernard Law Montgomery, 1943. Their relationship had not improved by 1944 (USNA).

Count von Schwerin was given a second chance to command a regiment largely because senior field grade officers were needed on the Eastern Front, and he took full advantage of the opportunity. He led his unit in the battles of Tichvin, Volkhov, and Staraja Russa and in the Siege of Leningrad. He earned the Knight's Cross at Schlüsselburg, where he cut the last remaining land route from Leningrad to the rest of Russia. On July 23, 1942, he was named acting commander of the 8th Jäger Division (also on the northern sector), a post he held until November 13, when he received his own division: the 16th Panzer Grenadier (formerly Motorized Infantry), on the southern sector of the Eastern Front. He had made a fine professional comeback. Meanwhile, he was promoted to major general on October 1, 1942. Schwerin continued to fight courageously in Russia, earning the Oak Leaves and Swords, as well as a promotion to lieutenant general on June 1, 1943.

In the spring of 1944 Schwerin's "Greyhound" Division (which was now in remnants) was transferred to France, where it merged the much larger 179th Reserve Panzer Division to form the 116th Panzer Division. Schwerin remained in charge. It was not sent to Normandy until late July.

By now, Count Gerd von Schwerin was an outspoken defeatist and, together with Dr. Speidel, was involved in the anti-Hitler conspiracy. He handled the 116th Panzer poorly during the Mortain counterattack and may have deliberately withheld it from the battle. General von Funck asked the commander of the 7th Army, SS General Hausser, for permission to relieve Schwerin of his command. Hausser agreed in principle but felt that the timing was bad. Schwerin was not relieved until on or about August 23, when Gerhard Müller, a one-armed veteran of the Afrika Korps, was sent to replace him. Müller, however, was not considered a good commander by the staff of the 116th, which basically mutinied against him—an event almost unique in the history of the Wehrmacht. For reasons of his own, Field Marshal Model briefly restored Schwerin to command. (Paris had just fallen, and Model probably decided that he simply did not have time to deal with the Greyhounds.)

Schwerin, meanwhile, led the 116th Panzer into the Siegfried line sector and was charged with defending the vital city of Aachen. The general, however, determined quite on his own that the city could not be successfully defended against the U.S. 1st Army. He decided to disobey Hitler and surrender the place and even sent a message to U.S. General Hodges.

Hitler, the military illiterate, was, for once, quite correct. Germany definitely needed for Aachen to be defended, and Hodges (like Patton) was nearly out of supplies. He had no plans to launch a major assault on Aachen in late August 1944. As a result, the Nazis were given more time to organize the defenses of western Germany, the Gestapo resumed its snooping, and Schwerin's plans were discovered. He was extremely fortunate that the Gestapo had not discovered that he knew about the plot of July 20 and that he escaped with his head for his unauthorized plan to surrender the Holy City of Aachen. He was, however, relieved of his command (again) on September 1, 1944, and was temporarily replaced by Colonel Heinrich Voigtsberger. Voigtsberger, however, was considered too closely allied with General von Schwerin, so he was replaced on September 14 by

Colonel (later Major General) Siegfried Waldenburg. As a divisional commander, this young general proved much superior to either Schwerin or Voigstberger, and he led the Greyhounds with considerable distinction for the rest of the war.[9]

◆

When Hitler sent the most of the panzer divisions to the west, he exposed Hill 112. The British and Canadians, assisted by the Polish 1st Armored Division, seized this critical position while Funck and Eberbach were fighting for Mortain. On the afternoon of August 8, in spite of overwhelming Allied air attacks, the 12th SS Panzer Division, spearheaded by the 101st SS Heavy Panzer Battalion, tried to retake it. They failed, and Michael Wittmann and his crew were killed near the town of St.-Aignan-de-Cramesnil. When last seen by German witnesses, his Tiger was under attack by five Shermans, probably belonging to the Sherbrooke Fusilier Regiment of the Canadian 2nd Armoured Division.

"Michael Wittmann died the way he lived—brave, inspirational and, as always, an example to his men," Kurt Meyer wrote later. "He displayed a true Prussian attitude to duty until his death. . . . However, the spirit of this brave officer lived on in his young tankers who fought and died with the same bravery as their old commander until the end of the struggle."[10] Wittmann was thirty years old.

The bodies of Wittmann and his men were discovered by a French road construction crew in the 1980s. They were reinterred in the La Cambe German war cemetery in 1993.

10

Falaise: Encirclement and Breakout

Gerd von Rundstedt was not the only general Hitler fired on July 2: Geyr von Schweppenburg was sacked as well. He was replaced as commander of Panzer Group West by one of Germany's most capable officers: Hans Eberbach.

✦

Heinrich Karl Alfons Willy "Hans" Eberbach was born in Stuttgart, Württemberg, on November 24, 1895. His father was a prominent businessman who died in 1905. His mother remarried the following year, to one of the partners in the firm, but both were killed in an accident in late 1907. This left the twelve-year-old Eberbach a ward of the firm, which immediately packed him off to a senior boarding school.

The nineteen-year-old orphan joined in the 180th (10th Royal Württemberg Guards) Infantry Regiment as a Fahnenjunker on July 1, 1914.[1] He fought in Belgium and France, was promoted to second lieutenant on February 25, 1915, and was given command of a platoon. On September 25 an enemy rifleman shot his nose off, and he was captured by the French. In part because of his wound,

General of Panzer Troops Hans Eberbach, commander of the 5th Panzer Army, Panzer Group Eberbach, and 7th Army on the Western Front, 1944. A brilliant commander, he was captured by the British at the end of August 1944.

he was repatriated to a hospital in Switzerland in December 1916 and returned to Germany during a prisoner exchange in September 1917. He was sent to a convalescent home in Tübingen, where his nose was partially rebuilt. (It never was the same again, however, and he avoided having photographs taken of his profile whenever possible.) In January 1918 he returned field duty as a platoon leader in the 116th Infantry Regiment—part of the German army in Macedonia.

Eberbach was transferred to Turkey in the summer of 1918 and was appointed a liaison officer to the Turkish 8th Army in Palestine on June 1, 1918. He fought in the battles there and, on September 20, was given command of the rearguard of the Turkish army during the retreat from the Holy Land. The British captured him on September 23.

Eberbach spent the next year languishing in POW camps. He was finally released on November 16, 1919, and returned to Stuttgart, where he was informed that, despite his solid record, he would not be selected for the Reichsheer. Instead, Eberbach joined the Württemberger State Police force as a first lieutenant on December 13, 1919, and was officially discharged from the army the following month.

Eberbach became a pioneer in the use of motorized vehicles, including motorcycles, automobiles, and armored cars, for police work. When Hitler began expanding the army in 1935, Eberbach returned to active duty as a major and assumed command of the 12th Antitank Battalion, which was also stationed at Schwerin in Pomerania, in Wehrkreis II.[2] It was part of the newly formed 12th Infantry Division. Eberbach was promoted to lieutenant colonel in 1937.

Because of his previous experience in motorized police units, Eberbach was named commander of the newly formed 35th Panzer Regiment of the 5th Panzer Brigade of the newly organized 4th Panzer Division at Würzburg in October 1938. He was promoted to colonel on June 1, 1939, and led his regiment in the Polish campaign and in the first twelve days of the French campaign. On May 22, 1940, Eberbach's close friend, Colonel Hermann Breith, the commander of the 5th Panzer Brigade, was seriously wounded and acting command of the brigade devolved on Eberbach.[3] He led the 5th Panzer for the remainder of the French campaign and in the Russian campaign the following year, where he pushed almost to the gates of Moscow.

On January 6, 1942, Eberbach succeeded Colonel Dietrich von Saucken as acting commander of the 4th Panzer Division.[4] The situation at this time was indeed critical. The Wehrmacht was pushed back as far as Orel, and Eberbach was constantly on the defensive or launching counterattacks throughout the month. On February 2 he was wounded in the shoulder and arm while directing a counterattack. He was rushed back to a base hospital at Smolensk, was placed in Führer Reserve, and was sent to a specialist in Würzburg. On March 2 he resumed command of his division. He was promoted to major general on April 1.

Eberbach led the 4th Panzer Division until November 22, 1942, and was on his way back to Germany undergo further treatment for his health, when the war forced him into a completely new situation.

From November 19 to 23, the huge Soviet counterattacks north and south of the German 6th Army overran the 3rd and 4th Romanian armies and cut off the 6th Army in Stalingrad, on the Volga. The XXXXVIII Panzer Corps, which had been assigned to the Romanians as a support, was engulfed in the onslaught and virtually destroyed. Lieutenant General Ferdinand Heim, the commander of the XXXXVIII Panzer, had made a *sauve qui peut* (every man for himself!) retreat across the Don. Heim was summarily recalled, court-martialed for dereliction of duty, and thrown in prison. He was replaced by Major General Hans Cramer, sent post haste from the Panzer Inspectorate in Berlin.[5] Cramer, however, was not up to the assignment. Otto von Knobelsdorff, a veteran lieutenant general, was named Cramer's successor, but he had gone on leave in October and his whereabouts were unknown. An officer at the Panzertruppenamt recommended that Eberbach be rushed in to take up the slack. Eberbach relieved Cramer on November 26.

Although weary and ill, Hans Eberbach took charge of the deteriorating situation. In keeping with his orders and his inclination to hold firm, he dug in his few tanks as pillboxes and deployed every soldier he could lay hands on—even the bakery and signal personnel of the headquarters. A Soviet probe against his unsecured southern flank on November 27 was repulsed by the general himself, leading a flying squad of motorcyclists and a few half-tracks. He remained in command until Knobelsdorff finally arrived on November 30. The next day Eberbach returned to Germany, where he checked into the military hospital for a three-week series of tests and treatments. He was then sent home for a rest. Here he learned that he had been promoted to lieutenant general on January 1, 1943.

Heinz Guderian, who had just been named inspector general of panzer troops, appointed Eberbach his deputy on February 28, with the responsibility of the Home Army's panzer units, including training, inspection, doctrine, production, and development.[6] In the beginning of autumn, however, Eberbach called on Guderian and declared that he (Eberbach) was ready for a couple of months' duty at the front to get firsthand information about the panzer formations. On October

15, 1943, Eberbach (who had been promoted to *General der Panzertruppen* on August 1) relieved the veteran General of Panzer Troops Joachim Lemelsen in temporary command of the XXXXVII Panzer Corps on the southern sector of the Russian Front.[7] On the 22nd, General Lemelsen returned from his leave to arrange the handing over of command of the XXXXVII to its permanent holder, General of Panzer Troops Erhard Raus. General Eberbach, meanwhile, had received an urgent call from his old commander, Colonel General Hermann Hoth, and reached his headquarters at Makarovka, despite Soviet air attacks.

Hoth was deeply concerned. Huge Soviet forces were breaking into the Kiev salient in spite of German resistance, and the city would fall unless some miracle took place. What was worse, however, was that the commander of the powerful XXXXVIII Panzer Corps, General Knobelsdorff, was cracking up. In a desperate state of mind, Knobelsdorff flew to Führer Headquarters to tell Adolf Hitler about the deteriorating military situation. (At Rastenburg, Knobelsdorff would be relieved of his command and sent home to rest and recuperate; he would not be reemployed until February 1944.) Eberbach hurried to XXXXVIII Panzer Headquarters and, by October 25, had managed to stall the Soviet assault. He continued to command the corps until November 25, when Guderian recalled him to Berlin, where he resumed his staff duties.

In early 1944 after conversations with Rundstedt, Rommel, and Geyr, Eberbach became involved in the controversy then raging in France about the disposition of the panzer units and the D-Day invasion.

The eastern generals, by far the majority, recommended the posting of the mobile forces in a central location from which they could launch a powerful counterattack against any Allied force moving inland from the invasion beaches. This seemed sensible—and would have been in Russia because the Red Air Force was not a major factor in the struggle. In the West, however—as Rommel was intensely aware—the Allied air forces would immediately establish aerial domination and smash any major armored concentrations in their assembly areas. Only by posting the panzer divisions near their intended victims could one realistically hope to defeat the Allies on or near the beaches and throw them back into the sea.

Always open-minded, Eberbach came down in favor of Rommel's solution: put the panzers as close to the coast as possible. This would reduce the length of time that they would be exposed to Allied fighter-bombers.

Among the other eastern generals in the West and in Berlin, Eberbach's opinions created consternation: he was "one of them" and his boss, Heinz Guderian, shared Geyr's reserve theory and had so informed the Führer. As a result, for the first time, a certain coolness entered the relationship between Eberbach and Guderian. Because of this, Eberbach suggested that it be best to let him return permanently to active field duty during May.

There is an old adage that states, "One should be careful what one wishes for." Eberbach's request was not acted on for several weeks. Then, on July 2, he was given command of Panzer Group West in Normandy, where the Allies had landed hundreds of thousands of men and where the floodgates were creaking.

✦

As the focus of the battle shifted to the western flank, where the Americans broke out of Normandy on August 1, Montgomery's primary task suddenly changed. His job now was to keep the pressure on Panzer Group West, by launching frontal attacks on its divisions, which would prevent Kluge and Eberbach from withdrawing them or reinforcing the hard-pressed 7th Army. He was not completely successful in the effort because the scales had finally fallen from the eyes of the men in Rastenburg. OKW had at last concluded that the Normandy invasion might not be a diversion after all, and they were at last sending Kluge reinforcements in the form of static infantry divisions from the 15th Army. One of these was the 326th Infantry Division, commanded by Victor von Drabich-Wächter. It replaced the 2nd Panzer Division in the front lines near Caumont on July 22. Monty attacked it again on August 2.

✦

Victor von Drabich-Wächter was born in Strassburg, Alsace (now Strasbourg, France), on August 18, 1889. He was the son of a German officer from Silesia. He became a Fahnenjunker in the Lower Silesian 7th Grenadier Regiment in 1910. Commissioned the following year, he spent almost all of World War I with his regiment on the Western Front, where he served as a company commander (1914), regimental adjutant (late 1914–1916), and company commander again (1916–18). He fought at Les Éparges and Verdun and was seriously wounded in Lorraine in 1914. Drabich was accepted into the Reichsheer and was adjutant and company commander in the 12th Infantry Regiment at Halberstadt, Saxony-Anhalt (1920); on the Staff of the Prussian 3rd Infantry Regiment at Deutsch-Eylau (now Ilawa, Poland); on the Staff, 7th Infantry Regiment at Oppeln (now Opole, Poland) (1920–22); adjutant of the 7th Infantry Regiment (1922–25); and company commander in the Prussian 8th Infantry Regiment at Frankfurt/Oder (1925–30). He was adjutant to the Infantry Commander II at Stettin (1930–33) and was a department head and later office group chief at the powerful HPA from 1933 to 1942. He was promoted to major general (1940) and lieutenant general (August 1, 1942). When Hitler sacked Bodewin Keitel (the brother of the field marshal) as chief of the HPA, Drabich-Wächter (one of his principle deputies) was also involuntarily retired. He was in Führer Reserve from October 1, 1942, until June 1, 1943, when he was finally let out of Hitler's doghouse and was recalled to active duty. He assumed command of the 326th Infantry Division at Narbonne, France, on June 1, 1943. The division was a composite unit, with men from all over western and southwestern Germany. It was transferred to northern France in February 1944 and was placed in 15th Army's reserve.

The 326th Infantry Division was transferred to Normandy and went into the front line on July 22, 1944. Viktor von Drabich-Wächter fought against the British and Canadians and was killed in action at La Mesnil, near Caumont, Normandy, on August 2, 1944.

✦

In the meantime, on August 10, under heavy American pressure, Hans von Funck's XXXXVII Panzer Corps Headquarters evacuated St.-Martin and headed for Briouze. Traveling over damaged roads full of destroyed German vehicles and dodging the ever-present Jabos, General von Funck and Captain von Zydow made the trip of fourteen miles in just under nine hours. The cars of Marwitz and Herschel, the corps chief of operations, were not as fast or fortunate; both were hit by fighter-bomber attacks. Marwitz was severely wounded and Lieutenant Colonel Herschel was killed.

Funck was at once assigned an officer from the Army Group B's staff as his operations officer—Major Artur von Eckesparre, who temporarily also had to double in brass as corps chief of staff. On August 12, under intense Allied attack, the headquarters evacuated Briouze under cover of darkness and took over a ruined farmhouse at Vieux Ponts, a few miles away.

Hitler's second Mortain offensive was never launched because Panzer Group Eberbach was pushed back to the west and the tactical situation became more and more hopeless. Funck and Eberbach, joined on August 14 by SS Lieutenant General Willi Bittrich of the II SS Panzer Corps, were able to stabilize a new defensive line along the Orne River, from Le Ferte Meis through Écouché to Fromentel, but by the morning of August 15 it was undeniable that even maintaining a defense was now out of the question, for 5th Panzer and 7th armies were in danger of being encircled in the Argentan-Falaise area. Nevertheless, Army Group B passed along the latest Führer Order, dated August 13. It insisted blithely on the attack "past Alençon westward." Funck privately informed Eberbach that his divisions were incapable of any such flight of fancy; "Leibstandarte" possessed only thirty battleworthy tanks while 2nd Panzer could field twenty-five and 116th only fifteen. Of 9th Panzer Division, Colonel Max Sperling commanded the equivalent of a company, with no tanks and no guns left in running order. His battle group was merged with 2nd Panzer Division for tactical purposes. (Map 15 shows the developing Falaise Pocket on August 15.)

On August 15, while Eberbach was conferring with Schwerin near Pomme-inville, near Argentan, Funck at Cheneuville received an order from Army Group B to report to the town of Necy for a senior general's conference with Field Marshal von Kluge. He went, to find Hausser, Eberbach, and Dietrich—but no Kluge. After a three-hour wait, the generals returned to their respective commands and the disasters continued on all sectors.

Kluge turned up late that evening, after a harrowing series of escapes from fighter-bomber attacks on his car; he was nervous and far more aware of the real state of affairs than ever before. He had, he told Funck, already suffered a serious

Map 15. The Falaise Pocket, August 13, 1944

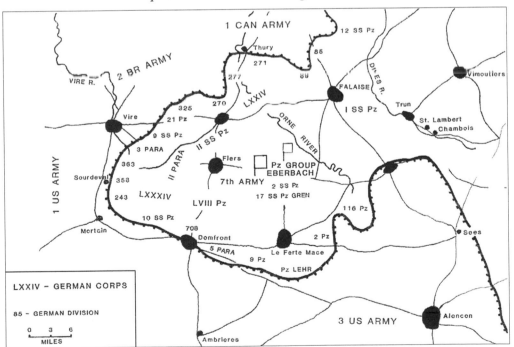

accident in Russia owing to a Soviet air attack on his command vehicle and had spent several months in the hospital as a result. The Americans were far more dangerous, he felt.

The baron sympathized but was adamant in his opinion that only an evacuation of the Falaise "finger" could save the two armies almost encircled within it. The field marshal promised to pass on all the recommendations to OKW in Berlin—for all the good it would do.

On August 16 and 17 the generals of both of the armies ordered all supply service and rear area troops to move as quickly as possible out of the rapidly forming pocket. Falaise fell on August 17th, and Army Group B ordered the II SS Panzer Corps out to a reserve position, but this was cancelled by the collapse of defenses southwest of Falaise, where the Allied troops were rapidly approaching Trun. At the same time, the battered 116th Panzer (the Greyhound Division) was forced out of its positions east of Argentan, allowing a Canadian column to reach and capture Le Bourg-St.-Léonard.

On August 18 Field Marshal Walther Model, who had now replaced Kluge, conferred with the senior generals outside the pocket and gave the order for the withdrawal. The next four days were terrible for the Germans. Although a small gap in the Allied lines was held open, the U.S. and Canadian forces could and did dominate the area with artillery fire and aircraft attacks.

Thanks to lack of supplies, practically all the guns, tanks, and trucks of the XXXXVII Panzer Corps—what remained of them—had to be abandoned. Funck and his staff officers accompanied Lieutenant General von Lüttwitz and his surviving officers with a tight group of three armored cars, preceded and followed by King Tiger tanks for the final breakout at night on August 21.

The convoy of vehicles, covered with riding troopers, surged to safety and reached the Seine. Lüttwitz was wounded in the attack on the hills but, after a brief pause at a field hospital, reported back to duty. They then proceeded to the Metz sector and the West Wall.

Günther von Kluge, meanwhile, was in no hurry to return to Germany. He had been summoned to Berlin and had reason to believe that he would be arrested because of his association with the conspirators of July 20. He did not leave La-Roche-Guyon until an American detachment reached the opposite bank of the Seine and brought the area under mortar fire. He then got in a car and headed east but instructed his driver to stop at Verdun, the site of some of his World War I battlegrounds. Here he spread out a blanket and bit down on a cyanide capsule.

Kluge left behind a letter to Hitler, urging him to make peace. After he read it, the Führer ordered Kluge's state funeral canceled. He was, however, permitted a military honor guard. He was buried at Böhne (near Rathenow), but his grave was destroyed after the war. The month after Kluge's death, both his son and his brother, Lieutenant General Wolfgang von Kluge, were relieved of their duties and later discharged from the army "for political reasons."

✦

The British efforts to break through to meet the Americans cut the 21st Panzer Division in half. Fortunately for the survivors of the 21st, the commander of the encircled forces was Joseph Rauch, a man of considerable guile and experience.

Unlike this brother regimental commanders in the 21st Panzer Division, and almost every other senior officer in Normandy, Rauch did not receive his commission in the usual way. He rose through the enlisted ranks and did not even receive a commission until sixteen years after his initial enlistment. He nevertheless rose to the rank of major general and distinguished himself in Normandy.

Joseph Rauch was born on February 27, 1902, in Kinding in the Eichstätt District of Bavaria. He enlisted in the Bavarian 7th Engineer Battalion in Munich in 1919 and, after twelve years of service, was discharged as a sergeant in 1931. Four years later Hitler officially began his military expansion and faced a serious shortage of officers. Ideally, 7 percent of the army's personnel needed to be officers. In 1935 Germany could not even manage 3 percent. Rauch was offered the opportunity to returned to active duty that year as a territorial (reserve) first lieutenant, and he immediately did so. He was given command of a company in the 84th Engineer Battalion, a bridging unit. He was not given active duty status, however, until September 1, 1939—the day the war began.

Rauch rose rapidly in rank after 1939. He commanded a company in the Bavarian 268th Engineer Battalion of the 268th Infantry Division, which served in the Saar sector. On April 1, 1940, he was transferred to Silesia, where he commanded the 8th Engineer Replacement Battalion. On June 29 he assumed command of the 27th Engineer Battalion of the Bavarian 27th Infantry Division, which was then in France. This turned out to be a major advancement for him, for on November 1, 1940, this division was converted into the 17th Panzer, and Rauch's unit became the 27th Panzer Engineer Battalion.

Rauch led his battalion on the central sector of the Russian Front in 1941 and 1942, fighting at Smolensk, Kiev, Bryansk, Tula, and Orel. Promoted to lieutenant colonel in 1942, he was given command of the 110th Panzer Grenadier

Regiment of the 11th Panzer Division on the southern sector of the Eastern Front. After a successful retreat, Rauch was apparently wounded on January 4, 1943; in any case, he did not return to active duty until May 15, 1943, when he was named commander of the 192nd Panzer Grenadier Regiment of the 21st Panzer Division, which was then forming in France. He was promoted to colonel on April 1, 1944.

Joseph Rauch did an excellent job commanding his regiment (and later battle group) in Normandy, the retreat across France, and in the West Wall. When half of the 21st Panzer Division was encircled at Falaise, Rauch assumed command of the encircled units and successfully broke out of the pocket. The colonel himself led the way.

✦

Army Group B lost another excellent commander on August 20, Theodor Wisch.

Theodor "Teddi" Wisch was born in Wesselburenerkoof, near Wesselburen, Holstein, on December 13, 1907. He joined the SS in 1930 and was commissioned SS second lieutenant in 1933. He was a captain and company commander in the LSSAH when the war began and remained in the unit from 1930 to 1944, rising from SS private to SS major general (effective January 30, 1944). He commanded the 2nd SS Motorized Regiment "LAH" (later the 2nd SS Panzer Grenadier Regiment) from 1942 to 1943 and on October 22, 1943, became commander of the division. In the meantime he saw action in Poland, the Netherlands, Belgium, France, the Balkans, the Eastern Front (two tours), and Italy.

On August 20 Wisch was critically wounded in both legs. His men got him out of the pocket and to a military hospital, where both of his legs had to be amputated. He lived but never returned to active duty.

✦

Lieutenant General Paul Mahlmann's 353rd Infantry Division of the 7th Army was surrounded near Falaise and broke out of the huge pocket with the II Parachute Corps. Perhaps half of the survivors of the division escaped capture. Because of Allied pressure, the 353rd was allowed only a brief respite. It was back at the front in September, controlling a miscellaneous assortment of five local security battalions, an infantry replacement-training regiment, and a Luftwaffe field unit of battalion strength. It was redesignated a Volksgrenadier division in October.

✦

Meanwhile, Lieutenant General Schack's 272nd Infantry Division arrived to reinforce the sagging 5th Panzer Army south of Caen in late July 1944.

Friedrich-August Schack was born on March 27, 1892, in Schmiedeberg am der Netze, Posen Province. He joined the army as a war volunteer in the 1st Hussars Regiment in 1914 and received a commission as a second lieutenant in the 195th Infantry Regiment in September 1915. After serving on the Western Front in World War I (where he was wounded), Schack was selected for retention in the Reichsheer and from 1938 to 1940 commanded the 15th Machine Gun Battalion at Brieg, Silesia (now Brzeg, Poland), and in the Polish campaign. Promoted to regimental commander, he led the 392nd Infantry Regiment (early 1940–42) in Lorraine, Norway, Finland, and the Far North sector of the Eastern Front. He was commandant of the War School at Potsdam (October 1, 1942–March 29, 1943) and, after a short divisional commanders' course, commanded the 216th Infantry Division on the Eastern Front (May 7–October 3, 1943) before assuming command of the 272nd Infantry Division at Antwerp on November 17, 1943—the day it was formed. He was promoted to lieutenant general on January 1, 1944. He had previously been promoted to lieutenant colonel (1937), colonel (October 1, 1940), and major general (July 1, 1943).

The 272nd Infantry Division repulsed several heavy British attacks but was encircled at Falaise in August 1944. Schack led the breakout and the subsequent retreat to the Siegfried line. Although he did an excellent job, General Schack had a highly excitable nature even in normal times and was definitely suffering from combat fatique by the time he and the remnants of his division reached the West Wall. He was nevertheless promoted to the command of the LXXXI Corps at Aachen on September 4—a move that turned out to be a mistake.

✦

Also trapped in the Falaise Pocket was one of the luckier men to fight in the war. Colonel von Gersdorff, the new chief of staff of the 7th Army, was a man who was very fortunate to escape death at the hands of the British, Canadians, Americans, Germans—and himself.

Baron Rudolf-Christoph von Gersdorff was born in Lueben, Silesia (now Lubin, Poland), on March 27, 1905. He joined the army as an officer cadet in 1923 and was commissioned second lieutenant in the 7th Cavalry Regiment in Breslau in late 1926. He remained here until 1935, when he was transferred to the 8th Cavalry Regiment at Brieg, Silesia, as a squadron commander. He began his General Staff training at the War Academy in 1938. This process was cut short by

Germany's mobilization on August 26, 1939. He was Ia of the 14th (later 12th) Army during the Polish campaign. He became Ic of the XII Corps (November 1, 1939), Ia of the 86th Infantry Division (May 6, 1940), Ic of Army Group Center (April 1, 1941), chief of staff of the LXXXII Corps (February 1, 1944), and chief of staff of the 7th Army (July 29, 1944). He was in Führer Reserve from September 18, 1943, to January 1944, when he underwent a stomach operation in Breslau. He was promoted to lieutenant colonel in 1942, colonel on January 1, 1943, and major general on January 30, 1945.

Gersdorff was a member of the anti-Hitler conspiracy. After his wife died of natural causes, he, for a time, had no desire to live. He approached his colleagues in the German Resistance and volunteered to commit suicide—and take Adolf Hitler with him. Gersdorff outfitted himself as a human bomb and primed it to detonate. He used an acid detonator since a ticking colonel would have alerted Hitler's bodyguards. Unfortunately, it is not possible to use such a device with complete accuracy, insofar as the timing is concerned. Gersdorff therefore decided to remain close to the Führer until the bomb exploded. He was only a few feet from the dictator when Hitler suddenly turned on his heels and left the room, and Gersdorff had to hurriedly rid himself of the activated time bomb. He found a restroom, where he defused the bomb and flushed part of it down the toilet. He then sat down on the commode in a state of nervous exhaustion. He later stated that a man could do something like that only once.

After the July 20, 1944, plot failed, Gersdorff was fortunate enough not to be identified by the Gestapo. He was, however, severely injured during the Battle of the Falaise Pocket, where he escaped hails of American artillery fire and attacks by fighter-bombers with a minor wound, only to be struck by lightning. His men, however, managed to get him to safety.

✦

While Gersdorff, Mahlmann, and Schack escaped the deteriorating pocket at Falaise, not every German was so lucky. Otto Elfeldt is a case in point.

Otto Elfeldt was born in Bad Sülze, Mecklenburg, on October 10, 1895, and joined the army as an officer cadet in the 20th Foot Artillery Regiment in June 1914. Elfeldt spent most of World War I on the staff of the regiment, fighting on the Marne, in Champagne, at Verdun (1916–17), on the Côtes de Meuse, on the Aisne, and at Chemins des Dames. In late 1917 Lieutenant Elfeldt was attached to the Headquarters, XIV Corps, as an artillery signals officer. He returned to the 20th Artillery as a regimental adjutant in May and held that post until the end of the war. He joined the Reichsheer in 1920 and served in artillery units until 1939, mainly with the 2nd Artillery Regiment at Stettin, Pomerania (1920–34). He was meanwhile promoted to second lieutenant (1915), first lieutenant (1925), captain (1929), major (1935), and lieutenant colonel (1938). Promotions to colonel (June 1, 1940), major general (January 1, 1943), and lieutenant general (August 8, 1944) would follow. Elfeldt served as commander of the II Battalion/56th Artillery Regiment in Hamburg-Wandsbek (1935–39), commander of the 619th Artillery Regiment on the northwestern coast of Germany (1939), on the staff of Army Group A (1939–40), chief of staff to the general of artillery at OKH (1940–42), and commander of the 302nd and 47th Infantry Divisions (November 26, 1942, to November 12, 1943, and December 27, 1943, to July 30, 1944, respectively). Elfeldt led the 302nd on the southern sector of the Russian Front and the 47th in France, where it was posted near Pas de Calais as part of the 15th Army. It was still there when General Elfeldt was summoned to Normandy.

Elfeldt became acting commander of the LXXXIV Corps in Normandy after Kluge fired General von Choltitz at the end of July. There was nothing he could do, however, to prevent the disaster that was even then overtaking 7th Army. Elfeldt led the LXXXIV in the Battle of the Falaise Pocket. During the breakout of August 20, he joined Kurt Meyer and the remnants of the 12th SS Panzer Division—the only more or less intact formation left in LXXXIV Corps. Elfeldt and his staff company formed the rearguard during the breakout. Meyer escaped, but Elfeldt and his detachment became separated from the main body and blundered into the Polish 1st Armored Division. He was captured near St. Lambert during the night of August 20–21. Not enough of the corps staff escaped to justify rebuilding it, so it was officially disbanded shortly thereafter.

◆

The retreat of Army Group B from the Falaise Pocket was covered by General of Infantry Erich Straube's LXXIV Corps.

Erich Straube was born in Elsterwerda, Saxony, on December 11, 1887. He became an officer cadet in 1907 and was commissioned in the 62nd Infantry Regiment in early 1909. A major when the Nazis came to power, he was promoted to lieutenant colonel (1933), colonel (1935), major general (June 1, 1939), lieutenant general (June 1, 1941), and general of infantry (June 1, 1942). He commanded the 82nd Infantry Regiment in Göttingen, Lower Saxony (1936–38); the War School at Munich (1938–39); and the 268th Infantry Division (August

General of Infantry Erich Straube, the tough commander of the LXXIV Corps. A forgotten hero of the Battle of the Falaise Pocket, he commanded the rear guard of Army Group B during the breakout from the encirclement and escaped with a sizable portion of his command—a feat of tactical brilliance. He was commander of the 1st Parachute Army at the end of the war.

26, 1939–1942) in the Saar, against the Maginot line, in occupied Poland, and on the central sector of the Russian Front, including the battles of Brest-Litovsk, Smolensk, Yelnya, Vyasma, Tula (near Moscow), and Juchnov, among others. He gave up command on January 6, 1942, and, after a leave, took charge of the XIII Corps on the Eastern Front (April 21, 1942–February 20, 1943), on the Don and at Voronesch. He was on inactive duty status from February 2 to August 1, 1943, when he assumed command of the LXXIV Corps in Brittany, which had been formed four days before.

Straube's LXXIV Corps was transferred to Normandy in late June and was inserted in the German line between the I SS Panzer and II SS Panzer Corps. It defended the excellent defensive terrain in the Villers-Bocage/Mount Pincon sector and initially controlled the 277th, 276th, and 326th infantry divisions. Later, when the XXXXVII Panzer Corps was pulled out of the line and sent west to launch the Mortain offensive, it took over part of the Caumont Gap sector, along with the 326th Infantry Division and elements of the 21st Panzer Division.

During the Battle of the Falaise Pocket, Straube's corps was given the unenviable position of covering the retreat of the entire army group. It controlled six battered divisions: the 276th Infantry (Lieutenant General Curt Badinski), the 277th Infantry (Colonel Wilhelm Viebig), the 271st Infantry (Lieutenant General Paul Danhauser); the 84th Infantry (Lieutenant General Erwin Menny); the 326th Infantry (Colonel Dr. Erwin Kaschner); and the 363rd Infantry (Lieutenant General Augustus Dettling).

✦

Curt Badinski was born in Grebenstein (ten miles northwest of Kassel), Hesse, on May 17, 1890. He became a Fahnenjunker in the 9th Jäger Battalion in 1910 and was commissioned the following year. He was later promoted to first lieutenant (1916), captain (1923), major (1933), lieutenant colonel (1936), colonel (1938), major general (February 1, 1942), and lieutenant general (March 1, 1943). He commanded the machine gun company of the 9th Jäger in 1914 and fought on the Western Front from 1914 to 1917. He became battalion adjutant in early 1915 but was severely wounded on June 29. He resumed his duties after he recovered but was again machine gun company commander in 1917. Later that year he was sent to Macedonia and became adjutant of the 22nd Infantry Brigade, a post he held until early 1919. Selected for retention in the Reichsheer, he spent the Weimar Era in infantry units, including tours of duty as a company commander in the 6th Infantry Regiment at Lübeck (1920–26) and the 2nd Infantry Regiment in Allenstein, East Prussia (now Olsztyn, Poland) (1926–32). He was a tactics instructor at the War School at Dresden (1933–36) and led the I/16th Infantry Regiment at Oldenburg in northwest Germany (1936–39). When the Third Reich mobilized on August 26, 1939, Badinski was given command of the 489th Infantry Regiment, which he led in France in 1940. From then until April 1941, the 489th was on occupation duty in Denmark; then it was sent to East Prussia, and it crossed into the Soviet Union on June 22, 1941. By October it had suffered more than 50 percent casualties. In January 1942 Badinski was sent to the Moscow sector, where he assumed command of the 23rd Infantry Division, which was down to an infantry strength of slightly more than a thousand men. Badinski led it until July 10, 1942, when he apparently fell ill. He returned to duty on September 1 as commander of the 269th Infantry Division, of which his old regiment, the 489th Infantry, was a part. This division had been sent to Bergen, Norway, where it partially rebuilt. Badinski remained here until November 1943, when he assumed command of the 276th Infantry Division in Germany.

The 276th Infantry Division was sent to Dax, France, in January 1944, and was involved in the Normandy fighting from mid-June. It was trapped in the Falaise Pocket on August 20–21 and virtually destroyed; a small part of the division did break out, but General Badinski was captured on August 21. After Falaise, the High Command considered disbanding the 276th but eventually decided to rebuild it in West Prussia as a Volksgrenadier division. The division was so disorganized and scattered that a successor to General Badinski was not named until September 4.

Wilhelm Viebig was born in Horst, Mecklenburg–West Pomerania, on June 3, 1899, and entered the service as a Fahnenjunker in 1916. Commissioned Leutnant in the 3rd Field Artillery Regiment in 1917, he fought on the Russian Front and in France in World War I, served in the Reichsheer, and was a major commanding the Brandenburger II/23rd Artillery Regiment in Potsdam in 1937. His subsequent career was not particularly distinguished. He was named commander of the 257th Artillery Regiment when Germany mobilized on August 26, 1939, and fought in Poland and in France (against the Maginot line), but was not promoted to lieutenant colonel until the spring of 1940 and did not become a colonel until 1942. In the meantime he served on Manstein's artillery staff (something of a demotion), commanded the 23rd Artillery Regiment on the central sector of the Eastern Front (1941–42), and led the 93rd Panzer Artillery Regiment of the 26th Panzer Division in Russia and Italy (1942–44). He assumed command of the 277th Infantry Division on August 10, 1944, but was not promoted to major general until January 1, 1945.

During the Battle of the Falaise Pocket, Viebig's division was crushed. He escaped with twenty-five hundred men—only a thousand of whom were combat troops. He and his division were sent to Hungary, where the division was rebuilt as a Volksgrenadier unit. This process was completed in time for the 277th to participate in the Battle of the Bulge.

Paul Danhauser was born in Regensburg, Bavaria, on August 2, 1892, and joined the Imperial Army as a Fahnenjunker in 1911. He attended the War School in Munich and was commissioned second lieutenant in the 15th Bavarian Infantry Regiment in 1913. He was appointed platoon leader and food supply officer for the replacement battalion of the 4th Bavarian Brigade when World War I began on August 2, 1914. He saw action on the Western Front and became battalion adjutant in November. His unit was taken over by the 1st Bavarian Replacement Regiment later that month, and Danhauser served with this command for the rest of the war, becoming regimental adjutant, company commander, and acting battalion commander. He was promoted to first lieutenant in 1917.

Selected for the Reichsheer, Danhauser joined the 20th Infantry Regiment in his hometown at the beginning of 1920 and remained with it until October

1932, serving as an orderly officer, regimental adjutant (1923–25), company commander (1925–30), and battalion staff officer. Promoted to captain in 1923 and to major ten years later, he was attached to the naval infantry from 1932 to 1935 as a tactics instructor at Swinemünde and Flensburg. From the spring of 1935 to October 1936, Danhauser was a group leader in the field equipment inspectorate of the General Army Office in the Defense Ministry. On October 12, 1936, however, he assumed command of the III Battalion of the 106th Infantry Regiment at Würzburg. Promoted to lieutenant colonel in 1936 and to colonel in 1938, he was on the regimental staff when Germany mobilized on August 26, 1939. At that time, he was named commander of the 214th Infantry Replacement Regiment at Hanau, Hesse, about fifteen miles east of Frankfurt/ Main. During the Polish campaign, however, he was attached to the staff of the XIII Corps and took part in the battles of Bzura and Warsaw, before returning to Hanua.

On August 20, 1940, after the French campaign, Danhauser became commander of the 36th Infantry Regiment of the excellent 9th Infantry Division, but he held the post for only six weeks. On October 5 he returned to Hanau, where he assumed command of the newly formed 427th Infantry Regiment. He led this unit in the invasion of the Soviet Union and fought at Rzhev, Smolensk, Vitebsk, in the drive on Moscow, and against Stalin's winter offensive of 1941–42. On February 14, 1942, he was named commander of the 256th Infantry Division, which he also led on the central sector of the Eastern Front, fighting at Smolensk and Rzhev. He was promoted to major general on April 1, 1942, and lieutenant general on March 1, 1943.

General Danhauser left Russia in late November 1943 and traveled to northern Bavaria, where the 271st Infantry Division was forming. This unit included the remnants of the 137th Infantry Division (which had been smashed in Russia), as well as four training and two eastern battalions. Danhauser formally assumed command on December 10. The 271st was sent to the Netherlands in early 1944 and, despite the fact that it was considerably understrength, it was sent to southern France, where it occupied a sector of the Mediterranean coast in June 1944.

Because Rommel and Rundstedt were begging for infantry divisions in Normandy, General Danhauser and his men were ordered to the Caen sector and replaced the 10th SS Panzer Division in the line on July 17. They fought well, but the 271st Infantry Division was trapped in the Falaise Pocket, where it was largely destroyed. Danhauser, however, broke out with the remnants of his command. The division was then sent to Holland, where it was rebuilt as a Volksgrenadier division.

✦

On July 29 Erwin Menny and his 84th Infantry Division arrived in Normandy, where it opposed Montgomery's drive on Falaise.

Erwin Menny was born in Saarburg on August 10, 1893. He joined the army as a Fahnenjunker and was commissioned in the 22nd Dragoons in February 1914. He fought in World War I, served in the Reichsheer, and was promoted to lieutenant colonel in 1937. He was named commander of the XVIII Antitank Command in late 1938. He was promoted to colonel on April 1, 1939. During World War II, he commanded the 81st Replacement Rifle Regiment (1939–40), the 69th Rifle Regiment (1940–41), and the 15th Rifle Brigade of the Afrika Korps. In this position he played a prominent role in the capture of Tobruk. Promoted to major general on April 1, 1942, he became acting commander of the 18th Panzer Division on the Eastern Front on September 15, 1942. He was promoted to lieutenant general on October 1, 1943, and successively assumed command (or acting command) of the 333rd Infantry Division (July 10, 1943), the 123rd Infantry Division (October 17, 1943), and the 72nd Infantry Division (November 1–20, 1943)—all on the southern sector of the Eastern Front.

General Menny was sent to the Dieppe area of northern France in February 1944 and was charged with the task of forming the 84th Infantry Division. By D-Day this mission was largely accomplished, and the 84th was in 15th Army's reserve, just behind the Channel coast. On July 29 Erwin Menny and his 84th Infantry Division arrived in Normandy, where it opposed Montgomery's drive on Falaise. The division was destroyed in the Falaise Pocket on August 20, and General Menny was captured by the British on August 21, 1944.

✦

Erwin Kaschner had been in command of the 326th Infantry Division for only five days when he had to fight his way out of the Falaise Pocket.

Dr. **Erwin Kaschner** was born in Görlitz on October 14, 1897. He entered the service as a war volunteer in the 130th Infantry Regiment in June 1915 and was awarded a reserve commission in the 203rd Reserve Infantry Regiment in 1917. He served as a platoon leader and orderly officer until July 29, 1918, when he was wounded and captured by the British. He was released from the POW camps and discharged at the end of 1919. Kaschner returned to school in 1920 and earned a PhD in agriculture from the University of Breslau in 1926.

He became a warrant officer in the 6th Infantry Regiment at Lübeck in 1927. As Hitler began to secretly expand the army, he applied to have his commission restored and became a captain in 1934. He was a company commander in 1938 and was a major when the war broke out. Upon mobilization (August 26, 1939), he was given command a battalion in the newly formed 486th Infantry Regiment, which he led in the Saar, against the Maginot line, and in the first battles on the Eastern Front. Later he commanded the regiment itself (August 17, 1941–September 1943) and participated in the battles of Brody, Zhitomir, Kiev, Bryansk, and Orel, among others. He assumed command of the 461st Infantry Regiment, also on the Eastern Front, in September 1943. After attending the monthlong Division Commanders' Course in the summer of 1944, he assumed command of the 326th Infantry Division on August 15, 1944, and led it for the rest of the war.

Although Kaschner succeeded in escaping the Falaise Pocket, his division was completely smashed. In late August it was collecting its stragglers in the St.-Quentin–Somme River area but was soon sent to a safer region (Galanta, Hungary), where it was rebuilt as a Volksgrenadier division. Meanwhile, Lieutenant General August Dettling made a courageous escape from the Falaise Pocket with the remnants of his command.

August Dettling was born in Stuttgart, Württemberg, on August 7, 1893. He entered the service as a Fahnenjunker in the 180th Infantry Regiment of the 26th Reserve Division in 1911, attended the War School at Danzig, and was commissioned on November 19, 1912. He spent all but three months of World War I with his regiment, serving as a battalion adjutant, company commander, machine gun officer, acting regimental adjutant, and acting battalion commander. In the process, he fought in the Vosges, in Artois, on the Somme, in the Hindenburg line, in Flanders, and at Arras and Cambrai. He was wounded at least once and was promoted to first lieutenant in 1916.

Dettling was selected for the Reichswehr and spent the years 1921 to 1933 with the 13th Infantry Regiment in Ludwigsburg (seven miles north of Stuttgart), where he spent three years as a company commander and four years as regimental adjutant. He was promoted to captain in 1922 and to major on April 1, 1933. The following October he was named adjutant to the Artillery Leader V, which can also be translated as V Artillery Command. The Staff, Artillery Leader V, became Staff, 15th Infantry Division, at Würzburg in 1935, and Dettling stayed on as adjutant. He took command of the I/56th Infantry Regiment at Ulm in October 1936, and when Germany mobilized in 1939, he became commander of the 195th Infantry Regiment of the 78th Infantry Division. Meanwhile, he was promoted to lieutenant colonel in 1935 and to colonel in 1938.

August Dettling led his regiment on the Upper Rhine and in the conquests of Belgium and France. He was given command of the 523rd Infantry Regiment of the 297th Infantry Division in mid-December 1940 and commanded it on the Eastern Front, fighting at Kholm, Zhitomir, Uman, Kiev, and Kharkov, among other battles. Promoted to major general on November 1, 1941, he was named commander of the 183rd Infantry Division on January 20, 1942. He continued to serve on the Russian Front and fought in the Battle of Moscow, at Gshatsk, Spas-Demensk, and Kiev, among other places. By October 1943 his division had suffered so many casualties that it was merged with two other divisions (the 217th Infantry and the 339th Infantry) to form Corps Detachment C. Dettling, who had been promoted to lieutenant general on January 1, 1943, was dubbed corps detachment commander; however, on November 15 he was sent home on leave. The following month he was sent to Poland, where he assumed command of the 363rd Infantry Division, which was in the process of forming.

The 363rd was a six-grenadier-battalion unit made up largely of veterans from the Eastern Front. It was transferred to the Jutland peninsula of Denmark in March and April 1944, and then to Rouen, France. It was transferred to Normandy just in time to be caught up in the Battle of the Falaise Pocket.

The 363rd Division was crushed in the Falaise battles. General Dettling was wounded but nevertheless retained command and led his division in a desperate breakout attempt. It was partially successful. Dettling escaped, along with twenty-five hundred of his men. They were sent to the Wildflecken Troop Maneuver Area in lower Franconia, where they formed the nucleus of the 363rd Volksgrenadier Division.

✦

Even though he formed the rear guard, Erich Straube somehow escaped in the darkness, reached German lines, reformed what was left of his LXXIV Corps, and took it into the West Wall.

On August 20, 1944, there were still remnants of other units that were not members of Straube's LXXIV Corps. One of these was a remnant of the 12th SS Panzer Regiment of the Hitler Youth SS Panzer Division. It was led by SS Lieutenant Colonel Max Wünsche.

✦

Max Wünsche was blond, handsome, and looked as though he belonged on a Nazi recruiting poster. He was born in Kittlitz, Schleswig-Holstein, on April 20, 1915. After finishing high school, he attended a business school and eventually became a department head in an accounting firm. In November 1932 he became a member of the Hitler Youth, and in the spring of 1933 he joined the SS-VT. He attended an army noncommissioned officer training course at Jüterbog (the home of the Artillery School) and an SS officers' training course at the SS-Junkerschule at Bad Tölz. He graduated in 1936 and was promoted to SS second lieutenant on April 20, 1936. Wünsche then became a platoon leader in the LSSAH.

On October 1, 1938, Wünsche became an orderly officer in Hitler's personal guard detachment, the Begleitkommando des Führers. A fanatical believer in the Führer, Wünsche defended him even after the war and openly questioned that the murder of the Jews during World War II was systematic.

After the Polish campaign, Wünsche transferred back to the Leibstandarte and became a platoon leader in Kurt Meyer's motorcycle company. He fought in the Netherlands, where he was wounded on May 15, 1940. During the Battle of France, Wünsche commanded the motorcycle company (15./Leibstandarte SS Adolf Hitler) because Meyer was wounded. He returned to his duties at Führer Headquarters in June but was dismissed from his post after a dispute with one of Hitler's butlers in late 1940. He returned to the LSSAH as Sepp Dietrich's adjutant in December 1940.

During the invasion of Russia, Wünsche was twice named acting Ia of the division. In February 1942 he was appointed commander of the division's assault gun battalion. He was instrumental in repulsing several Soviet breakout attempts.

Max Wünsche returned to Germany in June 1942, in order to attend the abbreviated (three-month) General Staff course in Berlin. He then went back to Russia, where he was named commander of the I Battalion of the newly formed 1st SS Panzer Regiment in October 1942. He particularly distinguished himself in the 3rd Battle of Kharkov (March 1943).

Wünsche was promoted to SS first lieutenant (1938), SS captain (May 25, 1940), SS major (September 1, 1942), and SS lieutenant colonel (January 30, 1944). He was named commander of the 12th SS Panzer Regiment of the 12th SS Panzer Division "Hitlerjugend" in June 1943.

Max Wünsche trained his regiment well. Between June 7 and mid-July 1944, it was credited with destroying 219 enemy tanks. Wünsche was awarded the Oak Leaves on August 11. (He had been awarded the Knight's Cross after Kharkov.) During the night of August 20–21, however, he was trapped in the Falaise Pocket. He broke out on foot but was shot in the calf in the process. He and his adjutant hid out until August 24, when they were captured.

The Falaise Pocket was cleared by August 24. After Falaise, most of the German generals were no longer trying to defend Fortress Europe. They were simply trying to escape.

11

The Fall of France

After the Battle of the Falaise Pocket, from the German point of view, France seemed doomed. To salvage the western portion of his empire, Adolf Hitler summoned the officer he considered his best general and the man he consistently chose for the most difficult and dangerous missions: Field Marshal Walter Model.

✦

Walter Model was perhaps the most capable of the Nazi generals. He was born in Genthin, Saxony-Anhalt, on January 24, 1891, the son of a music teacher of very modest means. He joined the army in 1909 as a Fahnenjunker in the 52nd Infantry Regiment and almost quit because of the harshness of the training, but his uncle persuaded him to continue. Sent to the Western Front with his regiment, he became adjutant of the I Battalion before he was severely wounded near Arras in May 1915. Promoted to first lieutenant in 1915, he took part in the early stages of the Battle of Verdun before being sent to an abbreviated General Staff course in 1916. He served on the staff of the 5th Infantry Division and fought at Verdun again (late 1916) and in the Vosges and Champagne districts (1917), where the 5th was lightly engaged. Model was promoted to captain in November 1917 and served on the staff of the Guards Ersatz Division during the summer offensive of 1918; he ended the war with the 36th Reserve Division in the Somme sector.

Model served in "the war after the war," during which he was engaged in putting down Communist insurrections in the Ruhr. Here he met Herta Huyssen, his future wife. She gave him three children: Christa, Hella, and Hansgeorg, a future West German general. He was selected for the Reichsheer in 1919 and first established a reputation for himself by writing a small book about Field Marshal August Gneisenau (1760–1831). Later he became known as an expert on technical and training matters. Physically he was tough, shorter than average, somewhat thickset, with a close-cropped "whitewall" haircut, and he sported a monocle, which he wore constantly. Most of all, he astonished everyone he knew with his incredible energy.

*Field Marshal Walter
Model, the Führer's fireman
(USAMHI).*

Model was assigned to the 2nd Infantry Regiment (1920) (where he commanded a company) and the 3rd Infantry Division (1925). He progressively was a General Staff tactics instructor (1928), chief of the training branch at the Truppenamt (the clandestine General Staff) (1930), a battalion commander at Allenstein, East Prussia (1932), and chief of the technical office (late 1933). A pro-Nazi, he annoyed General Ludwig Beck, the chief of the General Staff, during the Sudetenland Crisis of 1938 by constructing duplicates of Czech fortifications and then proving that German forces could successfully attack them. He was nevertheless promoted to major (1929), lieutenant colonel (1932), colonel (1934), and major general (March 1, 1938). Humorless and with no friends, he was blunt, outspoken, an uncomfortable subordinate, and a very difficult superior—especially to his officers.

Model was chief of staff of the IV Corps during the Polish campaign and was chief of staff the 16th Army during the French campaign of 1940. Promoted to lieutenant general on April 1, 1940, he led the 3rd Panzer Division in Russia until October 1, 1941, when he became commander of the XXXXI Panzer Corps. He was promoted to general of panzer troops on October 1, 1941. Then, on January 12, 1942, he was given command of the 9th Army, which was nearly surrounded just west of Moscow. Model saved the 9th Army, despite being outnumbered

4 to 1. He also dealt with Hitler's interference in his operations in a manner almost no other general ever got away with.

During the winter of 1941–42, the Soviets were obviously regrouping to launch another offensive aimed at wiping out the Rzhev salient, which they had nearly surrounded. Model asked for reinforcements, and Hitler and OKW agreed to give him a panzer corps—but they also told him where to place it—in the spot they thought the Reds would strike. Model refused to accept this kind of interference in his operations, so he flew to Führer Headquarters to meet with Hitler. After a brief argument, General Model screwed his monocle into his right eye, looked down on the dictator as if he were an insect, and coldly asked, "Führer, who commands 9th Army—you or I?" Hitler's mouth fell open. No one had spoken to him in this manner for years. Before Hitler could regain his intellectual balance, the general told the former corporal in no uncertain terms that he (Model) knew much more about the local situation than did anyone at Führer Headquarters, and that included Hitler himself. They, after all, knew the terrain only from maps, whereas he had actually been there. Furthermore, he insisted on being allowed to conduct the battle as he saw fit. The flabbergasted dictator backed down immediately.

"Did you see that eye?" a wide-eyed Hitler later asked a member of his entourage. "I trust that man to do it [stop the Soviets]. But I wouldn't want to serve under him!"

Stalin's men attacked exactly where Model said they would and were slaughtered by the newly arrived panzer corps. And the pattern was set. Not even Hitler was allowed to interfere in the military operations of Walter Model.

Model was seriously wounded on September 1, 1942, when a Soviet bullet cut his pulmonary artery. He returned to duty in January 1943 and led the 9th Army in the Battle of Kursk, where his strategy was largely responsible for the German defeat. He nevertheless was given command of the 2nd Panzer Army (while simultanouesly leading the 9th). In the spring of 1943 Model conducted a skillful withdrawal from the Rzhev salient, inflicting heavy losses on the Red Army in the process. On March 31, 1944, he was given command of Army Group North. Later he commanded Army Groups South (later North Ukraine) and Center, before being sent to the Western Front. Known as "the Führer's Fireman," he was given only the most difficult assignments, and he often mastered them. He was promoted to field marshal on March 1, 1944.

✦

On August 15, 1944, Hitler ordered Model to report to La-Roche-Guyon to assume command of OB West and Army Group B. Model arrived on the evening of August 17 and discovered that he had inherited a disaster. He salvaged as much as he could from the Falaise Pocket (about half of Army Group B escaped) and retreated to the German border. The Allies closed the pocket at 6:00 a.m. on August 21. Army Group B had lost approximately ten thousand killed and forty to fifty thousand missing or captured. Fewer than fifty thousand men escaped. Naturally, the losses were heaviest in the combat units. Lüttwitz's 2nd Panzer, for example, lost 90 percent of its armor in Normandy and was down to its last fifteen tanks when the general—who was ignoring his wounds—personally led the remnants of the division out of the pocket. He was followed by half of the Greyhounds of the 116th Panzer Division. The other half—including its last ten tanks—was destroyed near Trun.

After Falaise, Army Group B was a complete wreck. A partial inventory of the battlefield revealed that the two German armies and Panzer Group Eberbach had lost 220 tanks, 160 assault guns (including self-propelled artillery), 700 towed artillery pieces, 130 antiaircraft guns, 130 half-tracks, 5,000 motorized vehicles, and 2,000 wagons. At least 1,800 horses had been killed in the pocket, and another 1,000 were captured by the U.S. 90th Infantry Division alone. Between them, the seven panzer divisions that escaped the pocket escaped with only 62 tanks and 26 guns; they had lost 1,300 tanks in Normandy. Panzer Lehr, the 10th SS Panzer, the 116th Panzer, and the 9th Panzer divisions had no "runners" (operational tanks) left at all. All totaled, the German armies in Normandy had lost at least 50,000 men killed and 200,000 captured, and tens of thousands of others were isolated in various "fortresses" or on the Channel Islands. Clearly, the German grip on France was broken.[1]

Hitler, of course, wanted Model to hold Paris. He ordered that an obstacle line be established south of the city to slow the Allied advance. To command this blocking force, he selected Hubertus von Aulock.

◆

Hubertus von Aulock was born in Kochelsdorf on October 2, 1891. He joined the army as a Fahnenjunker and was commissioned in the 22nd Infantry Regiment in 1912. He served with this unit throughout World War I and spent the entire conflict on the Western Front, fighting in France and Flanders as a platoon leader, company commander, and battalion adjutant. He joined the Freikorps in "the war after the war" and was discharged from the army in 1920 as an honorary captain. Not interested in a military career, he was nevertheless recalled to active duty on August 26, 1939, when the Third Reich mobilized for World War II. Initially he was headquarters commandant of the 403rd Corps Supply Command. Aulock was promoted to major on October 1, 1939, and to lieutenant colonel on July 1, 1942. In the meantime he was headquarters commandant of the III Corps during the French campaign (1940) and, from November 1940 to April 1, 1941, was acting commander of the 800th Special Purposes Instructional Regiment "Brandenburg." In May 1941 he was appointed to the staff of the military commander, Northwest France, and remained with this headquarters until the autumn of 1944.

On August 15, 1944, Hubertus von Aulock became commander of the ad hoc Battle Group von Aulock, with which he was ordered to defend Paris. He was officially promoted to major general of reserves on August 21, 1944, bypassing the rank of colonel altogether. Choltitz gave Aulock enough soldiers to man the line south of Paris: twenty-five to thirty thousand men from Lieutenant General Baron Hans von Boineburg-Lengsfeld's 325th Security Division—but they were rear area troops, accustomed to the luxurious duty in Paris, not to the rigors of combat. Choltitz himself remained in the city with five thousand men, supported by fifty guns and about sixty airplanes.

With his low-quality troops, Aulock could do little to even delay the Allied advance on Paris. After the city fell, he tried to escape with the remnants of his command, but he was captured on September 2, 1944, before he could reach the Siegfried line.

◆

As the Allies approached the City of Light, Hitler signaled Model and demanded that it be held. The monocled general immediately sat down and wrote out a list of the reinforcements he would require to hold the city. Hitler could not fill even 10 percent of his requirements. Rather than argue with Model—always a fruitless adventure—he ordered the city be destroyed. Model passed the order on to General von Choltitz, who ignored it. Not wanting to go down in history as the destroyer of Paris, he surrendered the place on August 25. Model immediately drafted court-martial charges against him.

The field marshal, meanwhile, retreated across the Seine, closely pursued by the Allies (Map 16). In the process he lost much of his remaining force. General of Panzer Troops Walter Krüger came up with a plan to salvage part of the German army. He sent about a hundred officers from his LVIII Panzer Corps to block the roads and to rally the troops streaming to the rear. He experienced some success in this effort and no doubt would have experienced more, had not the Allied pursuit been so rapid.

◆

Walter Krüger was born in Zeitz, Saxony-Anhalt, on March 23, 1892, and joined the army as an infantry officer cadet in 1910. He transferred to the cavalry after receiving his commission in 1911. A member of the 19th Hussar Regiment, he distinguished himself in World War I, fighting on the Meuse, on the Marne, and in Flanders in 1914. Transferred to the staff of the Saxon 24th Reserve Division, he later commanded an infantry company in the same division and served in Flanders and in the Battle of the Somme. He underwent a brief General Staff training course and ended the war as a battalion commander.

Krüger spent the interwar years in the mounted branch, serving with the 19th and 12th Cavalry Regiments (1919–29), as IIa (chief personnel officer) of the 2nd Cavalry Division (1929–31), and on the staff of the cavalry inspectorate in the Defense (later War) Ministry (1931–37). In November 1937 he assumed command on the 10th Cavalry Regiment, but this unit was disbanded on mobilization on August 26, 1939, and Krüger (now a colonel) was given command of the 171st Infantry Regiment, a unit of Saxon reservists. It seems to have been

Map 16. The Allied Drive to the Seine

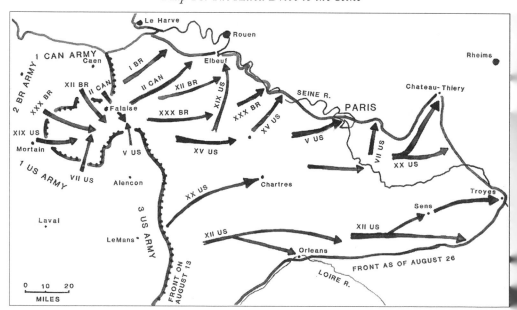

involved in mopping up Polish stragglers in October 1939 but did not see any major fighting. Krüger, meanwhile, recognized that the future did not lie with the horse. He arranged to be transferred to the staff of the 1st Rifle Brigade of the 1st Panzer Division, where he trained as a panzer officer. He assumed command of the brigade on February 15, 1940, and led it in Luxembourg, southern Belgium, and France, taking part in the battles of Sedan and Dunkirk in the process.

Krüger and his brigade spent the winter of 1940–41 in East Prussia and crossed into the Soviet Union on June 22, 1941. Krüger, meanwhile, was promoted to major general on April 1, 1941, and assumed command of the 1st Panzer Division on July 17, 1941.

The 1st Panzer was involved in heavy fighting from the beginning of Operation Barbarossa. Between June 22 and August 6, 1941, it lost 44 of its 155 tanks. By February 1942 it had only 18 runners remaining. It nevertheless played a major role in the defense of the Rzhev salient. In July 1942 the 1st Panzer—along with the 2nd Panzer Division—destroyed 218 Soviet tanks and 592 guns near Pushkev. The following month the 1st Panzer alone destroyed 65 superheavy KV-1 and KV-2 Soviet tanks in two days.

Krüger's division was withdrawn to Germany to rest and rebuild in January 1943. It was then sent to the Balkans, where it subdued the Italian 11th Army after Rome defected from the Axis in September 1943. The following month it was rushed back to the Eastern Front, where it slowed the Soviet advance west of Kiev. Krüger, meanwhile, was named commander of the LXVIII Reserve Panzer (later Panzer) Corps in southern France in October 1943. He became a lieutenant general on October 1, 1942, and a general of panzer troops from May 1, 1944. Krüger led his corps in Normandy, at Mortain, and in the retreat to the West Wall.

On August 24–25 Krüger tried to form a defensive line northeast of Paris, between the Oise and the Seine. Army Group B, however, had assigned LVIII Panzer Corps to the 5th Panzer Army. Krüger did not even know where the army's command post was located and was unable to reach it by radio or telephone. Feeling isolated, Krüger withdrew toward Compiègne. On August 26 Collins's VII Corps attacked the LVIII Panzer near Meaux and forced it to withdraw. It was pursued by the U.S. V Corps (Major General Leonard T. Gerow), which captured Compiègne (forty-five miles northeast of Paris) on August 31 and, on September 1, crossed the Aisne River between Compiègne and Soissons. The retreat continued and halted in front of the West Wall only because the Americans ran out of fuel and supplies.

✦

During the last week of August, Montgomery's army group pushed into the zone of the 15th Army and smashed General of Infantry Johann Sinnhuber's LXVII Corps, which was defending along the French coast between the Seine and the Somme.

Johann Sinnhuber was born in Wilkoschen, East Prussia, on March 27, 1887. He joined the army as a Fahnenjunker in April 1907 and was commissioned in the 52nd Field Artillery Regiment in 1908. He fought in World War I, served in the Reichsheer, and was a lieutenant colonel commanding the 21st Artillery Regiment at Elbing, West Prussia (now Elblag, Poland), in 1934. He was named commander of Arko 18 in Liegnitz, Lower Silesia (now Legnica, Poland), in 1938 and led it in Poland (1939) and France (1940). On May 21, 1940, as the Wehrmacht drove on Dunkirk, Sinnhuber was given command of the 28th Infantry Division, which he led in Belgium, France, and the drive on Moscow. The division suffered such heavy casualties that it had to be withdrawn to France, where it was rebuilt as a light (later jäger) division. It was sent back to the Eastern Front and was involved in the storming of the Soviet naval base of Sevastopol in the Crimea. The 28th was then sent north, where it was involved in the Battle of Volchov and the Siege of Leningrad. Sinnhuber led the division until May 1, 1943. After a furlough, he assumed command of the LXXXII Corps in northern France on July 10, 1943. He was promoted to colonel (1935), major general (1939), lieutenant general (April 1, 1941), and general of artillery (October 1, 1943).

Because he was unable to check an entire Allied army group with a handful of static infantry regiments, Sinnhuber was relieved of his command on September 1.

✦

On August 22 Hans Eberbach met with Field Marshal Model at the command post of the 5th Panzer Army in Cantelour, west of Rouen. (All units south of the Seine were now under the command of Dietrich's 5th Panzer Army.) Eberbach told Model that he had disbanded the small Panzer Group Eberbach staff and was now a general without a command. He requested permission to go to the Army Personnel Office in Berlin, where he intended to ask to be given a panzer corps on the Eastern Front. Model, however, named him commander of the 7th Army instead, replacing Hausser, who had been wounded.

The 7th Army was in bad shape. Its staff had been decimated at Falaise and needed rehabilitation. Model ordered Eberbach to take charge of the remnants of nine infantry divisions north of the Seine and to begin to rebuild them.

Major General von Gersdorff, 7th Army chief of staff, was already working with the staff of the 5th Panzer Army and a few field administration headquarters. He had done good preliminary work in reconstructing the divisions that had escaped the pocket. Only a nucleus of each division had managed to escape, however. "Around each of these cores, stragglers were collected," Eberbach recalled. "Each soldier crossing the Seine was stopped and given a slip with information as to where the division was assembling, how he was to reach that point, where he would receive food, pay, and clothing. Patrols were also sent out to pick up individual stragglers behind the lines and give them their directions. Some of the men had no rifles. Some of the men had even lost their uniform jackets in the course of their flight or in the numerous trucks that had been set on fire. However, all were perfectly willing and obeyed orders without a murmur. Thus, units were quickly formed in the assembly areas, each such unit amounting to a division, ranging in numbers from 1,500 to 2,500 men."[2] However, these units lacked heavy weapons and had almost no antitank weapons. Most of the divisions had only one or two pieces of artillery.

Initially, the 7th Army was assigned three corps headquarters: LXXIV (General Erich Straube), LXXXIV (Lieutenant General Otto Elfeldt), and II Parachute Corps. However, on August 23 the II Parachute Corps was ordered to proceed to Nancy with the remnants of its two divisions for the purpose of rehabilitation; LXXXIV Corps was destroyed in the Falaise Pocket; and Straube's headquarters was reassigned to 5th Panzer Army, in order to take over a defense sector on the Seine. The 7th Army thus found itself compelled to try to execute its mission without corps staffs. Of the seven divisions assigned to it, all combat effective units of company strength and upward, and in particular all guns, were assigned to Straube, and thus were attached to 5th Panzer Army.

After detaching all combat effective units, the remaining seven divisions had only 1,500 to 2,500 men each. Eberbach ordered that each form a reinforced regiment, if possible. This was very difficult because the units lacked weapons and had virtually no radios left.

On August 28 Eberbach drove to the 15th Army Headquarters in Tourcoing, in order to consult there with Colonel General Salmuth and to request help. Salmuth, however, had been relieved of his command and replaced by General of Infantry Gustav-Adolf von Zangen, who promised Eberbach that he would speedily send him the guns from the bunkers in Dieppe.

Everything now depended on how long Dietrich and Model could delay the Allies south of the Seine. Model hoped they could hold until September 7. He then planned to give the command of the 5th Panzer Army to Eberbach. Dietrich would be sent back to Germany, to assume command of the 6th Panzer Army, which had not yet been organized. The defense on the Seine and south of the river, however, collapsed almost immediately. The date for Eberbach's assumption of command of the 5th Panzer Army was therefore moved up to September 3. The northward retirement of the frontline units was to take place in nightly increments of fifteen kilometers each. "However," Eberbach wrote later, "once the German front had been deprived of the Seine obstacle, enemy tanks quickly succeeded in piercing the thinly held German lines and it proved impossible to hold the lines of resistance ordered." The infantry divisions, he added, had lost most of their antitank guns south of the Seine and were and exposed to annihilation. "Everything depended upon whether the British would advance slowly and methodically or, in realization of our weakness would seize their opportunity to effect a large-scale breakthrough."[3] The High Command decided to turn command of the 5th Panzer Army over to Hans Eberbach on September 1.

The general reached the command post of the 5th Panzer Army at noon on August 30. When he arrived, General Adolf Kuntzen was giving a report to the effect that his corps (LXXXI) had been broken through about forty-five kilometers southward on that morning and was retreating. Similar reports arrived from the corps on the left flank. No reserves were available to fill the gaps.

Eberbach requested Model's approval for the transfer his command post north of the Somme, as it seemed too seriously threatened in its present position. He emphatically refused to allow this before September 1, however, because of troop morale. Eberbach did not press the issue.

General Gause (Sepp Dietrich's chief of staff), Model, and Eberbach then discussed the situation in the zone of the LXXXI Corps. They had no reserves, and the only panzers in the entire army zone were five Tiger tanks, the remnants of one battalion. They decided to send them to Kuntzen. It is significant that the deterioration of the Wehrmacht's resources had reached the point that three German generals, including the commander-designate of a panzer army, were concerning themselves with the deployment of a mere five tanks.

Eberbach arose at about 5:00 a.m. on August 31. At 5:30 a.m, he and Gersdorff had breakfast with Dietrich and Gause, who were ready to leave. After breakfast, Eberbach saw from the map that, according to a message received during the night, an enemy spearhead had advanced to within fifteen kilometers (ten miles) south of the headquarters. He asked Gause about this. He confirmed that a message to that effect had been received during the night but added that the person reporting had no doubt just been seeing ghosts. Eberbach inquired whether anything had been done—whether any reconnaissance had been undertaken. He was told that reconnaissance had not been considered necessary.

The army general then accompanied Sepp Dietrich to his car. Before he had even entered the car, tank and machine gun fire erupted in the immediate vicinity. Dietrich and his staff sped away, and the British—who obviously correctly assumed that there was someone important in the staff car—pursued him for some miles. It was, in fact, a race. Dietrich escaped only because his car was faster than the British reconnaissance vehicles.

Eberbach's attempt to get away in a Volkswagen was fruitless, and he was apprehended by members of the British 11th Armoured Division at 7:30 a.m. Only his chief of staff, Colonel von Gersdorff, and his Ia, Major Gemmerich, succeeded in escaping by heading across country on foot. They made good their escape and eventually joined General of Panzer Troops Erich Brandenberger, who had been charged with the task of rebuilding the 7th Army. Dietrich remained in command of the 5th Panzer until September 12, when he was replaced by General of Panzer Troops Baron Hasso von Manteuffel. Dietrich was given command of the 6th (later 6th SS) Panzer Army.

✦

Karl Casper was born in Rehden, Lower Saxony (in northwest Germany, about forty miles southwest of Bremen), on February 23, 1893. He entered the army when World War I began as a Fahnenjunker in the 129th Infantry Regiment. He fought in East Prussia and Poland before transferring to the West Prussian 61st Infantry Regiment on the Western Front, where he fought in the Somme sector in France. Severely wounded in August 1915, he did not return to active duty until November 6. Thirteen days later he was promoted to second lieutenant. In September of the following year, he became a company commander. A month later he was chosen to command the elite assault company of his division (the 35th Infantry). Casper was named adjutant of the I Battalion/61st Infantry Regiment in February 1917 and was again a company commander in June. In the process, he fought at St.-Quentin, Flanders, and Ypres. He was named regimental adjutant in April 1918.

Despite a solid record of accomplishment, Casper was not selected for the Reichswehr and, in 1920, entered the police service in Berlin. He was on the staff of the Brandenburg Police School (1922–28), district police chief in

Recklinghausen (1928–33), and with the state police at Essen (1933–35). He was promoted to major of police in 1935 and rejoined the army at the same rank later that year. He became commander of I/13th Infantry Regiment in 1936 and directed it on the Saar Front in 1939. He commanded a battalion in the Silesian 174th Infantry Regiment for two months and on February 6, 1940, assumed command of the 118th Infantry (later Motorized) Regiment, which he commanded in France and Russia, where he took part in the drive on Leningrad, the Battle of Moscow, and the defense against Stalin's Winter Offensive of 1941–42. On October 27, 1942, he took command of the 335th Infantry Division in France. The 335th soon returned to the Eastern Front, however, and Casper fought in the Donetz battles and in the Ukraine. He was seriously wounded near Stalino on September 7, 1943, and did not return to duty until the beginning of 1944, when he assumed command of the 48th Infantry Division on the Belgian coast. He had, meanwhile, been promoted to lieutenant colonel (1937), colonel (October 1, 1940), major general (October 1, 1940), and lieutenant general (August 8, 1943). Casper led the 48th Infantry for the rest of the war, except for a brief period in October 1944, when he was on leave for medical reasons.

Karl Casper was a good general with a poor division. His 48th Infantry included a great many Poles and other non-Germans. It was inexperienced, poorly trained, and not particularly loyal to the Third Reich. It was swept aside by Patton at Chartres in August. Given its poor morale and lack of vehicles and equipment, Casper did a good job just to get away from the American Shermans and motorized infantry.

✦

Hugo Sperrle was born in Ludwigsburg, Baden-Württemberg (about seven miles north of Stuttgart), on February 7, 1885. He entered the army as a Fahnenjunker in the 126th Infantry Regiment in 1903. Promoted to second lieutenant in 1904 and first lieutenant in 1912, he underwent pilot training in 1913 and 1914. He was a pilot in the 4th Flying Battalion when World War I began. Promoted to captain in late 1914, he spent almost the entire war in aviation positions, including a tour as commander of the aerial observers' school at Cologne. He also spent three months taking the abbreviated General Staff training course at Sedan. Sperrle crashed behind German lines on February 23, 1916, and spent six weeks in the hospital. At the end of the war, he was commander of all aviation units attached to 7th Army.

During the Reichswehr era, Sperrle remained in the army, where he was promoted to major (1926), lieutenant colonel (1931), and colonel (1934). He served as aviation adviser to the staff of the 5th Infantry Division at Stuttgart (1920–24), in the Organizations Department of the Defense Ministry (1924–29), as commander of the III Battalion of the Baden 14th Infantry Regiment at Konstanz (1929–30), on the staff of the Prussian 8th Infantry Regiment at Frankfurt/Oder (1930–33), and as commander of the regiment (1933–34). He transferred to the secret Luftwaffe in 1934 and was named Higher Aviation Commander 2 in Berlin in 1935. He commanded the V Air District in Munich (1935–36), before leading the Condor Legion in the Spanish Civil War from November 1, 1936, to October 31, 1937. During this period, he invented the terror bombing raid. When he returned to Germany, he was named leader of the Luftwaffe's 3rd Command Group, which became the 3rd Air Fleet on February 1, 1939. Meanwhile, Sperrle was promoted to major general (1935), lieutenant general (1937), and general of fliers (1937). He played a major role in defeating France in 1940 and was promoted to field marshal on July 19, 1940, bypassing the rank of colonel general altogether. He was less successful in the Battle of Britain. In a critical meeting of the German air marshals in early September 1940, however, it was Sperrle who advocated continuing attacks against the British Fighter Command, instead of terror bombing London and other cities. Had his strategy been adopted, it is likely that Germany would have won the Battle of Britain.

Hugo Sperrle was one of the causes of the German defeat in the West in 1944. An effective commander until 1940, he "went to seed" in France and allowed himself to become corrupt and lazy. He enjoyed a life of luxury and neglected many aspects of his job, including pilot training. By early 1944 he was losing as many airplanes to accidents as to enemy action, largely because many of his pilots simply did not know how to land their airplanes. His air fleet was characterized by a huge ground and rear area organization, which was completely out of proportion to the few airplanes it was able to commit against the Allies. Hitler considered relieving him in early 1943 but did not—which was a mistake. He was finally sacked on August 24, 1944, because many of his men simply ran away from the battle, rather than putting up the slightest resistance. In many cases they also left behind secret documents and files, which they made no attempt to destroy. Many of these were discovered by astonished German soldiers as they withdrew toward the Seine, the Somme, or the German border. Their reports to Berlin were the straw that broke the camel's back, insofar as Hugo Sperrle was concerned.

✦

Joseph "Beppo" Schmid was born in Göggingen (near Augsburg), Bavaria, on September 24, 1901, and first saw action as a volunteer in General Ritter Franz von Epp's Freikorps in 1919. He entered the army as a Fahnenjunker in the 19th Infantry Regiment in Munich in 1921, attended the War Schools at Munich and Ohrdruf (1922–24), and was commissioned second lieutenant on December 1, 1924. While at Munich, Schmid became a Nazi, befriended Hermann Göring, and participated in the Beer Hall Putsch on the side of the Nazis. From 1925 to 1933, he was a platoon leader in the 21st Infantry Regiment at Nuremberg. He underwent General Staff training at the War Academy in Berlin (1933–35) and transferred to the Luftwaffe in July 1935. Initially assigned to the Operations Department of the General Staff of the Luftwaffe, he became chief of intelligence from April 1, 1939, to October 14, 1942. He was a complete failure in this position, as his estimates were always far wide of the mark, and he played a major role in the German defeat during the Battle of Britain. He nevertheless rose rapidly in rank, thanks to his friendship with Hermann Göring. Schmid was promoted to major (1936), lieutenant colonel (1938), colonel (July 19, 1940), major general (March 1, 1943), and lieutenant general (July 1, 1944). He commanded the Hermann Göring Panzer Division in Tunisia (1942–43), where he was flown out of the collapsing pocket on Göring's personal orders.

Beppo Schmid commanded the XII Air Corps (September 15, 1943–March 1, 1944) and the I Fighter Corps on the Western Front (April 1 to November 30, 1944). He was thoroughly defeated by the U.S. and Royal air forces on the Western Front in 1944. Even so, he was promoted to the leadership Luftwaffe Command West (as the downgraded 3rd Air Fleet was called) from December 12, 1944, to April 27, 1945, and was in charge of Luftwaffe operations on the Western Front.

✦

Otto Dessloch succeeded Hugo Sperrle as commander of the 3rd Air Fleet. Born in Bamberg, Lower Franconia, on June 11, 1889, Dessloch joined the army as an officer cadet in 1910 and was promoted to second lieutenant in 1912. He went to war as a platoon leader in the Bavarian 5th Chevaulegers (Cavalry) Regiment but was wounded within three weeks. Instead of returning to his unit, Dessloch volunteered for aerial observer and then pilot training. He eventually served with fighter squadrons on the Western Front and in October 1916 was forced to make an emergency landing in Switzerland, where he was interned. He made his way back to Germany in early 1917 and spent much of the rest of the war as a flying school commandant or as an air base commander. In "the war after the war" he served with Freikorps von Epp, where he commanded his own flying battalion. Selected for the Reichsheer, Dessloch was a signals officer with the 46th Infantry Regiment at Rendsburg, Schleswig-Holstein, and with the 21st Infantry Regiment at Nuremberg (1920–21). He spent the years 1921 to 1926 stationed at his hometown of Bamberg, as a staff officer and squadron commander in the 17th Cavalry Regiment. He returned to aviation in 1926, however, and was involved in secret flight training in Russia. Tours as an aviation adviser on the staff of the 7th Infantry Division at Munich (1927–32) and as a staff officer with the 18th Cavalry Regiment at Bad Cannstatt (near Stuttgart) followed.

Otto Dessloch transferred to the secret Luftwaffe in December 1933. He commanded the pilot school and air base at Cottbus (1933–35). On April 1, 1935, he was named commander of all land-based pilot schools. He then commanded the 155th Bomber Wing at Ansbach (1935–36), the 158th Bomber Wing (1936–38), the 32nd Air Division (1939), and the 6th Air Division in the Polish campaign (1939). In October 1939 he transferred to the flak branch and commanded the II Flak Corps (1939–42) and I Flak Corps (1942–43) in France and on the Russian Front. He became commander in chief of the 4th Air Fleet in southern Russia on September 4, 1943. He assumed command of the 3rd Air Fleet in France on August 21, 1944. Meanwhile, he was promoted to first lieutenant (1916), captain (1921), major (1932), lieutenant colonel (1934), colonel (1936), major general (1939), lieutenant general (July 19, 1940), general of flak artillery (January 1, 1942), and colonel general (March 1, 1944).

Like Hitler and Model, Dessloch wanted Paris destroyed. He even advocated bombing Paris *before* the German army evacuated it. After Choltitz surrendered the city, Dessloch did bomb it, in a night raid. By that time, however, 3rd Air Fleet had only a handful of bombers, and Dessloch's raid killed only a few hundred people. In its heyday, an attack by 3rd Air Fleet would have killed thousands.

Dessloch commanded the 3rd Air for only a month. On September 22, 1944, he returned to the East as commander of the 4th Air Fleet.

✦

Meanwhile, the LXXIV Corps (Straube), the LVII Panzer Corps (Krüger), and the I SS Panzer Corps (Keppler) were struggling to get back to the Siegfried line. They almost did not make it. On September 3 all three corps were surrounded at Mons by the U.S. 1st Army. They immediately turned to the senior corps commander, Erich Straube, who had commanded the rearguard at Falaise. Straube led an immediate breakout. All three corps headquarters escaped, although most of the men did not. The Germans, for once, were not showing much interest in fighting. Twenty-five thousand Germans were captured, including Lieutenant General Rüdiger von Heyking, the commander of the 6th Parachute Division. The 18th Luftwaffe Field Division was reduced to a strength of three hundred men. Map 17 shows the Western Front on September 15, as the Wehrmacht retreated into the Siegfried line. By this time, most of France was liberated, although a few of the ports had not yet been cleared of German forces. The most significant of these were in Brittany.

Map 17. The Western Front, September 5, 1944

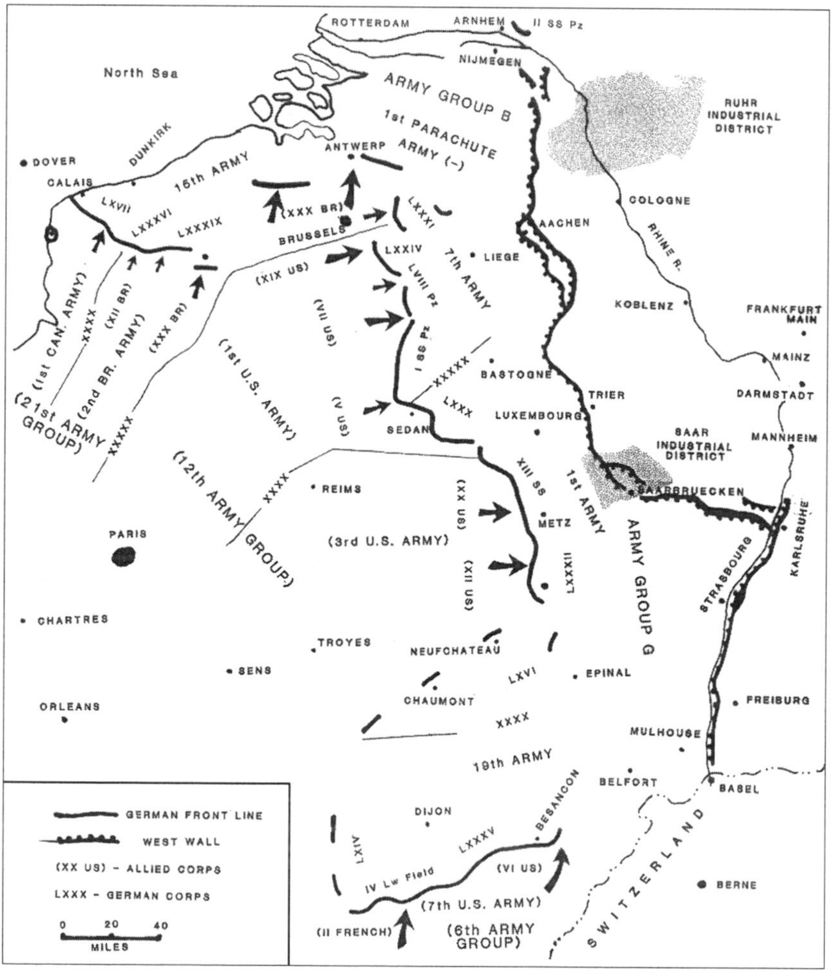

12

The Fall of Brittany

On July 25 the Allies launched Operation Cobra. Five days later the U.S. 4th Armored Division captured Avranches. Patton pushed the advanced elements of his newly activated U.S. 3rd Army into Brittany on August 1. He assigned the task of capturing Brittany to Gen. Troy Middleton, the veteran commander of the U.S. VIII Corps. They sent the motorized U.S. 83rd Infantry Division to capture the twin ports of St.-Malo and Dinard on the northern coast. At the same time, the U.S. 4th Armored and 8th Infantry divisions were ordered to capture Rennes, in the center of the peninsula. The 4th Armored was then to drive southwest to Quiberon Bay, cut off Brittany from the rest of France—and the XXV Corps from the rest of the Wehrmacht. Meanwhile, the U.S. 6th Armored and 79th Infantry divisions were instructed to drive two hundred miles due west of Avranches, to capture Brest, the best port in the region and the grand prize of the Brittany campaign. Initially, Patton and Middleton kept the U.S. 5th Armored, 83rd Infantry, and 90th Infantry divisions in reserve. (Map 18 shows the American conquest of Brittany.)

The task of defending Brittany fell to General of Artillery Wilhelm Fahrmbacher's XXV Corps.

◆

Wilhelm Fahrmbacher was born in Zwiebrücken in the Rhineland-Palatinate on September 19, 1888, and joined the 5th Bavarian Field Artillery Regiment as a Fahnenjunker in 1907. He attended the War School in Munich, graduated in 1909, and was commissioned second lieutenant in the Bavarian 4th Field Artillery Regiment in 1910. He went to war as a battalion adjutant but was wounded in Lorraine on August 24. Back on duty by mid-September, he fought on the Somme and in Artois. In 1916 he became a battery commander in the Bavarian 21st Field Artillery Regiment and fought at Verdun and in Russia and Romania, before returning to France as the regimental adjutant of the 4th Bavarian Field Artillery in early 1917. He ended the war as adjutant of the Bavarian 5th Artillery Command (Arko 5), fighting in the Battles of Picardy and

Map 18. The Conquest of Brittany

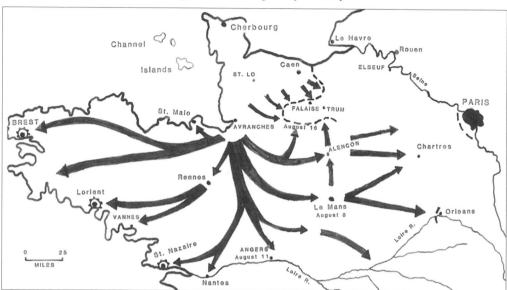

the Somme. After the war he commanded a panzer platoon in a border brigade before joining the Reichswehr in 1919. He was a squadron commander in the 7th Transport Battalion in Munich from 1920 to 1926. After serving with the 7th Artillery Regiment (also in Munich) from 1926 to 1928, he was assigned to the Weapons Office in the Defense Ministry (1928–31). Later he commanded the II Battalion of the 7th Artillery (1931–34) and returned to the Army Weapons Office as a department chief (1934–38). In March 1938 he was sent to Karlsruhe on the French border as commander of Arko 35.

On August 15, 1938, Fahrmbacher became commander of the 5th Infantry Division at Ulm, Baden-Württemberg. He led his division on the Western Front (1939–40) and in the conquest of France (1940). From October 20, 1940, to March 1, 1942, he commanded the VII Corps and fought on the central sector of the Eastern Front, including the battles of Bialystok, Smolensk, Vyasma, Moscow, and Gshatsk. Placed in Führer Reserve for two months, he recovered from the strain and exhaustion of the Eastern Front and was sent to northwestern France, where he assumed command of the XXV Corps at St.-Nazaire, Brittany, on May 1, 1942. Later Fahrmbacher moved his headquarters to Pontivy. Meanwhile, he had been promoted to first lieutenant (1915), captain (1918), major (1928), lieutenant colonel (1932), colonel (1934), major general (1937), lieutenant general (June 1, 1939), and general of artillery (October 20, 1940).

On June 6 Fahrmbacher had 100,000 combat effectives. Of these, about one-third were still on the peninsula on August 1. (This figure excludes thirty thousand men of the 319th Infantry Division. The 319th Infantry garrisoned the Channel Islands, which Hitler was convinced the Allies planned to invade. He steadfastly refused to allow Kluge or Fahrmbacher to use these men for the defense of Normandy or Brittany. The Allies never invaded, and the 319th Infantry surrendered on May 11, 1945. Most of its men did not fire a shot in anger while they were on the Channel Islands.)

To defend Brittany, Fahrmbacher had only two full-strength divisions: the 343rd Infantry and the 2nd Parachute. Both were posted to the Brest area. He also had the remnants of the 91st Air Landing and 77th Infantry divisions (which had been pushed out of Normandy) and weak elements of the 265th Infantry Division and Lieutenant General Karl Spang's 266th Infantry Division. The 266th was at Morlaix while the 265th garrisoned Lorient, St.-Nazaire, and Nantes. In all, Fahrbacher had only ten reliable infantry battalions, four unreliable eastern battalions, and about fifty thousand immobile noncombat troops, including sailors and air force service personnel.

◆

The Americans advanced rapidly into Brittany and isolated the fortress of St.-Malo on August 3, 1944. The garrison commander, Colonel Andreas von Aulock, put up a determined defense.

Andreas von Aulock, the brother of Major General of the Reserves Hubertus von Aulock, was born in Kochelsdorf, Upper Silesia, on March 23, 1893. He joined the army in 1912 as a lieutenant in the 95th (6th Thuringen) Infantry Regiment. During World War I, he fought in Belgium and on the Eastern Front (then in Poland), where he was a company commander. Sent to the Western Front in 1916, he was on the regimental staff at Verdun (1916–17) and Flanders (1917–18). He joined the Freikorps after the war. Discharged in 1920, Aulock was a European representative of General Motors between the wars. He returned to active duty as a captain of reserves in 1937 and was assigned to the III/87th Infantry Regiment. In March 1939 he became a battalion commander in the 212th Infantry Regiment of the 79th Infantry Division, which served in the Saar (1939–40), in the conquest of France (1940), and in the Soviet Union (1941–43). Aulock, meanwhile, assumed command of the 226th Infantry Regiment, which he led in Stalingrad. This regiment, however, was on detached duty and was not encircled with the division in November 1942. Aulock and his unit were in the Kuban in 1943, when he was promoted to colonel. Sent west in early 1944, he was briefly on the staff of Wehrmacht Command Netherlands until February 15, 1944, when he was named commandant of St.-Malo.

When St.-Malo was isolated by the U.S. 3rd Army on August 3, Hitler named Aulock fortress commander under his personal command. Despite having limited resources, Aulock made the Americans fight for every yard. He did not surrender the city until August 17, 1944, and was awarded the Oak Leaves to the Knight's Cross that same day. He was investigated for burning St.-Malo but was exonerated—the fires had been started by American artillery fire. Aulock had, in fact, done everything he could to prevent suffering among the French civilians trapped in the city.

✦

Karl Spang was born in Mergentheim (now Bad Mergentheim), Baden-Württemberg, on January 22, 1889. He joined the army as a Fahnenjunker in the 49th Field Artillery Regiment in 1905, fought in World War I, and served in the Reichsheer. He was named commander of Arko 5 in Stuttgart in 1937 and was promoted to major general in 1938 and to lieutenant general on April 1, 1940. He commanded German forces on the Lower Rhine, including the ad hoc Division Spang (1939–40). Later he led the 337th Infantry Division (November 15, 1940–May 2, 1941), a rear area command in the Crimea (December 1941–May 1942), and the 585th Rear Area Command in southern Russia (May–October 1942). He also commanded an ad hoc battle group in the street fighting in Stalingrad (October 1942). Flown out of the pocket on or about December 31, 1942, he was deputy rear area commander of Army Group Don until January 12, 1943, when he was either wounded or fell ill and was not reemployed until that summer, when he assumed command of the 266th Infantry Division. Formed in the Münsingen Maneuver Area on May 20, 1943, this static division consisted partially of veterans from the Eastern Front. Five of its infantry battalions, however, were filled out mainly with eastern troops, which Admiral Friedrich Ruge assessed as having "very little combat value."[1] All the 266th's units lacked heavy weapons, and its artillery units were equipped with captured Soviet guns. It was on coastal watch duty in Brittany from August 1943 until the Normandy Front collapsed in August 1944.

Not having enough vehicles to effect a rapid retreat, Spang's 266th Infantry Division was easy game for the U.S. 4th Armored Division as it swept up the Brittany peninsula. General Spang ordered his remaining battalions to head for the relative safety of Brest or St.-Malo. Most of the division was captured before it could reach St.-Malo, as was General Spang, who led it throughout its existence—although remnants of the 266th did manage to escape to Brest, where they were absorbed by another unit. They defended against the Allied siege and were destroyed by September 19.

After virtually destroying the German 77th Infantry Division south of Avranches, the spearheads of Major General John S. Wood's U.S. 4th Armored Division headed for Rennes, a commercial city of eighty thousand that linked Brittany to the rest of France. It was the capital of Brittany, and no fewer than ten major highways ran through the city. After racing forty miles southwest of Avranches, the Americans reached the northern suburbs on the afternoon of August 1. They found the city defended by Colonel Eugen König, the commander of the 91st Air Landing Division.

✦

Eugen König was born in Trier on September 19, 1896, entered the service as a war volunteer in 1915, and earned a battlefield commission in the 189th Infantry Regiment in 1917. He served as a platoon leader, battalion adjutant, and company commander until September 27, 1918, when he was captured by the British. After being released from the POW camps, he was discharged from the army in 1920 as a second lieutenant of reserves. He became a civil servant in the 1920s but returned to active duty as a first lieutenant of reserves in 1936. Nine years later he was a lieutenant general. Assigned to the 352nd Infantry Regiment of the 246th Infantry Division when Germany mobilized on August 26, 1939, he served as regimental adjutant, commander of the II Battalion, adjutant of the 246th Infantry Division, and commander of the 352nd Infantry Regiment. He served in the Saar (1939–40), in France (1940), and on the Eastern Front (February 1942–spring of 1944), where he spent a year fighting in the Rzhev salient as part of Model's 9th Army. On November 3, 1943, he assumed command of Division Group 251—the former 251st Infantry Division, which had been downgraded. Ordered back to Germany, he began a monthlong division commanders' course on May 1, 1944, and then reported to OB West as a potential division commander. On June 10 he succeeded Colonel Bernhard Klosterkemper as commander of the 91st Air Landing Division. He spent the next seven weeks fighting in hedgerow country, where his division was gradually crushed. During the last week of July, the remnants were pushed into Brittany. König led them back to Rennes, where he took charge of all German forces in the city.

✦

The spearheads of the U.S. 4th Armored Division reached the northern suburbs of Rennes on the afternoon of August 1. They were met by two Luftwaffe 88mm batteries, supported by infantry, machine guns, and *panzerfausts* (individual-carried, shoulder-fired, single-shot disposable antitank weapons). They put up surprisingly stiff resistance, so the Americans halted and awaited reinforcements. While they waited, two German army replacement and training battalions (about nineteen hundred men) arrived from Le Mans. König issued panzerfausts to many of them and sent them to the front lines.

His timing was excellent. Combat Command A of the 4th Armored Division launched a prepared attack on the city that night. It was beaten back with severe losses, including eleven Sherman tanks.

At this point, General Wood correctly decided that it would be a mistake to involve his armored division in urban fighting. He contained Rennes with motorized infantry and awaited the rest of his division (which was strung out along forty miles of highway between Avranches and Rennes), as well as the U.S. 8th Infantry Division. He wanted to continue the advance with some of his tanks but was overruled by the more conservative General Middleton, who ordered both American divisions to attack the city.

By 11:00 p.m. on the night of August 3, Rennes was ablaze and the 91st Air Landing Division was partially surrounded. At the last minute SS General Hausser, the commander of the 7th Army, signaled König and gave him permission to break out. König burned his excess supplies and slipped out of town with his last two thousand men at 3:00 a.m. on the morning of August 4. Using back roads and moving cross-country, he was able to avoid the rapidly moving Americans, who operated almost exclusively on the major highways. As a result, Colonel König was able to reach the fortress of St.-Nazaire and safety on August 9.

Eugen König had proved that he was a competent tactician and a good divisional commander. He was promoted to major general effective September 1, 1944.

Meanwhile, General Ramcke, Erwin Rauch, and his men prepared to defend Brest from the American outslaught.

◆

Hermann-Bernhard Ramcke, the son of a farmer, was born in Schleswig (near the Danish-German border) on January 24, 1889. He joined the Imperial Navy as an enlisted man in 1905 at age sixteen. During World War I, he first saw action aboard the *Prinz Adalbert*, doing cruiser duty in the North and Baltic Seas (August 1914–April 1915). He spent the rest of the war serving in the naval infantry in Flanders (mainly in the 2nd Marine Infantry Regiment), was wounded five times, and earned a commission. He was in the hospital recovering from wounds when the war ended. Transferred to the army and promoted to first lieutenant in 1919, Ramcke served as a company commander in the Freikorps in the Baltic, where he fought alongside the White Russian Army and was shot through the right shoulder. He remained in the Reichswehr (as an army officer) and held a number of positions, most notably company and battalion commander in the 2nd Infantry Regiment at Allenstein, East Prussia (now Olsztyn, Poland) (1927–35). Meanwhile, he married the daughter of Lieutenant General Paul Goeldner (1875–December 13, 1945). They had eight children, the oldest of whom was Hermann. He immigrated to the United States in the 1950s and has two children and three grandchildren—all Americans.

Ramcke served on the staff of the commandant of the Grossborn Troop Maneuver Area (1936–38) and commandant of the Riesa Troop Maneuver Area (1938–40). During the Polish campaign, he was attached to the XXII Motorized Corps as an observer. On September 10, near Magierow, he coaxed a 109-man Polish motorized engineer company to surrender. A grateful General von Kleist personally decorated him with the Bar to his Iron Cross, 1st Class.

Ramcke was named commander of the 69th Infantry Replacement Regiment in Soest, northern Westphalia, in January 1940. Although he was promoted to colonel on February 29, 1940, Ramcke was not satisfied with his career progression or with missing the campaigns in Norway and France—and Poland also, where he was merely an observer. (Part of the problem was his own abrasive personality and the fact that he was a demanding subordinate. Rommel had his fill of Ramcke in North Africa in 1942 and complained several times about his insatiable demands for special treatment for his paratroopers.) Seeing little prospect for advancement in the army, Ramcke transferred to the paratroopers in July 1940 and went to jump school at the age of fifty-one. Named chief of training of Kurt Student's XI Air Corps, he jumped into Crete on May 21, 1941, the day after the invasion began. He assumed command of the 1st Parachute Regiment and Group West when he learned that General Meindl had been seriously wounded. He helped secure the Maleme Airfield (a move that saved the 7th Air Division) and, together with the 5th Mountain Division, took Canea on May 27. He was awarded the Knight's Cross and instantly became a rising star in the parachute branch.

After Crete, Ramcke was given command of an ad hoc parachute unit (later designated the 2nd Parachute Brigade) and was charged with training the Italian

Folgore Parachute Division, which was earmarked for the airborne invasion of Malta (1941–42). After this plan was cancelled, the Ramcke Brigade was sent to Egypt, where he briefly served as acting commander of the 90th Light Division (September 8–17, 1942).[2] He fought in the Second Battle of El Alamein (October 23–November 4, 1942). Cut off in the desert when the Afrika Korps was virtually destroyed, he hijacked the vehicles of a British convoy and made his way back to German lines with most of his command. For this miraculous escape, Adolf Hitler personally decorated him with the Oak Leaves to the Knight's Cross.

On February 13, 1943, Hermann Ramcke was then given command of the 2nd Parachute Division in Italy. When the Italians attempted to defect from the Axis on September 8, 1943, Ramcke led his division against the Italian army outside of Rome and fought against General Giacomo Carboni's Italian Motorized Corps. One of Ramcke's battalions made a combat jump in an effort to capture General Mario Roatta, the chief of the Italian General Staff. The battalion (II/6th Parachute Regiment) captured the headquarters and twenty-five hundred men, but Roatta and his senior staff officers had already fled. Ramcke himself was seriously injured when his staff car was run off the road by an Italian fighter-bomber. He was medically evacuated back to Dresden and could not return to active duty until early 1944. On February 17 he resumed command of the 2nd Parachute Division, which was now on the Eastern Front and engaged in withdrawing to the Bug. Ramcke fell ill during this operation; he turned command of the division over to Lieutenant Colonel Hans Kroh and returned to Germany on March 17. He returned to duty on May 5 or 6, 1944. At this time, his division was stationed at the Wahn Maneuver Area near Cologne, but the following month it was sent to Brittany, following the D-Day landings. It took up positions south of Brest, in the extreme western part of the peninsula.

◆

Also encamped in the Brest area was Lieutenant General Erwin Rauch's 343rd Infantry Division.

Erwin Rauch was born in Berlin on October 19, 1889. He joined the army as a Fahnenjunker in the 35th Fusilier Regiment in 1908, fought in World War I, and was discharged in late 1920. He returned to active duty as a major in 1934 and, in late 1938, was named commander of the East Prussian 2nd Infantry Regiment. He led the 2nd in Poland and France. In October 1940 he assumed command of the 422nd Infantry Regiment, which he led in the initial battles on the northern sector of the Eastern Front. He assumed command of the 123rd

Infantry Division on August 6, 1941, during the advance to Leningrad. Rauch's division was on the southern flank of the army group, covering fifty miles of frontage, when it was attacked by four Soviet armies in January 1942. The 123rd was largely destroyed, although elements escaped to the west or into the Demyansk or Kholm pockets. The division was not completely reunited until early 1943. Partially rebuilt in northern Russia, it was sent to the southern sector later that year and suffered heavy casualties in the battles of the lower Dnieper. Rauch gave up command of the 123rd on January 15, 1944, and assumed command of the 343rd Infantry Division in France on February 1. In the meantime he had been promoted to lieutenant colonel (1934), colonel (1937), major general (1941), and lieutenant general (November 1, 1942).

✦

Unlike Ramcke, and to a lesser extent Rauch, Hans von der Mosel, the commandant of Brest, had not had a particularly distinguished career. He did, however, end it well.

Hans von der Mosel was born in Bodenbach, Rhineland-Palatinate, on May 3, 1898. He joined the Saxon 101st Grenadier Regiment as a Fahnenjunker in 1916 and was commissioned in 1917. He fought on the Somme and in the Champagne sector and was selected for the Reichsheer in 1920. He did not excel after 1920 and, in 1939, was a major, commanding air defense troops at the Altwarp training grounds. He commanded a battalion in the 234th Infantry Regiment in Belgium (1940), in the II Battalion of 156th Infantry (later Motorized) Regiment in Russia (1942), and the 548th Infantry Regiment in central Russia (1942) and France (1943). The High Command and Army Personnel Office, however, decided not to give him another field command. He became commandant of Brest on May 1, 1943.

✦

Ramcke's principal subordinate in the 2nd Parachute Division was Hans Kroh.

Born in Heidelberg, Baden-Württemberg, on May 13, 1907, **Hans Kroh** entered the Brunswick (Braunschweig) Police service in 1926. On April 1, 1933, shortly after Hitler secured the passage of the Enabling Act and established his dictatorship, Kroh was promoted to second lieutenant of police. He became a first lieutenant of police on August 1, 1933. (Such a rapid promotion suggests Nazi Party connections.) In any case Kroh became a platoon leader Police Battalion Wecke (later State Police Group "General Göring") in early 1933 and remained there until October 1, 1935, when the group evolved into Regiment General Göring of the Luftwaffe. Kroh was now made a company commander in the I (Jäger) Battalion, but he was not promoted to captain until after he completed parachute training in 1937. At that time he became a company commander in the IV (Parachute) Battalion of the Regiment "General Göring." He was appointed a company commander in the I/1st Parachute Regiment on April 1, 1938, and joined the staff of the 7th Air Division on January 1, 1939. After serving in the Low Countries, Kroh assumed command of the I/2nd Parachute Regiment on August 1, 1940, and remained in command of this battalion until February 28, 1943. He was promoted to major in 1941 and to lieutenant colonel in early 1943 and fought in Crete, Egypt, and Tunisia. He was acting commander of the Ramcke Parachute Brigade (November 30, 1942–February 18, 1943) and was commander of the 2nd Parachute Regiment from March 1, 1943, to August 11, 1944. He became a full colonel on April 6, 1944. Kroh simultaneously served as acting commander of the 2nd Parachute Division from November 20 to December 11, 1943, and from March 17 to early May 1944.

◆

As the Americans approached Brest, Hitler sent Ramcke, Mosel, and Erwin Rauch orders to fight to the last round, and they proceeded to do so. U.S. Maj. Gen. Robert W. Grow's 6th Armored Division attempted to take the fortress by coup de main on August 7 but was beaten back. Grow issued a surrender ultimatum on August 8, but it was rejected by Mosel. He launched an all-out attack on the fortress the following day but was again thrown back.

By attempting to capture Brest quickly, the Americans allowed Hermann Ramcke to slip into the fortress from the south with his 2nd Parachute Division on August 9, bringing the strength of the garrison to around forty thousand men. From this point on, Brest was *his* battle.

On August 12 Hitler formally appointed Ramcke commandant of the fortress, Mosel became his chief of staff, and Hans Kroh became acting commander of the 2nd Parachute Division. Meanwhile, Middleton brought up the U.S. 2nd, 8th, and 29th Infantry divisions.

The Battle of Brest was fierce. Seeking to minimize the casualties among their ground forces, the Americans made liberal use of their numerically superior artillery, as well as of their air superiority. Friction developed between Middleton and Patton, who was already having serious supply problems and did not want to lavish ammunition on a garrison two hundred miles behind the front lines.

Middleton, however, refused to attack until Patton guaranteed his minimum supply needs and, in the end, got his way. It would take thirty thousand tons of ammunition (mostly artillery ammunition) to subdue Brest.

The Germans fought with great determination—especially the 2nd Parachute, which added to the awesome reputation the German paratroopers already enjoyed. The 343rd Infantry Division and Mosel's miscellaneous formations (of which nothing was expected) did not perform at the same level as Ramcke's elite veterans, of course, but they did fight well and exceeded expectations by a wide margin. For this reason, Hans von der Mosel was promoted to major general on September 1. Ramcke received a special promotion to general of paratroopers two weeks later.

Mosel surrendered the city on September 18. General Rauch was taken prisoner the same day. The next day the U.S. 8th Infantry Division reached Ramcke's headquarters at Pointe des Capucins on the Crozon Peninsula, just west of Brest. Under a flag of truce, U.S. Brig. Gen. Charles Canham, the deputy commander of the division, approached Ramcke and demanded his surrender. The German asked to see Canham's credentials. The American—who had had about enough of German paratroopers—responded angrily. "These are my credentials!" he snapped, pointing to a nearby detachment of American infantry. Ramcke capitulated. Being of a practical turn of mind, he had already packed several suitcases for the trip into the POW camps. He even brought along his fishing gear.

About thirty-eight thousand German soldiers surrendered at and near Brest on September 18–20. Four thousand of them were wounded. More than a thousand had been killed during the siege. The city of Brest was destroyed in house-to-house fighting. The Old City was partially razed. More important for the Third Reich, the harbor facilities were completely destroyed. The fall of Brest would do nothing to solve Patton's supply problems.

✦

After General Marcks was killed near St.-Lô, Fahrmbacher briefly served as acting commander of the LXXXIV Corps in Normandy in June 1944. Returning to Brittany, he and 25,000 of his men were cut off in the port city/fortress of Lorient by the rapid U.S. advance into the peninsula but held the city until the end of the war. Had the Americans not overestimated his strength, they would almost certainly have overrun his defenses. But they estimated that he had 500 guns, which was 303 more than he actually had, so they did not attack. Fahrmbacher did not surrender Lorient until May 10, 1945.

✦

Meanwhile, General Hans Junck and his men were isolated on the Channel Islands.

Hans Junck was born in Leipzig, Saxony, on September 16, 1893. He entered the army as a Fahnenjunker in the Saxon 12th Field Artillery Regiment in 1913, trained at the War School at Neisse, and was commissioned on August 12, 1914. He spent World War I serving with his regiment, which fought in Belgium and France, and was a battery commander on October 15, 1918, when he was seriously wounded. (This was at least his third wound of the war.) After being released from the hospital in the spring of 1919, Junck joined the Reichswehr and (except for attending an occasional army school) spent the entire January 1921 to October 1932 period with the Prussian-Saxon 4th Artillery Regiment in Dresden. In 1928 he earned an advanced engineering degree from the Technical College at Dresden. He served in the Defense Ministry (1932–33) and was a group director in the Army Weapons Office (1933–37). Transferred to Schwerin, Mecklenburg-Vorpommerin (West Pomerania), he commanded the I Battalion of the Prussian 2nd Artillery Regiment (1937–38) and served on the regimental staff (1938–39). He returned to the Army Weapons Office as a department chief (1939–42) and was an army acceptance inspector (1942–43). Promoted to first lieutenant (1918), captain (1926), major (1934), lieutenant colonel (1937), and colonel (February 1, 1940), he finally went to the field in June 1943, when he was named commander the 609th Special Purposes Artillery Regiment on the northern sector of the Eastern Front and supported I Corps south of Leningrad. He served as acting commander of the 253rd Infantry Division from June 17 to July 30, 1943, and was the leader of the 125th Artillery Command (Arko 125), supporting 3rd Panzer Army on the Eastern Front, from September 1943 to April 1944. During the period January 21 to February 7, 1944, he also served as acting commander of the elite 4th Panzer Division. He had been promoted to major general on November 1, 1943.

Hans Junck was sent back to Germany on April 25, 1944, to take some leave and to attend a two-week divisional commanders' course. On June 8, 1944, he reported to OB West in Paris as an excess divisional commander, but no such post was immediately available. On July 30, after Lieutenant General Otto Elfeldt was named commander of the LXXXIV Corps, he replaced Elfeldt as commander of the 47th Infantry Division in Normandy, but this job lasted only until August 3, when the permanent commander, Major General Carl Wahle, arrived.

Meanwhile, Lieutenant General Walter Duevert was relieved of command of the 265th Infantry Division in Brittany, and Junck was named his successor.

✦

Walter Duevert was born in 1893 in Görlitz, Saxony, the eastern half of which is now Zgorzelec, Poland. He had been an up-and-coming young general when the invasion of the Soviet Union began. Earmarked to become one of the senior generals in the German High Command, he commanded of the 13th Panzer Division in all of the major battles on the southern sector of the Eastern Front until February 1942, when he suffered a nervous breakdown from which he never completely recovered. After being allowed a few months to recuperate, he was given command of the 20th Panzer Division, also on the Eastern Front. It was soon determined, however, that his nerves could no longer stand the strain of combat. Duevert was unemployed from October 1942 until June 1, 1943, when he was given command of the 265th Infantry Division in occupied France. As the Allies broke out of Normandy and threatened Brittany, it was obvious that the 265th Infantry would soon be committed to battle. Before this happened, General Duevert suffered yet another nervous breakdown on July 27, 1944. He was sent back to Germany and medically retired on November 30.

✦

Hans Junck assumed command of the 265th Infantry Division on August 3, 1944, and was leading it in combat within two weeks. The 265th was not an outstanding division. It had been formed from the 403rd Security Division, which had fought Soviet partisans in the rear areas of Army Groups Don and South, and it had two battalions of eastern troops. Part of the division had been sent to the 7th Army in Normandy as a battle group, where it had been destroyed. Another kampfgruppe had been sent to Russia in 1943 and never returned. Junck was nevertheless able to withdraw the remnants of his division, along with other miscellaneous units, back into the isolated French port of St.-Nazaire, which Hitler dubbed a "fortress" on September 26. A determined American attack would no doubt have ended in the capture of the place, but, after the heavy casualties they suffered in Brest, this was something General Patton decided not to do. St.-Nazaire remained isolated—and guarded by a few U.S. and French battalions—until the end of the war.

13

What Happened to the Defenders of Fortress Europe?

The battle for Fortress Europe was a traumatic moment in the lives of all of those who fought in it, and it ended many of them. This chapter describes the lives of those who survived.

✦

In his retirement, **Erwin von Witzleben** remained involved in the anti-Hitler conspiracy and was earmarked to be supreme commander of the Wehrmacht in the post-Hitler government. He arrived at the Bendlerstrasse, the headquarters of the Replacement Army, at about 4:30 p.m. on July 20, 1944, ordered General Joachim von Kortzfleisch, the pro-Nazi commander of Wehrkreis III, arrested, and replaced him with Lieutenant General Baron Karl von Thüngen-Rossbach. He also sent a telegram to Stülpnagel in Paris, ordering him to arrest all of the SS and SD men in Paris, and he sent Kluge a telegram stating, "The Führer is dead. Carry out your instructions as planned." He signed it, "Witzleben, Supreme Commander of the Wehrmacht." Kluge was taken aback and momentarily prepared to join the putsch, but his OB West chief of staff, General Blumentritt, managed to get through to Major General Helmuth Stieff, the chief of the Organizational Section of OKH, who told him the truth: Hitler was only slightly wounded.[1]

About 10:00 p.m. that night, it became obvious that the assassination attempt had failed and that the plot was falling apart. Witzleben chewed out General Beck and Colonel von Stauffenberg and declared that he would not participate in such a badly organized affair. He dissociated himself from the conspiracy altogether and returned to the Seesen estate near Potsdam, where he was arrested the next day.

Field Marshal von Witzleben was expelled from the army by the so-called Court of Honor (see below). He was tried before Judge Roland Freisler's People's Court. He seemed to have aged ten years during his two weeks in Gestapo captivity. The Gestapo had taken away his false teeth and belt, and his pants were now too large for him, so he had to pull them up constantly. "You dirty old man!" Freisler screamed at him. "Why do you keep fiddling with your trousers?" The specially selected audience of Nazis cackled with malicious delight. When Witzleben was foolish enough to attempt to give the Nazi salute, the judge yelled at him: "The Hitler salute is only given by citizens whose honor is still unimpaired."[2] Witzleben was, of course, convicted of treason and sentenced to death. He was taken to Plötzensee Prison in Berlin and hanged naked that same day. The event was filmed for Adolf Hitler's amusement.

✦

Gerd von Rundstedt's third retirement was very short. He was outraged by the attempt to assassinate Adolf Hitler, and he agreed to serve on the army's so-called Court of Honor, which expelled officers involved in the coup from the military so that they could be arrested by the Gestapo and tried by the Nazi Volksgerichtshof (People's Court). Here most of them were physically tortured by the SS, verbally abused by the judge, and subsequently executed via slow strangulation.

By early September it was obvious that holding the jobs of OB West *and* commander in chief of Army Group B had proved too much for Rundstedt's successor, Field Marshal Model—as Model himself had predicted. In addition, Rundstedt had proved his loyalty to the Führer by his actions on the Court of Honor. He became OB West for the second time on September 4, 1944. Almost simultaneously, the Western Front stabilized because the Allies had outrun their supply lines. Eisenhower then diverted the bulk of his fuel and supplies to Montgomery, who launched an ambitious airborne-ground operation designed to breach the Rhine River, outflank the Siegfried line and capture the Ruhr Industrial District, without which Germany could not wage war. This offensive was defeated by Field Marshal Model at Arnhem.

Hitler, meanwhile, decided to launch a "last chance" offensive in the Ardennes. He built up while Rundstedt checked the Allies in the Siegfried line battles from September to December. Rundstedt, however, opposed the offensive from the beginning. Frankly stating that the plan was "stupid," he simply handed the operation over to Model, who did not believe in it either. Once the order was given, however, Model did his best to carry it out. Rundstedt was very annoyed when the Allied media dubbed the attack "the Rundstedt Offensive."

The Battle of the Bulge began on December 16, 1944. Although it raged into January 1945, Army Group B was effectively defeated by December 26. Germany had lost at least seventy-five thousand men and almost six hundred tanks and assault guns. Worst still, the morale of the German *soldat* in the West was broken. The war was lost.

Eisenhower began his final offensive on February 2, 1945. The Allies broke through the Siegfried line on February 20, and Rundstedt—hampered as always by interference from Berlin—fell back across the Rhine. On March 7 the U.S. 9th Armored Division captured the Ludendorff Railroad Bridge at Remagen, breaching the Rhine River line. Bonn fell the next day, and on March 9 Hitler relieved Gerd von Rundstedt of his command. He was as defeated as his men. He was replaced by Field Marshal Albert Kesselring.

Rundstedt was captured by members of the U.S. 36th Infantry Division on May 2, 1945, at the resort of Bad Tölz, where he was undergoing treatment for arthritis. He was investigated as a war criminal and suffered his second heart attack during interrogation. It was determined that he had cooperated with the Einsatzgruppen (SS murder squads) during the Russian campaign and was scheduled to be tried by a British military tribunal; however, he was released in July 1948, owing to ill health. Gerd von Rundstedt retired to Hanover, where he died on February 24, 1953.

Friedrich Christiansen remained commander, Armed Forces Netherlands, until April 7, 1945. From November 10, 1944, to January 28, 1945, he was simultaneously commander of the 25th Army. On October 2, 1944, on General Christiansen's orders, a raid was conducted on the Dutch town of Putten in retaliation for the killing of one of his officers by the Dutch Resistance. The town was burned, several civilians were shot, and 651 males were deported as slave laborers. Most of these men never returned. In 1948 Christiansen was tried by the Dutch for the raid and was sentenced to twelve years imprisonment. He was released on December 19, 1951, owing to ill health. He died in Innien, Holstein, on December 3, 1972—nine days before his ninety-third birthday.

Hans von Salmuth was relieved of the command of the 15th Army on August 25, 1944, because he had known about the plans for the anti-Hitler putsch but had failed to report it. Arrested by the Allies at the end of the war, he was tried for war crimes in Russia. Among other things, he had cooperated with Himmler's Einsatzgruppen in their actions against the Jews. He was convicted in 1948 and was sentenced to twenty years in prison, but he was released in 1953. He died during the night of December 31, 1961–January 1, 1962, in Wiesbaden.

General of Infantry **Günther Blumentritt** gave up his post as chief of staff of OB West on September 9, 1944. He was acting commander of the XII SS Corps (October 19, 1944–January 1945), acting commander of the 25th Army (January 29–March 28, 1945), and acting commander of the 1st Parachute Army (March 28–April 10, 1945). He ended the war as commander of the ad hoc Army Blumentritt (April 10–May 5, 1945). He was commander in chief of Schleswig-Holstein under the British from May 6 to June 1, when he was taken into custody. Later handed over to the Americans, he was released from the POW camps on January 1, 1948. In his retirement he wrote a laudatory biography of Rundstedt. He died in the city of his birth on October 12, 1967.

✦

Max Pemsel, the former chief of staff of Dollmann's 7th Army, took command of 6th Mountain Division in August 1944. He was the rearguard of XIX Mountain Corps on the Far North sector of the Eastern Front during the night of October 9–10, when strong Soviet amphibious forces landed in his rear and cut the Petsamo-Kirkenes Road, which was the only route of escape for the XIX Mountain. Pemsel not only repulsed strong frontal attacks from the Soviet 14th Army, he also counterattacked and regained control of the road, allowing his division and other units to escape. For this action, he was awarded the Knight's Cross. He was promoted to lieutenant general on November 9 (to date from November 1), proving that Berlin did not hold him responsible for the disasters in Normandy and that he was, in fact, a highly respected combat leader. He was named battle commandant of Berlin on April 4, 1945, but a snowstorm grounded him in Norway and, by the time he arrived in the capital, the post had been filled by another officer—much to Pemsel's relief. Jodl named him chief of staff of the Ligurian Army in northern Italy as a sort of consolation prize, and Pemsel (who pretended to be disappointed) left the doomed capital as quickly as he could. He took up his new duties on April 10 and narrowly avoided being killed by Italian partisans before he surrendered to the Americans near Lake Como on April 28, 1945. In 1956 he reemerged as a general in the West German Army and was commander of the VI Military District (Wehrbereich VI) in Munich. The following year he was named commander of the II Corps in Ulm. He retired as a lieutenant general (the equivalent of an American three-star general in the new rank structure) in 1961 and retired to Regensburg, where he died on June 30, 1985.

✦

Rudolf Hofmann was chief of staff of the 15th Army until November 6,

1944, when he became chief of staff of Army Group H under General Student. He became chief of staff of OB Northwest (northern Germany and Denmark) under Field Marshal Ernst Busch in April 1945. He was promoted to general of infantry on April 20, 1945, and surrendered to the British on May 8, 1945. Released from captivity in March 1948, he returned to his native Bavaria, where he died in Kainsbach on April 13, 1970.

Lieutenant General **Alfred Gause**, Rommel's longtime chief of staff, was in Führer Reserve from November 1, 1944, until April 1, 1945, when he was named commander of the II Corps in the Courland Pocket (in northern Latvia) on the Eastern Front. The men here were hopelessly cut off, and if Germany lost the war—as could now be anticipated by any reasonable person—they would end up in Soviet captivity. It is obvious that someone in the Army Personnel Office held Gause's previous association with Rommel against him. Gause did not receive his promotion to general of engineers, which would have been appropriate for his position. He surrendered his corps on May 10, 1945, and remained in Soviet prisons until 1955. Finally released, he retired to Karlsruhe, West Germany, where he died on September 30, 1967.

Despite his poor handling of Army Group B on D-Day, Lieutenant General **Hans Speidel** was retained as chief of staff by Rommel and his successors, Kluge and Model. Despite Field Marshal Model's efforts to protect him, Speidel was arrested on suspicion of being involved in the anti-Hitler conspiracy, but the Court of Honor did not expel him from the army; he therefore could not be executed, but he did spend the rest of the war in prison. He was freed by French troops on April 29, 1945, the day before Hitler committed suicide. After the war, Speidel became a professor of modern history at the University of Tübingen. In 1955 he became a lieutenant general in the West German Army and held high positions in NATO. Speidel retired as a full general on March 31, 1964, and died at Bad Honnef on November 28, 1984.

Admiral **Theodor Krancke**, the commander of Naval Group West, played an important role in suppressing the anti-Hitler revolt in Paris. He served as commander of Naval Group West until April 18, 1945, and ended the war as commander of Naval Group Norway (April 26–August 26, 1945). Released from prison in 1947, he retired to Wentorf (near Hamburg), where he died on June 18, 1973.

Edgar Feuchtinger continued to command the 21st Panzer Division in the battles of the Siegfried line. On Christmas Eve 1944 a Nazi official arrived at Headquarters, 21st Panzer Division, to investigate his behavior on D-Day and the night before. He was shocked to find that, while his division was fighting the Americans, the general had gone home for the holidays and was away without leave. The investigator saw to it that Feuchtinger was relieved of his command, arrested on January 5, 1945, taken to Fortress Torgau, and court-martialed. He was convicted, demoted to the rank of *Kanonier* (private), and sentenced to death on March 2. His high-ranking Nazi friends, however, secured him a reprieve and assigned him to the 20th Panzer Grenadier Division, then fighting on the Eastern Front. Once out of prison, Feuchtinger quickly deserted and fled to Celle, where he resided when the war ended. He later moved to Krefeld, where he convinced the American occupiers that he had been arrested and condemned because of his anti-Nazi principles and that he had, in fact, resisted the National Socialists. He then went to work for the U.S. Army. He was under investigation for corruption on January 21, 1960, when he died on a trip to Berlin.

In October 1944 **Hermann Oppeln-Bronikowski** was finally given command of his own panzer division—the 20th—on the Eastern Front. He did well in East Prussia and Hungary and was promoted to major general on January 1, 1945. A holder of the Knight's Cross with Oak Leaves, Swords, and Diamonds, he survived the war and settled in Hanover. He died in Gaissach (near Bad Tölz, Bavaria) on September 18, 1966.

Fritz Bayerlein continued in command of the Panzer Lehr until the end of the Battle of the Bulge, even though he was "in a complete daze," according to Theodor-Friedrich von Stauffenberg, Claus von Staffenberg's cousin, coauthor of *The Battle of Sicily*, and an authority on the panzer branch. Despite his popularity with certain Western historians immediately after World War II, Bayerlein's handling of the Panzer Lehr Division in Normandy was not outstanding, and his conduct during the Battle of the Bulge was exceptionally poor. He also accepted false intelligence reports about American troop strengths and movements from a pro-Allied Belgian, as well as bonus road directions. At one point, for example, he wasted valuable time trying to seduce a captured American nurse. At another point during the battle, Baron Hasso von Manteuffel, the commander of the 5th Panzer Army, was seriously considering relieving Baron von Lüttwitz of the command of the XXXXVII Panzer Corps, which had bogged down outside Bastone. Apparently he did not do so only because Bayerlein was the senior divisional commander in the XXXXVII Panzer, and Manteuffel thought he was inferior to Lüttwitz. (This according to Stauffenberg, who had a low opinion of Bayerlein.)[3]

Bayerlein was relieved of his command on January 25, 1945, but was assigned to the hard-pressed 7th Army as a reserve panzer officer. Here he was engaged in organizing stragglers into ad hoc formations. On March 6, 1945, however, General of Cavalry Count Edwin von Rothkirch und Trach accidentally drove into American lines and was captured. As the senior available officer, General Hans Felber gave Bayerlein command of the LIII Corps and ordered him to retake the Ludendorff Bridge at Remagen. He reacted slowly and failed. Field Marshal Model was so dissatisfied with Bayerlein's performance that he transferred all of the LIII Corps's armor to General of Infantry Carl Püchler's LXXIV Corps.[4]

Bayerlein surrendered to the U.S. 7th Armored Division on April 16, 1945. He was released from prison in 1947 and retired to Würzburg. Here he contributed to Chester Wilmot's exhaustive *The Struggle for Europe* but refused to assist Milton Shulman in *Defeat in the West*. Bayerlein also assisted B. H. Liddell Hart in the writing of *The Other Side of the Hill* and in editing *The Rommel Papers*. He also collaborated with Hans Karl Schmidt (aka Paul Carell) in the production of *Hitler Moves East*, *Foxes of the Desert*, *Scorched Earth*, and *Sie Kommen*. In influencing these historians, Friedrich von Stauffenberg later asserted, the less-than-candid Bayerlein succeeded in partially rewriting history.

Immediately after the war, Bayerlein went to work for the Americans, first as an automobile mechanic. He then spent ten years working the U.S. military intelligence service. In the 1960s he went into private business and eventually owned two oriental carpet shops in Würzburg. On January 30, 1970, Fritz Bayerlein died there of a liver disease he had contracted while serving in North Africa. He held the Knight's Cross with Oak Leaves and Swords.

◆

Wolfgang Pickert was promoted to general of flak artillery on March 1, 1945. He led the III Flak Corps on the Western Front until March 19, when he was named general of flak artillery to the commander in chief of the Luftwaffe (Göring). He surrendered to the Americans on May 8, 1945, and was a POW until January 5, 1948. He retired to Weinheim, ten miles north of Heibelberg in northern Baden-Württemberg, where he died on July 19, 1984, at the age of eighty-seven.

✦

Wilhelm Richter (who was suffering from combat fatigue) gave up his 716th Infantry Division in September and, after two months' rest, became deputy commander of an infantry division. Unemployed from December 25, 1944, to late January 1945, he was sent to Norway, where he assumed command of the 14th Luftwaffe Field Division on February 1. He surrendered to the British in May 1945. After his release from the POW camps in 1947 or 1948, he returned to Rendsburg, the home base of his former regiment, where he died on February 4, 1971.

✦

Lieutenant General **Bodo Zimmermann**, the chief of operations of OB West, held his position until the end of the war. He lived in Bonn after "Final Victory" and died in 1963.

✦

Baron Friedrich von der Heydte was promoted to lieutenant colonel and fought against the British in Operation Market Garden, for which he earned the Oak Leaves. In late October he was appointed commandant of the 1st Parachute Army's Battle School. In December 1944 he was given command of a poor quality kampfgruppe, which dropped behind American lines on December 17. (Heydte protested against the drop and even took his case to Field Marshal Model but to no avail.) The jump was scattered, did not accomplish any of its objectives, and was a bit of a disaster. The 6th Panzer Army, which was supposed to relieve it, never arrived, and Heydte—who was injured in the drop—surrendered to the Americans at Monshau on Christmas Day. He was released from the POW camps in 1947.

Heydte earned his PhD in 1950 and became a professor of civil and international law at the University of Mainz. He had a long and distinguished career as a professor of international law at the Ludwig Maximillian University in Munich. Shortly after the West German army was established, Heydte became a lieutenant colonel of reserves. He became a brigadier general (*Brigadegeneral*) of reserves in October 1962. He was elected to the Bavarian Provincial Parliament as a Christian Democrat in 1966 and served until 1970. He also wrote a book about his experiences in Crete, *Daedalus Returned*, which was published in 1958. Baron von der Heydte died in Aham an der Vils, near Landshut, Lower Bavaria, on July 7, 1994, at the age of eighty-seven.

✦

SS General **Werner Ostendorff** returned to duty on October 23, 1944, as commander of the 17th SS Panzer Grenadier Division, but left again in December to become chief of staff of Himmler's Army Group Upper Rhine. Ostendorff assumed command of the 2nd SS Panzer Division on the Eastern Front on February 10, 1945, and led it until March 9, when he was critically wounded by an incendiary shell during the fighting in Hungary. He died in the hospital at Bad Aussee on May 4, 1945. Ostendorff, who was a highly capable and well-liked officer, was one of the few SS officers to refuse to renounce his Christian faith. He left behind a wife, a son, and a daughter.

✦

SS Colonel **Otto Binge**, the commander of the 17th SS Panzer Grenadier Division until he was injured on August 30, was well educated and fluent in French but was not regarded as a good divisional commander on the Western Front because he was too ponderous. He returned to duty in October 1944 but was not given another command. He ended the war on the staff of the SS Main Leadership Office (Führungshauptamt). He died on June 13, 1982.

✦

On September 6, 1944, SS Major General **Kurt "Panzer" Meyer** was cut off by an American task force and was eventually captured by Belgian partisans, who handed him over to the Americans. He was temporarily succeeded as divisional commander by SS Lieutenant Colonel Hubert Meyer. Meyer was tried as a war criminal after the war, and he was convicted of killing eleven Canadian prisoners at his headquarters at the l'Ancienne Abbabye Ardenne on June 7, 1944. He was sentenced to death, but his sentence was reduced to life imprisonment in 1946, and after serving nine years' imprisonment, he was released in September 1954. Meyer's judges accepted some highly dubious evidence, and it seems quite likely that the Canadian prisoners were murdered by Meyer's subordinates without his knowledge. Meyer returned to Hagen, where he worked for the Andreas Brewery. In 1957 he published *Grenadier*, a wartime memoir. He suffered from ill health the last years of his life and died of a heart attack in Hagen on December 23, 1961—his fifty-first birthday.

✦

Wilhelm Mohnke, the commander of the 26th Panzer Grenadier Regiment of the Hitler Youth SS Panzer Division in Normandy, was named commander of the 1st SS Panzer Division "Leibstandarte Adolf Hitler" on August 20, 1944. He was promoted to *SS-Brigadeführer* (SS major general) on January 13, 1945. He was wounded in an air attack on February 6 and was replaced as divisional commander by SS Major General Otto Kumm. Upon recovery, Wilhelm was named commandant of the Reichchancellery in Berlin, a post he held when Adolf Hitler and Eva Braun committed suicide on April 30, 1945. His first order to his men was to shoot Martin Bormann if he created difficulties or refused to submit to Mohnke's authority (which he did not). Mohnke led the subsequent breakout, and although several of his people escaped, Martin Bormann was killed and Mohnke himself was captured. He remained in Soviet prisons until October 10, 1955. He thus escaped trial for the murder of Canadians in Normandy and also the Malmedy Massacre tribunal. He was also accused of having murdered Jews in Russia, but again was never tried for it. Protected by friends in the West German government, he ran a successful business and died a wealthy man in Barsbüttel, a suburb of Hamburg, on August 6, 2001.

✦

A solid and dependable commander in Russia, **Adolf Kuntzen** was not as successful on the Western Front in August 1944. Hitler held him partially responsible for the loss of France—a charge that had little justification. General Kuntzen was nevertheless relieved of his command on September 4, 1944, and he was never reemployed as a general. He had been promoted to general of panzer troops in 1941. He died in Hanover, Lower Saxony, on July 10, 1964.

✦

After Arnhem, General **Hans von Obstfelder** continued to command LXXXVI Corps until late 1944. He then led 1st Army (December 1, 1944–February 28, 1945), 19th Army (March 1–25, 1945), and 7th Army (March 25–May 4, 1945), all on the Western Front. After being released from the POW camps, Obstfelder resided in Kassel, Hessen, where he died in late 1976, at the age of ninety.

✦

When Lieutenant General **Erich Diestel** returned to duty from leave on November 18, 1944, he was named commander of the 331st Special Administrative Divisional Staff in the Netherlands (1944–45). He briefly commanded Corps Diestel (March 23–April 9, 1945) and was acting commander of Army Detachment Kleffel from April 10 until the end of the war. A POW until 1947, he lived near Goslar in the Harz in the 1950s and died in Bad Wiessee in the Bavarian Alps on August 3, 1973.

✦

Baron Heinrich von Lüttwitz, who had led the 2nd Panzer Division in Normandy with a considerable amount of success, became commander of the

XXXXVII Panzer Corps after Funck was unjustly placed in Führer Reserve on September 4, 1944. He was promoted to general of panzer troops on November 1, 1944. He was a very good divisional commander but was less successful commanding a corps, especially in the Battle of the Bulge. Lüttwitz led the XXXXVII Panzer Corps in the Battle of the Ruhr Pocket. Realizing that the war was lost, he did not try to offer fanatical resistance and, together with Bayerlein (now commander of the LIII Corps) and General of Infantry Erich Abraham (commander of the LXIII Corps), surrendered to the Americans on April 16. He was released from prison in 1946 and retired to Neuberg in Bavaria, where he again cultivated his horsemanship and acquired a stable from funds saved from his old estates, which were now lost. He died at Neuburg on October 9, 1969, at the age of seventy-three. His widow, two sons, and a daughter survived him.

✦

Heinz Lammerding was promoted to SS-Brigadeführer und Generalmajor der Waffen-SS on November 9, 1944. He had been wounded on July 26, 1944, and his replacement, SS Colonel Christian Tychsen, had been killed by soldiers of the U.S. 2nd Armored Division on June 28. SS Colonel Otto Baum then assumed the post of acting divisional commander. Lammerding resumed command on October 23.

Heinz Lammerding became chief of staff of Army Group Vistula on January 20, 1945. Its commander, Reichsführer-SS Heinrich Himmler, proved to be in completely over his head, and Lammerding secretly asked Colonel General Gotthard Heinrici, Guderian, and other leaders, to do whatever he could to get rid of Himmler. Himmler stepped down "for reasons of health" on March 20, 1945. The new commander, Heinrici, then promptly sacked Lammerding as well. He retired to Bad Tölz, the site of a former SS training academy, where he prospered financially working as an engineer. He died on January 13, 1971.

✦

Karl-Wilhelm von Schlieben, the commander of Fortress Cherbourg, was released from the prison camps in October 1947 and retired to Giessen, Hesse, where he died on June 18, 1964. He and his wife, Elenor, had six children.

✦

Colonel **Rudolf Bacherer**, the commander of the 77th Infantry Division, was captured on August 15, 1944, and remained a POW until August 15, 1948. He then returned to Baden and died in Bad Krotzingen, Baden-Württemberg, on July 6, 1964. Despite the failure of his gallant attack south of Avranches, he was awarded the Oak Leaves to the Knight's Cross on August 11, 1944. He had received the Knight's Cross in October 1943, for his work in Russia.

Admiral **Walter Hennecke**, the naval commander in Normandy, and the man responsible for the destruction of the Cherbourg harbor, was released from captivity on April 17, 1947, and died in Bad Lippspringe, North Rhine-Westphalia, on New Year's Day 1984.[5]

Since his native Königshütte was now part of Poland, **Robert Sattler**, the commandant of Cherbourg, settled in Seesen, Lower Saxony. He died on August 7, 1978, at the age of eighty-six.

From September 1944 to the end of the war, **Sepp Dietrich** led the 5th Panzer, 6th Panzer, and 6th SS Panzer armies and rose to the rank of SS colonel general. (On February 1, 1945, the 6th Panzer Army was officially redesignated 6th SS Panzer Army.) Sepp Dietrich led the 6th Panzer to its final defeats in Hungary and Austria. He even joked that they called it Panzerarmee 6 "because we have only six panzers left." He broke with Hitler after the fall of Vienna in early April, surrounded his headquarters with men loyal to him personally, and sent the Führer a dispatch inviting him to kiss his backside.

Dietrich surrendered his army to George Patton on May 8, 1945. After stays in several prisons, he, along with Fritz Krämer, Jochen Peiper, and dozens of others, were put on trial at Dachau for the murder of U.S. soldiers at Malmédy. Since Dietrich was not even in the same country at the time, it is difficult to explain how the U.S. Military Government Court found him guilty and sentenced him to life imprisonment. Among those who pled for leniency on his behalf were Field Marshal von Rundstedt, Heinz Guderian, Lieutenant General Wilhelm Speidel, and Siegfried Westphal, the last chief of staff of OB West.

Sepp Dietrich was released from U.S. custody on parole on October 22, 1955. His wife, meanwhile, had divorced him. He was soon pursued by the West Germans, however. The Munich *Landgericht* (Regional Court) found him guilty of being an accomplice to manslaughter in connection with the Blood Purge of the Brownshirts in 1934—and this time he really was guilty. He served seven months at Landsberg (where Hitler had been imprisoned in 1924) before being released in February 1958.

Dietrich spent his last years in poor health at Ludwigsburg, where he died of a heart attack (apparently in his sleep) on April 21, 1966. He had survived

Walter Model by exactly twenty-one years. Seven thousand former SS men and Wehrmacht veterans attended his funeral.

✦

SS General **Paul Hausser** led the 7th Army in Normandy until he was severely wounded during the breakout from the Falaise Pocket. As he was walking down a road, machine gun at the ready, an American artillery shell landed just to his front and a piece of shrapnel struck him in the neck. His men lay him on a panzer, which was one of the few German tanks to escape the pocket. Although Hausser reached safety, two-thirds of his command did not. A poor to mediocre army commander, his dry and sarcastic sense of humor did little to earn him friends in the party or the army; he was nevertheless promoted to the command of Army Group G when he returned to duty in January 1945. By now he was thoroughly disillusioned with Hitler and the Nazi leadership. He was sacked by Hitler on April 3, 1945, after a heated argument with the dictator, because he objected to one of the Führer's senseless hold-at-all-costs orders. Despite his long association with the Waffen-SS, Hausser was not subjected to a long imprisonment after the war. He remained a staunch defender of the Waffen-SS until his death in Munich on December 21, 1972, at the age of ninety-two.

✦

Promoted to *SS-Obergruppenführer und General der Waffen-SS* on August 1, 1944, **Willi Bittrich** made a number of unguarded, derogatory remarks about Himmler and the Nazi leadership. Also, in direct defiance of SS policy, he allowed church services to be held in his command. The Reichsführer-SS ordered him recalled to Berlin, but this move was blocked by Field Marshal Model, who protected him.

A brave and talented commander who was highly respected by his men, Bittrich won his most famous victory at Arnhem in September 1944, when he destroyed a British airborne bridgehead and crushed the British 1st Airborne Division. He led the II SS in the Battle of the Bulge and in Hungary (1945). He held the Knight's Cross with Oak Leaves and Swords (which was awarded on May 6, 1945, a week after Hitler's suicide and several days after Himmler had been stripped of his posts). He surrendered to the Americans at the end of the war, but they turned him over to the French, who held him until 1954. He was tried for war crimes committed in Bordeaux but was acquitted. He died in Wolfratshausen, Upper Bavaria, on April 19, 1979.

✦

SS Colonel **Sylvester Stadler**, who had been seriously wounded in Normandy on July 31, resumed command of the 9th SS Panzer Division October 10, 1944. Promoted to SS major general in late 1944 or early 1945, he led the 9th SS for the rest of the war and managed to surrender it to the Americans. He was only thirty-four years old when the war ended. Stadler died in August 23, 1995.

SS Lieutenant Colonel **Walter Harzer** led the KG 9th SS Panzer Division during the Battle of Arnhem, for which he was awarded the Knight's Cross. Harzer became chief of staff of the V SS Mountain Corps on the Eastern Front in October and assumed command of the 4th SS Panzer Grenadier Division "Police" on November 28. He was promoted to SS colonel two days later and to Oberführer in April 1945. He was active in SS veterans' affairs after the war and died of heart failure on May 29, 1982, in the city of his birth.

Heinz Harmel led the 10th SS Panzer Division at Arnhem, during the Siegfried line battles, at Strasbourg, in Saxony, and in Czechoslovakia. He was promoted to SS major general on September 7, 1944, and was relieved of his command on April 28, 1945, reportedly for refusing to lead his division in a suicide attack. He died in Krefeld on September 2, 2000, at the age of ninety-three.

◆

Fritz Krämer served as acting commander of the 12th SS Panzer Division "Hitlerjugend" from October 24 to November 13, 1944, when he followed Dietrich to the 6th Panzer Army as chief of staff. Dietrich was more impressed with Krämer than he was with Albert Gause, Rommel's former chief of staff. Dietrich allowed higher headquarters to dismiss Gause, who ended up on the Eastern Front. Krämer held this post until the end of the war. He was sentenced to ten years in prison during the Malmédy Massacre trials but did not serve the entire sentence. He died at Höxter, West Germany, on June 23, 1959.[6]

◆

After giving up command of the I SS Panzer Corps, General of Waffen-SS **Georg Keppler** led the III (*germanisches*) SS Panzer Corps on the Eastern Front from October 30, 1944, to February 4, 1945. He assumed command of the XVIII SS Corps on February 12 and led it until the end of the war, surrendering to the Americans on May 22, 1945. A POW until April 1948, he settled in Hamburg, where he ran a chemist shop. He died in Hamburg on June 16, 1966.

◆

While he recovered from his wounds, the Gestapo learned of Field Marshal **Erwin Rommel**'s involvement in the conspiracy of July 20. On October 14 Lieutenant General Wilhelm Burgdorf and his deputy, Major General Ernst Maisel, arrived at his home with a message from Hitler: commit suicide or stand trial. If he stood trial, they added, his family would also be held responsible for his anti-Hitler activities. A half an hour later, the Desert Fox bit a cyanide capsule. He is buried in Ulm.

◆

After he recovered from the wounds he received at Falaise, **Richard Schimpf** resumed command of the 3rd Parachute Division, which had been rebuilt in the Netherlands, on January 6, 1945. On March 8, 1945, Schimpf was captured by American forces near Bad Godesberg before he could escape across the Rhine. He was released from the POW camps just before Christmas 1945.

Schimpf worked as a civilian engineer until 1957, when he joined the Bundeswehr (the West German armed forces) as a major general (equivalent to a *Generalleutnant* in the 1933–1945 rank structure). Schimpf commanded the III Air District until July 31, 1962, when he retired from the military for the last time. He remained busy, however, teaching military technical affairs at the Technical University of Aachen. He died in Düsseldorf on December 30, 1972.[7]

◆

After recovering from the wound he suffered at Falaise, **Eugen Meindl**'s II Parachute fought the British at Cleve and Nijmegen. In 1945 Meindl fought at Venlo and defended the Wesel bridgehead on the lower Rhine. He surrendered his corps to the British in Schleswig-Holstein in May 1945. Released from prison in late September 1947, he died in Munich on January 24, 1951.

◆

Gerhard Grassmann commanded Higher Artillery Command (Harko) 309 during the Normandy fighting, during the Falaise encirclement, and in the retreat to and defense of the West Wall. He became commander of Harko 321 (supporting the 19th Army on the southern sector of the Western Front) on November 15, 1944. He held this post until the end of the war. A POW until June 1947, he settled in Aschaffenburg, Lower Franconia (in southwestern Germany), after the war and died there on September 27, 1975.

◆

Major General **Karl Sievers**, the commander of the defunct 16th Luftwaffe Field Division, was sent back to the Netherlands, where he assumed command of the 719th Infantry Division on July 30, 1944. This static unit was small by German standards. It had only two understrength infantry regiments; an artillery battalion instead of a regiment; engineer and signal companies, instead of battalions; and a mobile company, instead of reconnaissance and antitank battalions. Its staff called its artillery unit "the Artillery Museum of Europe," so old and diverse were its guns. The division saw action in the Battle of the Scheldt, where it suffered heavy casualties. Sievers, however, was no longer considered suitable to command a division. He was relieved of his command on September 30 and was never reemployed. He was nevertheless promoted to lieutenant general the next day. He lived in Göttingen after the war and died on November 9, 1961.

Hans von Luck commanded a battle group in Hitler's ill-fated attempts to break Patton's right flank in September 1944. He then led his kampfgruppe in the retreat to the West Wall, fighting in the western Vosges and in the battles around Saarbrücken and Saarlautern (Saalouis). After General Feuchtinger was arrested, the Army Personnel Office, which was now directed by the strongly pro-Nazi General of Infantry Wilhelm Burgdorf, selected Major General Werner Marcks—another strong Nazi—to replace him. For six days, Luck was acting commander of the 21st Panzer Division. When Marcks actually turned up, Luck returned to the command of his regiment. In this capacity he served in Operation Northwind (Himmler's badly managed offensive aimed at recapturing Strasbourg) and in the battles for the twin villages of Hatten-Rittershoffen, which involved some of the fiercest fighting of the war. The bitter house-to-house fighting in deep snow and brutal cold lasted almost two weeks until January 21, 1945, when the Americans finally withdrew. By this point, the 21st Panzer Division had lost sixteen thousand men since June 6, 1944—more than 100 percent of its strength on D-Day.

In February 1945 the 21st Panzer was transferred to the Eastern Front. The last Soviet offensive began on April 16. By nightfall on April 19, most of the 9th Army, including Luck's command, were virtually surrounded in the Halbe Pocket, about sixty miles southeast of Berlin. General Theodor Busse, the commander of the 9th Army, ordered Luck to spearhead a breakout to the west, across the Dresden-Berlin highway. He did not make it. Vastly outnumbered and pulverized by Stalin tanks, the battle group broke up. A few of the men managed to make it back across the Elbe and surrendered to the Americans. Colonel von Luck, however, was not among them. With a handful of men, he surrendered to the

Soviets on the morning of April 27, 1945—three days before Hitler committed suicide in Berlin.

As a POW, Luck quickly adjusted to prison life and learned Russian. In late 1949 he managed to impress a Soviet colonel who headed a committee responsible for discharging prisoners. Even though this man hated the "vons," as he called German aristocrats, he made an exception and decided to let Luck go. The former colonel was transported back to Germany and discharged at Hamburg on January 5, 1950. He was thirty-nine years old and almost penniless.

Luck started life anew in a Germany he hardly recognized. Initially, he got a job as a night receptionist at a hotel in Hamburg. Finally, however, he received an offer to work for a businessman who intended to set up a firm in Angola. Luck demurred and pointed out his lack of business experience. "The mechanics can be learned," his would-be employer responded. "Good management and reliability are innate."[8] He convinced Luck to accepted the offer, and the former colonel's business career began.

Like F. W. von Mellenthin and Hasso von Manteuffel, among others, Luck was a successful business executive and achieved prosperity as a coffee merchant. He met a lady named Regina, who married him and eventually gave him three sons. Then, in the 1960s, he was astonished to receive an invitation from the British Staff College at Camberley. They wanted him to speak about his experiences in Normandy. He was reticent because he realized that he had served an evil regime, but eventually he accepted. He found the young British officers did not hate him but rather were friendly and anxious to learn from him. Both Luck and the officers enjoyed his speech, and he was invited back regularly. He also spoke on a number of television shows and to other service academies, as well as at the University of Innsbruck and the University of New Orleans, where the coeds expected to meet a high-ranking and brutal Nazi officer. Instead, they were charmed by an Old World aristocrat.

Luck's last years were enjoyable, and he never missed an opportunity to visit a friend from his World War II days—even those who were French. He passed away at Hamburg on August 1, 1997, at the age of eighty-six. His wife and sons survive him.[9]

◆

Hans Schmidt, the commander of Kampfgruppe Heinz and the 275th Infantry Division in Normandy, was severely wounded in Hürtgen Forest, where he distinguished himself. He was still leading the 275th when the war ended.

Part of the division was at Flensburg (near Hamburg) when the Third Reich fell, although part of it was destroyed in the Halbe Pocket on the Eastern Front. General Schmidt surrendered to the Allies in May 1945. He settled in Weiden, Upper Westphalia, and died on November 28, 1971.

General **Paul Mahlmann**, the commander of the 353rd Volksgrenadier Division, led his division in the Siegfried line campaign, including the battles of Maastricht, Trier, and Düren. He particularly distinguished himself against the Americans in the Battle of the Hürtgen Forest, where he was wounded. As the German army retreated toward the Rhine, Mahlmann was relieved of his command on February 15, 1945, for reasons not made clear by the records; he may have been wounded again. In any case he held no further appointments. His division was destroyed in the Ruhr Pocket two months later. General Mahlmann lived in Munich after the war and died in 1963.

After he surrendered Paris, **Dietrich von Choltitz** was imprisoned in several locations, including Clinton, Mississippi. After being released from the POW camps in 1947, he retired to Baden-Baden, where he died of lung disease on November 5, 1966, after a long illness. He was highly respected throughout France, and his funeral was attended by several high-ranking French officers. He was buried in the Stadtfriedhof in Baden-Baden on November 9, on what would have been his seventy-second birthday.[10]

SS Colonel **Otto Baum** commanded the 2nd SS Panzer Division until October 23, 1944. After he led a good part of what was left of the division out of the LXXXIV Corps encirclement, he fought in the Mortain counterattack and in the Falaise breakout. He then took the division (which was now at regimental strength) back to the Siegfried line. He was awarded the Swords to the Knight's Cross with Oak Leaves and was promoted to SS-Oberführer on September 17, 1944. A capable commander, he stepped down as division commander when General Lammerding returned from the hospital. He was given his third division in late October 1944, when he assumed command of the 16th SS Panzer Grenadier Division "Reichsführer SS." Baum led the 16th SS in Italy and Hungary and surrendered his command to the British on May 5, 1945. He was released from the POW camps in 1948 and returned to the town of his birth, where he died on June 18, 1998.

Gustav Wilke led the 5th Parachute until September 1944, when he was ordered to organize the 9th Parachute Division. He led the new division on the Eastern Front and fought in the battles of Stargard, Stettin, Prenzlau, and the Küstrin Bridgehead. On March 10, 1945, he was sent to form a new 10th Parachute Division, which he briefly commanded on the Eastern Front, but he was replaced by Colonel Karl-Heinz von Hofmann in April. He surrendered to the Americans on May 5. He was released from the POW camps in July 1947 and died at Oberstdorf in the Bavarian Alps on March 14, 1977.[11]

✦

General of Panzer Troops **Baron Hans von Funck** and his pregnant second wife traveled to the small Harz Mountain resort town of Blankenburg, where he reopened the long-locked door of his pretty second residence on the town's outskirts. The general considered this place safe from both the Allied bombers and the Soviets. He was half right. To his astonishment—and for no particular reason—U.S.-Russian diplomats arbitrarily decided that the River Mulde would constitute a frontier and thus enclosed all of Anhalt within the Eastern Zone.

The Soviet authorities arrested General von Funck and arraigned him before a Soviet Military Court, which was enforcing a law promulgated by the Supreme Soviet Politburo in 1943: any German officer above the rank of colonel who served against the armies of the USSR was an enemy of the people of the Soviet Union. Minimum sentence: ten years in one of the gulags. He was released in the general amnesty of October 1955. Age fifty-four when he began his imprisonment, he was a weak, white-haired sixty-four when eventually repatriated to West Germany. He died on February 14, 1979, at the age of eighty-eight.

✦

Hitler sacked General of Panzer Troops **Baron Leo Geyr von Schweppenburg** on July 2, 1944, for submitting too honest a report. His forced retirement, however, lasted only a few weeks. On July 21, 1944, the day after the unsuccessful attempt on Hitler's life, Geyr's friend Heinz Guderian became the new chief of the General Staff of the Army. The following month Guderian managed to install Geyr as his successor as inspector general of panzer troops (August 7, 1944–May 8, 1945). Captured by the Americans at the end of the war, Geyr was released from the POW camps in July 1947. He became a prolific writer about military affairs. Until the end of his life, Geyr maintained that he was right and Rommel was wrong concerning the use of German strategic reserves in Normandy. It is difficult to follow his logic, however. He died at Irschenhausen on January 27, 1974.

✦

Lieutenant General **Count Gerd von Schwerin** was relieved of the command of the 116th Panzer Division on September 1, 1944, and was unemployed for more than three months. He still had friends in high places, however, and one of them was Colonel General Heinz Guderian, the chief of the General Staff and the father of Schwerin's former operations officer with the Greyhounds, Heinz Günther Guderian. As a result, when Lieutenant General Ernst-Günther Baade, the commander of the 90th Panzer Grenadier Division in Italy, was seriously wounded by an American sniper, Schwerin was chosen to replace him.

Schwerin commanded the 90th for only a little over two weeks. On December 26, General of Panzer Troops Traugott Herr, the commander of the LXXVI Panzer Corps in Italy, had to step down, in order to undergo an operation on his head. Schwerin was named his temporary replacement. When Herr returned to duty on February 15, 1945, however, he was named commander of the 10th Army, and Gerd von Schwerin was named his permanent replacement. Schwerin was promoted to general of panzer troops on April 1.

During the second week of April, the Anglo-Americans launched a huge offensive against Army Group C in Italy. By April 20 Schwerin's corps was largely destroyed. Rather than suffer any further unnecessary casualties, Schwerin surrendered most of the corps on April 25, earning the censure of OKW and Berlin, which was already surrounded by the Soviets. Hitler committed suicide five days later.

Colonel General Heinz Guderian, the chief of the General Staff from July 21, 1944, to late March 1945 (USAMHI).

Count Gerhard von Schwerin lived in Bonn after the war. He attempted to join the West German Army (the Bundesheer) in the mid-1950s but was not successful. He died in Rottach-Egern in Upper Bavaria on October 29, 1980, at the age of eighty-one.

✦

After his kampfgruppe broke out of the Falaise Pocket and reached the Siegfried line, Colonel **Joseph Rauch** of the 192nd Panzer Grenadier Regiment (21st Panzer Division) reported himself ill in September 1944. In late November, after he recovered from his illness, Rauch attended a brief divisional commanders' course and, on January 1, 1945, assumed command of the 18th Panzer Grenadier Division on the Eastern Front. He was promoted to major general on April 20, 1945. He surrendered to the Soviets at the end of the war and remained in Soviet prisons until 1955. He resided in Landsberg-am-Lech, Upper Bavaria, after the war. He died on August 14, 1984.

✦

Theodor Wisch, the commander of the 1st SS Panzer Division, lost both of his legs in the Battle of Normandy. He retired to Norderstedt, near Hamburg, where he learned to walk, very slowly, on artificial legs. Somewhat of a recluse in his later years, he died on January 11, 1995, at age eighty-seven. His family reportedly sold his medals almost immediately.

✦

General **Friedrich-August Schack**, the former commander of the 272nd Infantry Division, led the LXXXI Corps during the Battle of Aachen from September 4, 1944. Here he made several mistakes and showed definite signs of panic before General Brandenberger, the commander of the 7th Army, realized that he was suffering from exhaustion and combat fatigue. He relieved Schack without prejudice on September 21.

After two months rest, Schack returned to active duty on November 15, 1944, as acting commander of the LXXXV Corps, which he led on the Western Front until December 16. After a brief leave, he attended a monthlong corps commanders' course and assumed command of the XXXII Corps on the Eastern Front on March 26, 1945. Part of the 3rd Panzer Army, he fought on the Oder and in the retreat from Stettin and Pomerania. Promoted to general of infantry on April 20, 1945, he surrendered his command to the British on or about May 8, 1945. After being released from the POW camps in 1947 or 1948, he retired to Goslar in the Harz Mountains after the war and died there on July 24, 1968.

✦

Baron Rudolf-Christoph von Gersdorff was only one of two members of the staff of the 7th Army to escape capture when the British overran the headquarters on August 31, 1944. He escaped on foot, across country. The Gestapo never learned that he attempted to assassinate Adolf Hitler. Fortunate to survive the war, he surrendered to the Americans on May 9, 1945, and remained in the POW camps until November 1947. On August 16, 1967, he was injured in a horse-riding accident and was paralyzed for life. He died in Munich on January 26, 1980.

Lieutenant General **Otto Elfeldt**, the last commander of the LXXXIV Corps, was released from the POW camps on January 20, 1948, he lived at Bad Schwartau (between Lübeck and the Baltic Sea) after the war and died on October 23, 1982.

On December 15 General of Infantry **Erich Straube** was succeeded as commander of the LXXIV Corps by General of Infantry Carl Püchler. From December 17, 1944, until almost the end of the war, Straube led the LXXXVI Corps on the Western Front. He was named commander of the 1st Parachute Army on April 28, 1945, and surrendered on May 8. He retired to Osterode in the Harz and died on March 31, 1971.

✦

Lieutenant General **Kurt Badinski**, the commander of the 276th Infantry Division until he was captured at Falaise, was released from the POW camps in June 1947. He settled in Oldenburg, Lower Saxony (between Bremen and Groningen, the Netherlands), where he died on February 27, 1966.

✦

In early March 1945 Major General **Wilhelm Viebig**, the commander of the 277th Volksgrenadier Division, faced an impossible situation. With the German army in full retreat and in complete disarray and with his back to the Rhine River, he received a "stand fast" order from Führer Headquarters. Viebig ordered his combat units to continue their retreat across the river while he "stood fast" in his command post with a handful of men. (He preferred capture by the Western Allies to execution by the Nazis.) He was captured by the Americans on March 7, 1945, and was released from prison in May 1948. Later that year he became a riding instructor with the British Army of Occupation, a job he held until 1952, when he became a trainer for the riders of the German Olympic Team. He was a stable director in Warendorf, Westphalia, after that. He died in 1982.

✦

Lieutenant General **Paul Danhauser** reformed the remnants of his 271st Infantry Division in the Netherlands in the fall of 1944, where it absorbed the 576th Grenadier Division and was redesignated the 271st Volksgrenadier Division. The division was then sent to the Eastern Front and eventually to the war in Czechoslovakia. Danhauser, however, was named acting commander of Wehrkreis XII in Wiesbaden on October 10. He held this post until November 1, 1944, when he became chief of Army Field Equipment at OKH at Zossen. He escaped the fall of Berlin in April 1945 and surrendered to the Americans on May 8, 1945. Released from the POW camps in June 1947, he settled in Landshut, Bavaria, where he died on December 11, 1974.

✦

Lieutenant General **Erwin Menny**, the former commander of the 84th Infantry Division, was released from the POW camps and retired to Freiburg, where he died on December 6, 1949.

✦

August Dettling, the commander of the 363rd Infantry Division, took the remnants of his command to the Wildflecken Troop Maneuver Area, where it merged with the 566th Volksgrenadier Division to form the 363rd Volksgrenadier Division. Hurriedly sent to the Netherlands, it clashed with the U.S. 101st Airborne Division near Nijmegen in September 1944. The division held a sector in the Arnhem sector until the end of 1944 and in 1945 fought near Aachen, at Düren, on the Rhine, and in the Battle of the Ruhr Pocket. For reasons not made clear by the records, General Dettling was placed in Führer Reserve on February 15, 1945, and was never reemployed. He was captured by the Americans on May 16, 1945, and remained a POW until June 16, 1947. He retired to Ulm, where he died on May 6, 1980.

✦

In the fall of 1944 **Dr. Erwin Kaschner** took his 326th Infantry Division to Hungary, where it was rebuilt as a Volksgrenadier division, in part by absorbing the partially formed 579th Volksgrenadier Division. The 326th reappeared in mid-December on the Western Front in the Roer River battles, during which it helped hold the Hellenthaler Wald against the U.S. V Corps. Later it fought in the Ardennes offensive and was defending in the Eifel area south of St-Vith in January 1945. The following month the 326th was smashed in the Schnee Eifel, where the Americans described it as "dazed" and "disorganized." By March it was in "tiny remnants," retreating along with the German 7th Army. The survivors of the 326th Volksgrenadier ended up in the Ruhr Pocket, where they surrendered to the Americans in April. Kaschner, who had been promoted to major general on January 1, 1945, was captured by the Americans on April 28, 1945, two days before Hitler committed suicide. A prisoner of war until June 1946, he settled in Eutin, eastern Holstein, where he died on November 6, 1973.

✦

SS Lieutenant Colonel **Max Wünsche** was released from prison (apparently in 1948) and managed an industrial plant in Wuppertal, West Germany. A prosperous man and a member of the SS Veterans' Association, he died in Munich on April 17, 1995, at the age of eighty years.

✦

In September Hitler finally realized that commanding both OB West and Army Group B was too much to ask of anybody. On September 4 he recalled Rundstedt from retirement and named him commander in chief of OB West. Field Marshal **Walter Model** retained command of Army Group B.

Model played the major role in defeating Operation Market Garden, the British attempt to breach the Rhine. He inflicted heavy losses on the British 1st Parachute Division in the process. He then largely checked the Allied advances against the Siegfried line until December 16, 1944, when he launched the Battle of the Bulge. Although he believed "this thing doesn't have a damn leg to stand on," he nevertheless did all he could to make it succeed. After it failed, Model led Army Group B until it was surrounded in the Ruhr Pocket. Rather than surrender, he shot himself near Duisburg on April 21, 1945. He lay in an unmarked grave for years. He is now interred in a soldiers' cemetery on the edge of the Hürtgen Forest, not far from the grave of George S. Patton.

Although tactically brilliant, Model tended to oversupervise and was often too harsh in dealing with subordinate commanders, although never with enlisted men. A strongly Catholic and yet pro-Nazi officer, he was drinking heavily by the end of the war.

✦

Major General **Hubertus von Aulock** remained in the POW camps until December 1948. He died at Norderstedt (near Hamburg), Schleswig-Holstein, on January 18, 1979.

✦

General of Panzer Troops **Walter Krüger** continued to lead the LXVIII Panzer Corps on the Western Front, where he fought Hitler's ill-conceived Lüneville counterattacks in September 1944, in the Ardennes, and in the defense of the

Roer River. A good, solid corps commander but not a brilliant one, he was fired by Hitler on March 25, 1945, for his failure to check the Allied advance. After the Führer cooled down, however, Krüger was named commander of Wehrkreis IV, which was headquartered in Dresden, on April 10. In this post he had the painful duty of abandoning his native Saxony to the Soviets.

General Krüger surrendered to members of the U.S. 87th Infantry Division on May 10, 1945, along with two of his generals and most of its staff. He was released on June 26, 1947, and settled in Baden-Baden, Württemberg, on the western edge of the Black Forest. He died here on July 11, 1973, at the age of eighty-one.

✦

On April 1, 1945, General of Artillery **Johann Sinnhuber**, who had been unjustly relieved of the command of the LXXXII Corps in September, was recalled to active duty and commanded a battle group in the Hamburg-Bremen sector until mid-April. He retired to Augsburg, in the Swabian District of Bavaria, where he died on October 23, 1974.

✦

Lieutenant General **Karl Casper**'s 48th Infantry Division fought at Metz and later in the Siegfried line. Attacked by the U.S. 3rd Army in November, it finally collapsed altogether and was temporarily incorporated into the 559th Infantry Division. Reorganized as a Volksgrenadier division in Slovakia and eastern Austria, it was sent to the Eastern Front. It opposed the Soviet drive on Vienna and ended the war at kampfgruppe strength on the lower Danube. Casper surrendered the remnants of his division to the Americans in Austria on May 9, 1945, although part of it did fall into Soviet hands. It had fewer than two thousand men left, despite the fact that it had absorbed the remnants of the 171st Infantry Division. A POW until May 1948, General Casper lived for a time in Baden-Baden but died in Munich on August 25, 1970.

✦

After being relieved of command of the 3rd Air Fleet, Luftwaffe Field Marshal **Hugo Sperrle** was never reemployed. He was bitter over his perceived mistreatment at the hands of Hitler and Göring; in Sperrle's case, however, one can criticize them only for not acting sooner. Sperrle surrendered to the Western Allies on May 8, 1945, and was later tried as a war criminal at Nuremberg but was acquitted in 1946. Embittered after the war, he died in relative poverty in Munich on April 2, 1953.

✦

Luftwaffe Lieutenant General **Beppo Schmid** was captured by the British on April 27, 1945, and was a prisoner of war until April 1, 1948. He then took up residence in Augsburg, Bavaria, and worked with the U.S. Air Force's German Historical Monograph Project in Karlsruhe. He died suddenly on August 30, 1956.

Luftwaffe Colonel General **Otto Dessloch**, the man who bombed Paris, resumed his duties as commander of the 4th Air Fleet, which fought in Romania, Hungary, Yugoslavia, and Austria (September 1944–April 1945). He became commander of the 6th Air Fleet on April 27, 1945, and surrendered to the Western Allies on May 8, 1945. He was released from the POW camps in 1948. He died in Munich on May 13, 1977.

Andreas von Aulock, the defender of St.-Malo, was charged with war crimes for burning part of the city, but he was acquitted. The fire had been started by U.S. Navy gunfire. He retired to Wiesbaden, where he died on June 23, 1968.

Lieutenant General **Karl Spang**, the commander of the 266th Infantry Division in Brittany, was released from the POW camps in 1947 or 1948. He lived in Ellwangen, Baden-Württemberg, after the war and died on August 29, 1979.

Major General **Eugen König**'s 91st Air Landing Division eventually made its way back to the German border, where it fought in the battles of the Siegfried line. It had, however, suffered so many casualties in Normandy that it had to be disbanded. Its survivors were absorbed by the 344th Infantry Division on November 5. König was named commander of the 272nd Volksgrenadier Division in the Eifel (the German Ardennes) on December 13, 1944—the day an American offensive against the division began. König, however, was generally able to hold his positions. An able and effective commander, he was promoted to lieutenant general on March 1, 1945. As the Allies pushed into the Harz Mountains, he was named commander of the remnants of the 12th Volksgrenadier Division on April 12 while simultaneously retaining command of the 272nd. He surrendered to the Americans on April 18. He settled in Bitburg (in the Eifel) after the war and died on April 8, 1985.

General of Paratroopers **Hermann Ramcke**, the defender of Brest, was a prisoner of war in Clinton, Mississippi, for some time, after which he was transferred to French custody. Charged with war crimes in 1951, he escaped and made his way back to Germany, but he voluntarily returned to France shortly thereafter. He was sentenced to five years imprisonment but served only three more months. After his release, he settled in Kappeln (near Flensburg), Schleswig-Holstein on July 4, 1968.

◆

Lieutenant General **Erwin Rauch**, who commanded the 343rd Infantry Division at Brest, reportedly lived in Reicholzheim, Baden-Württemberg, after the war and died on February 26, 1969.

◆

Major General **Hans von der Mosel**, the commandant of Brest and Ramcke's chief of staff, settled in Nienburg/Weser (in Saxony-Anhalt) after the war. He died on April 12, 1969.

◆

After he surrendered the 2nd Parachute Division in the ruins of Brest, Colonel **Hans Kroh** remained in various POW camps until 1948. In 1956 he entered the Bundeswehr as a colonel. He was promoted to brigadier general on September 1, 1957, and assumed command of the West German 1st Air Landing Division the following day. He was promoted to major general on July 1, 1959, and retired on September 30, 1962. General Kroh died in Brunswick, Lower Saxony, on July 8, 1967.

◆

The Americans turned General of Artillery **Wilhelm Fahrmbacher**, after he surrendered Lorient at the end of the war, over to the French, who did not release him until August 1950. From 1951 to 1958 Fahrmbacher served as a military adviser to the Egyptian army. He retired to Garmisch-Partenkirchen, Upper Bavaria (on the Swiss border), where he died on April 27, 1970.

◆

Lieutenant General **Hans Junck** commanded the fortress of St.-Nazaire in Brittany from September 1944 until the end of the war. He was promoted to lieutenant general on January 30, 1945. He surrendered on May 11, 1945, the last German general in the West to do so. The French promptly accused him of war crimes and a trial was held in 1947, but Junck was acquitted of all charges. He was finally released on March 15, 1948. He settled in West Berlin, where he died on November 28, 1966.

✦

Walter Duevert, the former commander of the 265th Infantry Division, lived in Düsseldorf after being medically retired in 1944. He died in 1972.

✦

After his capture by the British outside Amiens in 1944, General **Hans Eberbach** was sent to the London District POW cage and later to the Island Number 11 camp but was transferred to Germany in the fall of 1947. He was released from prison on January 8, 1948. He spent most of the rest of his life working with or directing evangelical schools and charities. He reportedly spent his last few months in a retirement home. Hans Eberbach died on July 13, 1992, at the age of ninety-two.

APPENDIX 1
TABLE OF COMPARITIVE RANKS

U.S. Army	German Army and Luftwaffe
—	Reichsmarschall (Luftwaffe only)*
General of the Army	Field Marshal (Generalfeldmarschall)
General	Colonel General (Generaloberst)
Lieutenant General	General of Infantry, Panzer Troops, etc.
Major General	Lieutenant General (Generalleutnant)
Brigadier General	Major General (Generalmajor)
Colonel	Colonel (Oberst)
Lieutenant Colonel	Lieutenant Colonel (Oberstleutnant)
Major	Major (Major)
Captain	Captain (Hauptmann)
First Lieutenant	First Lieutenant (Oberleutnant)
Second Lieutenant	Second Lieutenant (Leutnant)
—	Senior Officer Cadet or Ensign (Fähnrich)
Officer Candidate	Officer Cadet (Fahnenjunker)
Master Sergeant	Sergeant Major (Stabsfeldwebel)
First Sergeant	—
Technical Sergeant	Technical Sergeant (Oberfeldwebel)
Staff Sergeant	Staff Sergeant (Feldwebel)
Sergeant	Sergeant (Unterfeldwebel)
Corporal	Corporal (Unteroffizier)
—	Lance Corporal (Gefreiter)
Private First Class	Private First Class (Obersoldat)
Private	Private (Soldat, Grenadier, Jäger, etc.)

* Held only by Hermann Göring (July 19, 1940–April 23, 1945).

U.S. Army	Waffen-SS
General of the Army	Reichsführer-SS
General	SS Colonel General (SS-Oberstgruppenführer)
Lieutenant General	SS General (SS-Obergruppenführer)
Major General	SS Lieutenant General (SS-Gruppenführer)
Brigadier General	SS Major General (SS-Brigadeführer)
—	SS Oberführer (SS-Oberführer)
Colonel	SS Colonel (SS-Standartenführer)
Lieutenant Colonel	SS Lieutenant Colonel (SS-Obersturmbannführer)
Major	SS Major (SS-Sturmbannführer)
Captain	SS Captain (SS-Hauptsturmführer)
First Lieutenant	SS First Lieutenant (SS-Obersturmführer)
Second Lieutenant	SS Second Lieutenant (SS-Untersturmführer)
Officer Candidate	SS Officer Cadet (SS-Fahnenjunker)
Master Sergeant	SS Sergeant Major (SS-Sturmscharführer)
First Sergeant	SS First Sergeant (SS-Hauptscharführer)
Technical Sergeant	SS Technical Sergeant (SS-Oberscharführer)
Staff Sergeant	SS Staff Sergeant (SS-Scharführer)
Sergeant	SS Sergeant (SS-Unterscharführer)
Corporal	SS Corporal (SS-Rottenführer)
Private First Class	SS Private First Class (SS-Sturmann)
Private	SS Private (SS-Mann)
—	SS Aspirant (SS-Anwärter)

German Army/Luftwaffe	German Navy (Officer Ranks Only)
Reichsmarschall (Luftwaffe only)	Grand Admiral (Grossadmiral)
Field Marshal (Generalfeldmarschall)	—
Colonel General (Generaloberst)	General Admiral (Generaladmiral)
General (General der . . .)	Admiral (Admiral)
Lieutenant General (Generalleutnant)	Vice Admiral (Vizeadmiral)
Major General (Generalmajor)	Rear Admiral (Konteradmiral)
Colonel (Oberst)	Captain (Kapitän zur See)
Lieutenant Colonel (Oberstleutnant)	Commander (Fregattenkapitän)
Major (Major)	Lieutenant Commander (Korventtenkapitän)
Captain (Hauptmann)	Lieutenant (Kapitänleutnant)
First Lieutenant (Oberleutnant)	Leutnant*
Second Lieutenant (Leutnant)	Leutnant zur See**
Officer Cadet (Fahnenjunker)	Seekadett

* Equivalent to lieutenant (j.g.) in U.S. Navy.
** Equivalent to ensign in the U.S. Navy.

APPENDIX 2
GERMAN STAFF POSITIONS

Chief of Staff (Not present below the corps level)

Ia — Chief of Operations
Ib — Quartermaster (Chief Supply Officer)
Ic — Staff Officer, Intelligence (subordinate to Ia)
Id — Director of Training (not present below army level)
IIa — Chief Personnel Officer (Adjutant)
IIb — Second Personnel Officer (subordinate to IIa)
III — Chief Judge Advocate (subordinate to IIa)
IVa — Chief Administrative Officer (subordinate to Ib)
IVb — Chief Medical Officer (subordinate to Ib)
IVc — Chief Veterinary Officer (subordinate to Ib)
IVd — Chaplain (subordinate to IIa)
V — Motor Transport Officer (subordinate to Ib)
National Socialist Guidance Officer (added 1944)
Special Staff Officers (Chief of Artillery, Chief of Projectors [Rocket Launchers], Chief Signal Officer, etc.)

NOTE: The Ia was referred to as the Generalstabsoffizier 1 (1st General Staff Officer or GSO 1), the Ib was the Generalstabsoffizier 2, the Ic was the Generalstabsoffizier 3, and the Id was the Generalstabsoffizier 4.

APPENDIX 3
GERMAN UNITS, RANKS, AND STRENGTHS

Unit	Rank of Commander*	Strength
Army Group	Field Marshal	2 or more armies
Army	Colonel General	2 or more corps
Corps	General	2 or more divisions
Division	Lieutenant General/ Major General	10,000–18,000 men** 200–350 tanks (if panzer)
Brigade***	Major General/ Colonel	2 or more regiments
Regiment	Colonel	2–7 battalions
Battalion	Lieutenant Colonel/ Major/Captain	2 or more companies (approximately 500 men per infantry battalion; usually 50–80 tanks per panzer battalion)
Company****	Captain/Lieutenant	3–5 platoons
Platoon	Lieutenant/ Sergeant Major	Infantry: 30–40 men Panzer: 4 or 5 tanks
Section	Warrant Officer/ Sergeant Major	2 squads (more or less)
Squad	Sergeant	Infantry: 7–10 men Armor: 1 tank

* Units were commanded by lower-ranking men as the war went on.
** As the war progressed, the number of men and tanks in most units declined accordingly. SS units usually had more men and tanks than Army units.
*** Brigade headquarters were rarely used in the German army after 1942.
**** Called batteries in the artillery (4 or 5 guns per battery).

APPENDIX 4
CHARACTERISTICS OF SELECTED GERMAN AND ALLIED TANKS OF WORLD WAR II

Model	Weight (in tons)	Speed (mph)	Range (miles)	Main Armament	Crew
BRITISH					
Mark IV "Churchill"	43.1	15	120	16-pounder	5
Mark VI "Crusader"	22.1	27	200	12-pounder	5
Mark VIII "Cromwell"	30.8	38	174	175mm	5
AMERICAN*					
M3A1 "Stuart"	14.3	36	60	137mm	4
M4A3 "Sherman"	37.1	30	120	176mm	5
GERMAN					
PzKw II	9.3	25	118	120mm	3
PzKw III	24.5	25	160	150mm	5
PzKw IV	19.7	26	125	175mm	5
PzKw V "Panther"	49.3	25	125	175mm	5
PzKw VI "Tiger"	62.0	23	73	188mm	5
RUSSIAN					
T34/Model 76	29.7	32	250	176mm	4
T34/Model 85	34.4	32	250	185mm	5
KV 1	52	25	208	176.2mm	5
JSII "Joseph Stalin"	45.5	23	150	122mm	4

**All American tanks were also in the British inventory. The British Shermans were sometimes outfitted with a heavier main battle gun. These Shermans were called "Fireflies."

APPENDIX 5
LUFTWAFFE AVIATION UNITS, STRENGTHS, AND RANKS OF COMMANDERS

Unit	Composition	Rank of Commander
OKL	All Luftwaffe units	Reichsmarschall
Air Fleet	Air Corps and Air and Flak divisions	General to Field Marshal
Air Corps	Air and Flak divisions plus various miscellaneous units	Major General to General
Air Division	2 or more wings	Colonel to Major General
Wings	2 or more groups	Major to Colonel Rarely Major General
Group	2 or more squadrons 30 to 36 aircraft	Major to Lieutenant Colonel
Squadrons	2 or more sections 9 to 12 aircraft	Lieutenant to Captain
Section	3 or 4 aircraft	Lieutenant

NOTES

Chapter 1: The Atlantic Wall

1. Between 1920 and 1935, Germany was divided into seven military districts, which were called *Wehrkreise*. Numbered I through VII, each Wehrkreis had one infantry division and assorted other units. The division bore the same number as the Wehrkreis. Each infantry division had two deputy divisional commanders: the *Infanterieführer* (infantry leader) and the *Artillieführer* (artillery commander). Wehrkreis III in Berlin, for example, controlled the 3rd Infantry Division, which included Infantry Commander III and Artillery Commander III. These terms are translated as Infantry Command III and Artillery Command III when referring to the unit or the headquarters, rather than to its commander.

2. Kurt von Schleicher was a "political" general who served as defense minister (1932) and as chancellor for fifty-seven days (1932–33). He was the last chancellor before Hitler but continued to plot a comeback until his murder. Bredow was the chief of Schleicher's ministerial office.

3. Witzleben was supported in his demand by his chief of staff, Colonel Erich von Manstein, as well as by two generals, Gerd von Rundstedt and Ritter Wilhelm von Leeb. The inquiry, however, was blocked by the pro-Nazi defense minister, Colonel General Werner von Blomberg.

4. Franz Halder (1884–1972) was born in Würzburg, Bavaria. He was chief of the General Staff from August 27, 1938, to September 24, 1942, when Hitler fired him. He was never reemployed and ended the war in a concentration camp. Earlier he had commanded the Bavarian 7th Infantry Division (1935–36) and was deputy chief of the General Staff. He was promoted to general of artillery on February 1, 1938, and to colonel general on July 19, 1940.

5. Günther Blumentritt, *Von Rundstedt: The Soldier and the Man* (1952), 21.

6. Brauchitsch was born in Berlin in 1881, the son of General of Cavalry Heinrich von Brauchitsch. His older brother, Major General Adolf von Brauchitsch

231

(1876–1935), retired in 1929. After being educated in cadet schools and serving as personal page for Empress Augusta Victoria, Brauchitsch was commissioned in the elite 3rd Foot Guards Regiment in 1900, but transferred to the 3rd Guards Artillery Regiment the following year. He attended the War Academy (1909–12) and spent World War I as a General Staff officer on the Western Front. He alternated between command and very responsible General Staff positions during the Weimar era and was a lieutenant general commanding the 1st Infantry Division and Wehrkreis I in 1933. He assumed command of Army Group 4 in 1937. This headquarters controlled all of Germany's panzer, light, and motorized divisions. He was named commander in chief of the army on February 4, 1938, and was promoted to field marshal on July 19, 1940. Brauchitsch accepted a bribe from the Nazis in exchange for his appointment as commander in chief, and his appointment effectively brought the army under Hitler's control. He was arrested by the Allies on August 26, 1945, at his estate in Rachut, Holstein, and died in Allied captivity in 1948.

7. Erich von Manstein (1887–1973) was considered by many (including this author) to be the greatest general Germany produced in World War II. His father and stepfather were both generals, and his uncle was Field Marshal Paul von Hindenburg. He attended cadet schools and entered the army as a *Fähnrich* (senior officer cadet) in the elite 3rd Guards Regiment of Foot in 1907. He was a lieutenant colonel when Hitler came to power; he became deputy chief of the General Staff and chief of operations of the army (1936–38); he commanded the 18th Infantry Division (1938–39), served as Rundstedt's chief of staff in the Polish campaign (1939), and originated the plan that led to the fall of France in 1940. During this campaign, he commanded the XXXVIII Corps. Later he led LVI Panzer Corps (1941), 11th Army (1941–42), and Army Groups Don and South (1942–44) on the Eastern Front. Hitler sacked Manstein and Field Marshal Ewald von Kleist on March 31, 1944. Kleist was never reemployed, though Manstein later worked as a consultant. Manstein was sentenced to eighteen years imprisonment as a war criminal in 1950 but was released owing to ill health in 1953.

8. Baron Leo Geyr von Schweppenburg, "Panzer Group West (mid-1943–July 15, 1944)," Foreign Military Studies MS # B-258 (unpublished manuscript, Office of the Chief of Military History, 1947); and Leo Geyr von Schwep-penburg, "Panzer Group West (mid-1943–July 15, 1944)," Foreign

Military Studies MS # B-466 (unpublished manuscript, Office of the Chief of Military History, 1947).

9. Desmond Young, *Rommel: The Desert Fox* (1965), 32 and 41.

10. The *Reichswehr* (armed forces) consisted of the *Reichsheer* (100,000-man army) and *Reichsmarine* (navy). Under the terms of the Treaty of Versailles, Germany had no air force. The Reichswehr was converted to the Wehrmacht in 1938.

11. The War School at Weiner-Neustadt was the former Maria Theresa Military Academy, which was founded in 1751, inside the imperial castle. It is still in operation.

12. Erwin Rommel, *The Rommel Papers*, ed. B. H. Liddell Hart (1953), 82–84; Young, *Rommel*, 76–77.

13. Georg Stumme was born in Halberstadt, Saxony (in central Germany), in 1886 and entered the service as an infantry Fahnenjunker in 1907. Later he transferred to the cavalry, fought in World War I, served in the Reichswehr, and rose to the command of the Prussian 1st Cavalry Regiment at Tilsit. He was Rommel's predecessor as commander of the 2nd Light/7th Panzer Division (1938–40). He commanded the XXXX Panzer Corps in France and Russia (1940–42), before he was sentenced to prison for a security violation. He was promoted to general of cavalry on June 1, 1940, but this rank was changed to general of panzer troops at Stumme's request a year later. Rommel requested that Heinz Guderian replace him as commander of Panzer Army Afrika and was not pleased with the selection of Stumme at all. Rommel left North Africa on September 23.

14. Michael Carver, *El Alamein* (1962), 177; I. S. O. Playfair and C. J. C. Molony, *The Mediterranean and Middle East*, vol. 4, *The Destruction of the Axis in Africa* (1966), 475–76.

15. *Rommel Papers*, 446–47.

16. Heinz-Hellmuth von Wühlisch was born in Oppeln, Upper Silesia (now Opole, Poland), in 1892 and entered the service as a Fahnenjunker in the 5th Hussars in 1912. He went to war with his regiment and was severely wounded in East Prussia on August 12, less than two weeks after hostilities began. Later he became an aerial observer and pilot and was wounded again in the fall of 1915. Selected for the Reichsheer, he served in the 5th Cavalry Regiment (1919–23 and 1929–32), underwent secret General Staff training (1923–25), and served in the Defense Ministry (1925–29 and 1933–34) and on the staff of the 2nd Cavalry Division (1932–33). He transferred to the

Luftwaffe in 1934 and held a variety of command and General Staff positions, including commander of the Air War Academy (1939–40) and chief of staff of the 1st Air Fleet (1941). He became chief of staff of the Armed Forces Commander, Netherlands, in late 1942. Promoted to lieutenant general on April 1, 1942, he committed suicide while in a Dutch prison in September 1947.

17. Metz, which is in the province of Lorraine (Lothringen in German), became part of France in 1552. It was awarded to Germany in 1871, at the end of the Franco-Prussian War, but was returned to France by the Treaty of Versailles in 1919. The Germans recaptured it in 1940, but it again became part of France in 1945.

18. David Irving, *The Trail of the Fox* (1977), 317–18, 334.

19. Friedrich Ruge, *Rommel in Normandy: Reminiscences*, trans. Ursula R. Moessner (1979), 122–23.

20. Dollmann's promotion dates were: first lieutenant (1910), captain (1913), major (1921), lieutenant colonel (1927), colonel (1930), major general (1932), lieutenant general (1933), general of artillery (1936), and colonel general (July 19, 1940).

21. Siegfried Westphal was a General Staff officer known for both his competence and arrogance. Born in Leipzig, Saxony, in 1902, he joined the army as an infantry Fahnenjunker on November 10, 1918—the day before the Armistice. He was commissioned in the 11th Cavalry Regiment in Neustadt, Upper Silesia, in 1922 and remained in cavalry or General Staff assignments virtually his entire career. During World War II, he was Ia of the 58th Infantry Division (1939–40), Ia of the XXVII Corps (1940), on the staff of the Franco-German Armistice Commission (1940–41), Ia of Panzer Group Afrika (later the 1st Italian-German Panzer Army) (1942–43), and chief of staff of OB West (1944–45). He was wounded in North Africa on May 31, 1942, did not return to duty until August 30, and (to his great pride) served as acting commander of the 164th Light Afrika Division from December 1 to 29, 1942. On June 5, 1944, the day after the fall of Rome, he collapsed with a nervous breakdown and did not return to duty until September 9. Promoted to general of cavalry on February 1, 1945, Westphal lived in Dortmund after the war. He died in Celle in 1982.

22. Wilhelm Keitel was born in Helmscherode, Hanover, in 1882. A weak-willed and none-too-bright lackey, he was exactly the kind of yes-man Hitler was looking for. He served as commander in chief of the High Command of

the Armed Forces from February 4, 1938, until the end of the war. He was arrested on May 13, 1945, and was hanged at Nuremberg on October 16, 1946.

Chapter 2: D-Day

1. See Theodor Krancke, "Invasionabwehrmassnahnen der Kriegsmarine im Kanalgebeit, 1944," *Marine-Rundschau* 66 (1969): 170–87.
2. Bernard Law Montgomery, *Normandy to the Baltic* (1958), 43.
3. Hans von Luck, *Panzer Commander: The Memoirs of Colonel Hans von Luck* (1989), 150.
4. Cornelius Ryan, *The Longest Day: June 6, 1944* (1959), 296; and Paul Carell, *Invasion—They're Coming! The German Account of the Allied Landings and the 80 Days' Battle for France*, trans. Ewald Osers (1966), 101. Paul Carell was the pen name of Paul Karl Schmidt (1911–97), the press chief of the Foreign Ministry from 1940 to 1945. Later he authored several popular books about the German armed forces in World War II.
5. Ryan, *Longest Day*, 298–299.
6. P. A. Spayd, *Bayerlein: From Afrikakorps to Panzer Lehr: The Life of Rommel's Chief-of-Staff Generalleutnant Fritz Bayerlein* (2003).
7. Carell, *Invasion*, 112.
8. Ryan, *Longest Day*, 297.
9. See Otto Jacobsen, *Erich Marcks, Soldat und Gelehrter* (1971).
10. Wolf Keilig, *Die Generale des Heeres* (1983), 382.

Chapter 3: The Battles for the Hedgerows

1. Historians do not all agree as to the exact date of Witt's death. Even Kurt Meyer, in his book *Grenadiers: The Story of Waffen SS General Kurt "Panzer" Meyer*, translated by Michael Mendé and Robert J. Edwards (2005) places it as June 16 (p. 238). I have accepted the date provided by the unit historian, SS Lieutenant Colonel Hubert Meyer, who was chief of operations of the division at the time. See Hubert Meyer, *The 12th SS: The History of the Hitler Youth Panzer Division*, translated by H. Harri Henschler (2005), vol. 1, 237–41.
2. Kurt Knispel, the leading panzer ace of World War II, was born in Salisfeld in the Sudetenland (now Salisou, Czech Republic) in 1921. He worked as an apprentice in an automobile factory until 1940, when he voluntarily enlisted in the panzer branch. Assigned to the 29th Panzer Regiment of the 12th Panzer

Division, he fought on the Eastern Front. Later he transferred to the 503rd Heavy Panzer Battalion, which was equipped with Tiger tanks. He briefly fought in Normandy, but most of his 168 confirmed and 27 unconfirmed tank kills were on the Russian Front. The only noncommissioned officer from the Panzerwaffe to be mentioned in a Wehrmacht communiqué, Kurt Knispel was killed in action on April 28, 1945—two days before Hitler committed suicide. A modest man who gave others credit before himself, Knispel was never commissioned and was never awarded the Knight's Cross.

Lieutenant Otto Carius was born in Zweibrücken, Rhineland-Palatinate, in 1922. He served in the 21st Panzer Regiment (20th Panzer Division), the 502nd Heavy Panzer Battalion, and the 512th Heavy Tank Destroyer Battalion, primarily on the Eastern Front. The 512th was transferred to Army Group B in 1945 and ended up in the Ruhr Pocket, so Carius surrendered to the Americans. He had 150 tank kills in World War II—perhaps more. At last report, he was still alive.

Captain Johannes Bölter was born in Mülheim in the Ruhr in 1915. He enlisted in the 10th Cavalry Regiment in 1933 but transferred to the 1st Panzer Regiment (1st Panzer Division) in 1935 and fought with it in Poland, France, and Russia. In March 1942 he transferred to the 502nd Heavy Panzer Battalion, which was equipped with Tiger tanks in 1943. Bölter destroyed at least 139 enemy tanks, not counting unconfirmed kills. He was transferred to Eisenbach as a company commander in the NCO School for Panzer Troops in late 1944 and ended the war commanding a battle group near Kassel. He died in the city of his birth in 1987.

Chapter 4: Cherbourg

1. William B. Breuer, *Hitler's Fortress Cherbourg: The Conquest of a Bastion* (1984), 114.
2. Gordon A. Harrison, *Cross-Channel Attack* (Office of the Chief of Military History, Dept. of the Army, 1951), 441.
3. Breuer, *Hitler's Fortress Cherbourg*, 235.

Chapter 5: Attrition

1. Kurt von der Chevallerie was born in Berlin in 1891. An infantry officer, he distinguished himself on the Eastern Front as commander of the 99th Light Division (1940–41) and the LIX Corps (1941–44). Named commander of the 1st Army on June 2, 1944, he was sacked by Hitler on September 5,

1944. He was in Kolberg, East Prussia, when the Soviets closed in during April 1945. He was last seen on April 18 and was almost certainly killed by the Soviets.

2. Rommel also gave Geyr's Panzer Group West the LXXXVI, II SS Panzer, I SS Panzer, and XXXXVII Panzer Corps. Hausser's 7th Army had only the II Parachute and LXXXIV Corps.

3. The "Der Führer" SS Regiment later became the 4th SS Panzer Grenadier Regiment of the 2nd SS Panzer Division "Das Reich." The "Deutschland" SS Regiment became the 3rd SS Panzer Grenadier Regiment of the 2nd SS Panzer Division. Both managed to surrender to the Americans at the end of the war.

4. Chester Wilmot, *The Struggle for Europe* (1952), 347.

5. Albert Seaton, *The Battle for Moscow, 1941–1942* (1981), 211.

6. Henning von Tresckow was born in Magdeburg on January 10, 1901. He joined the army as a Fahnenjunker in the 1st Guards Regiment of Foot in 1917 and was commissioned the following year. Discharged in 1920, he rejoined the army in 1926 as a member of the elite 9th Infantry Regiment at Potsdam. This unit was known throughout the army as "I. R. von 9" because of its high number of aristocratic officers and its almost hereditary officer corps. Tresckow was a company commander in 1939 but spent most of World War II in General Staff positions, serving successively as chief of operations of the 221st Infantry Division (1939–40), Army Group A (1940), and Army Group B (later Center) (late 1940–43), serving in Poland and on the Russian Front in the process. He briefly commanded the 442nd Infantry Regiment in the Kiev sector of the Eastern Front (October 15–November 12, 1943), before becoming chief of staff of the 2nd Army on November 20. He was promoted to major general on June 1, 1944, with a date of rank of January 30, 1944.

7. Hitler sacked Brauchitsch on December 19, 1941, and assumed the duties of commander in chief of the army himself. This made Halder the senior general left at OKH.

8. David Mason, *Breakout: Drive to the Seine* (1969), 169.

9. L. F. Ellis, *Victory in the West*, vol. 1, *The Battle of Normandy*, with G. R. G. Allen, A. E. Warhurst, and Sir James Robb (1962), 372.

10. Caesar von Hofacker was born in Ludwigsburg (seven miles north of Stuttgart) in 1896. He joined the 20th Ulan Regiment and fought in World War I but had no desire for a military career. He became a lawyer and worked for

United Steel Works in the 1920s and 1930s. Recalled to active duty in 1939, he became head of the Iron and Steel section in the military government of France before becoming Stüplnagel's right-hand man. After the coup failed, Hofacker planned to return to Germany and go underground, but he acted too late and the Gestapo arrested him on July 26, 1944. He was severely tortured but nevertheless defiantly verbally attacked Adolf Hitler when he was put on trial in front of Judge Roland Friesler's People's Court. Even his interrogators were impressed by his spirit and professed admiration for his immense courage. He was hanged in Berlin's Plötzensee Prison on December 20, 1944.

11. John Keegan, *Six Armies in Normandy: From D-day to the Liberation of Paris* (1983), 244.

Chapter 6: St.-Lô

1. "Richard Schimpf," in *The D-Day Encyclopedia*, ed. David G. Chandler and James Lawton Collins Jr. (1994), 481–82; and Rudolf Absolon, comp., *Rangliste der Generale der deutschen Luftwaffe nach dem Stand vom 20. April 1945* (1984), 41.

2. In addition to being a corps commander, Charles H. Corlett (1889–1971) was deputy commander of the U.S. 3rd Army, appointed by Patton. Owing to a blood circulation problem, however, he was forced to give up XIX Corps in the fall of 1944 and return to the states. Later he commanded the XXXVI Corps and retired as a lieutenant general. He had previously commanded the U.S. 7th Infantry Division in the Pacific. Leonard T. Gerow (1888–1972) was the former director of the War Plans Department and assistant chief of the General Staff. He later commanded the 15th Army in the last stages of World War II. He was later commandant of the Command and General Staff College (1945–48) and the U.S. 2nd Army (1948–50). He retired in 1950 as a full general.

3. Reinhard Stumpf, "Eugen Meindl," in *D-Day Encyclopedia*, 360–61; Absolon, *Rangliste der Generale der deutschen Luftwaffe*, 28; and Ernst Martin Winterstein and Hans Jacobs, *General Meindl und seine Fallschirmjägerz: Vom Sturmregiment zum II. Fallschirmjägerkorps, 1940–1945* (1976).

4. Meindl's son Klaus (born in 1924) fought with the paratroopers on the Eastern Front. Commissioned in 1943, Klaus served with the II Parachute Corps in Normandy, as a lieutenant with the 9th Parachute Regiment, 3rd Parachute Division. He was wounded and captured by the Americans near

Mons, Belgium, on September 4, 1944. Imprisoned in Texas, he moved to the United States in the 1950s, became an American citizen, and retired as a warehouse supervisor.

Chapter 7: Caen

1. The 321st Infantry Division was downgraded to Division Group 321 (a regimental sized formation) on November 2, 1943.
2. Luck, *Panzer Commander*, 5. Colonel von Luck's memoir is the source of much of this information. Also see "Colonel Hans von Luck," Obituary, *Times* (London), August 1997, kindly supplied to the author by Mr. Hardy of the Axis History Forum, August 28, 2001.
3. Rudolf Schmundt was born in Metz, Lorraine, in 1896. An infantry Fahnenjunker in 1914, he became chief adjutant to the Führer in early 1938 and rose from major to general of infantry between 1938 and 1944. He became chief of the Army Personnel Office on October 2, 1942. Considered decent but rather slow and politically naive by most of the other generals, Schmundt nevertheless did a good job as chief of the Army Personnel Office. On July 20, 1944, he was blinded by Colonel Claus von Stauffenberg's bomb during the unsuccessful anti-Hitler putsch. He died of his wounds in the hospital at Ratsenburg on October 1, 1944.
4. Dagmar's mother was one-fourth Jewish but was tolerated by the Nazis because she was the wife of a prominent businessman. She judged the situation correctly, however, and realized that this toleration would not continue indefinitely. Accordingly, she went to Switzerland on a vacation and never returned.
5. Luck succeeded Colonel Rolf Mämpel (1895–1955), a Knight's Cross holder from the Eastern Front, who had returned to Germany owing to illness.
6. Luck, *Panzer Commander*, 154.

Chapter 8: The Americans Break Out

1. William B. Breuer, *Death of a Nazi Army: The Falaise Pocket* (1985), 47.
2. Bayerlein even pulled in some of his reconnaissance units and outposts—thus moving them from north of the rectangle into the primary killing zone.
3. Mason, *Breakout*, 45.
4. Bayerlein commentary in *Rommel Papers*, 489–90.
5. Carell, *Invasion*, 235.
6. Larry Collins and Dominique Lapierre, *Is Paris Burning?* (1965), 24.

7. Ibid.

8. E. G. Krätschmer, *Die Ritterkreuzträger der Waffen-SS*, 3rd ed. (1982), 452–55. The 2nd SS Panzer lost two-thirds of its men during the Normandy fighting. Max Hastings, *Das Reich: Resistance and the March of the 2nd SS Panzer Division through France, June 1944* (1981), 217–18.

9. Florian Berberich, "Gustav Wilke," in *D-Day Encyclopedia*, 596; Absolon, *Rangliste der Generale der deutschen Luftwaffe*, 42.

Chapter 9: Counterattack

1. Albrecht Ludwig Otto Ernst, Freiherr von Funck, the older brother of the future panzer general, was born at Aachen on October 25, 1889, and was the oldest child in the family. He entered the army in 1908, fought in World War I, won the coveted *Erinritter* of the Order of St. John in 1917 and continued service under the Reichswehr through 1939, by which time he was a lieutenant colonel on the staff of the German ambassador to Belgrade. He later served as part of the Occupation Government in Yugoslavia, was captured by Tito's partisans at the end of the war, and died, a colonel, in a prison compound on October 17, 1945. Though he had married the *Freifrau* (Baroness) Lonnie von Gultlingen, in Ludwigsberg, Württemberg, on December 19, 1925, they had no children.

2. Theodor-Friedrich von Stauffenberg papers, in the author's private collection.

3. Walter Warlimont (1894–1976) joined the army as a Fahnenjunker in 1913. He was commissioned in the Prussian 10th Field Artillery Regiment in 1914 and fought in France and Italy in World War I, serving as a battery officer, brigade adjutant, and battery commander. He later served in the Märcker Freikorps (which was incorporated into the Reichsheer en masse) and was a General Staff by 1926. In 1929 he traveled to Great Britain and the United States, where he studied industrial mobilization in wartime. He was on the staff of the Industrial Mobilization Office in the Defense Ministry (1930–33). He later headed the office (1935–37) and was a liaison officer to Franco in Spain (1936–37). He commanded the II Battalion/34th Artillery Regiment in Kolbenz (1937–38) and the 26th Artillery Regiment at Düsseldorf (1938) before joining OKW's operations staff. He was deputy chief of the operations staff of OKW (and Jodl's deputy) from September 1939 to September 1944. He was promoted to major general in 1940, lieutenant general in 1942, and general of artillery on April 1, 1944. Even though he was wounded on July 20, 1944, Hitler and Jodl wrongly decided that he might have been

involved in the plot. He was placed in Führer Reserve in September 1944 and was never reemployed. Tried at Nuremberg, he was sentenced to life imprisonment in 1948 but was released in 1957.

4. Nikolaus von Vormann (1895–1959) was the former commander of the 23rd Panzer Division in Russia (1942–43). He led the 9th Army from June 27 to September 21, 1944. Sacked by Hitler, he was given command of fortresses in the Balkans and the Alps but never held another important field command.

5. Stauffenberg papers.

6. Panzer Group West was upgraded to 5th Panzer Army on August 5, 1944.

7. Keilig, *Die Generale des Heeres*, 319.

8. See Samuel W. Mitcham Jr., *Rommel's Desert Commanders: The Men Who Served the Desert Fox, North Africa, 1941–1942* (2007), for a more detailed account of the commanders who were sacked by the Rommel and their subsequent careers.

9. See Heinz Günther Guderian, *Das letzte Kriegsjahr im Westen: Die Geschichte der 116. Panzer-Division—Windhunddivision, 1944–1945* (1993).

10. Meyer, *Grenadiers*, 289–90.

Chapter 10: Falaise: Encirclement and Breakout

1. Like the Bavarian Army, the Royal Württemberg Army functioned independently of Berlin in peacetime. In time of war it was absorbed by the Imperial (Prussian) Army.

2. Georg Tessin, *Verbände und Truppen der deutschen Wehrmacht und Waffen SS im Zweiten Weltkrieg, 1939–1945* (1973–1980), 2: 234–35; Stauffenberg papers.

3. Hermann Breith (1892–1964) recovered from his wounds and later commanded the 3rd Panzer Division and III Panzer Corps on the Eastern Front. The 35th Panzer Regiment would meet a tragic end. In January 1945 it was cut off in East Prussia by the rapid advance of the Red Army. On April 16 it boarded the transport *Goya* for shipment back to the Reich, for the defense of Berlin. En route, the ship was torpedoed by a Soviet submarine and sank in four minutes. For all practical purposes, the 35th Panzer Regiment was wiped out.

4. Dietrich von Saucken (1892–1980) was an East Prussian cavalry officer who possessed incredible courage and the skill to match. As late as March 1945 he categorically (and rudely) refused to obey one of Hitler's orders to the dictator's face—and got away with it. Saucken ended the war as a general of

panzer troops, commanding the 2nd Army in East Prussia (March 1945). He was the last man to receive the Knight's Cross with Oak Leaves and Swords. He surrendered his army to the Soviets in May 1945 and spent the next ten years in Communist prison camps. He died in Munich.

5. Hans Cramer (1896–1968) was a veteran of the campaign in North Africa and was sent back to Africa as commander of the Afrika Korps in February 1943. After the German supply lines to Tunisia collapsed, Cramer surrendered his command to the British. He was subsequently promoted to general of panzer troops. Exchanged in 1944 because he was suffering from severe asthma, Cramer was a special adviser to Panzer Group West. After Rommel's involvement in the plot to overthrow Hitler became known, Cramer (who was close to Rommel) was involuntarily retired on August 17, 1944—effective July 20, 1944—the day of the failed attempt on Hitler's life. He lived in Minden after the war and died at Hausberge.

6. Heinz Wilhelm Guderian—the father of the Blitzkrieg—was born in Kulm, West Prussia, in 1888. Both his father and son became German generals. Promoted to general of panzer troops in late 1938 and to colonel general on July 19, 1940, he was relieved by Hitler for the German failure before Moscow and held no further commands but was inspector general of panzer troops (1943–44) and acting chief of the General Staff of the Army (July 21, 1944– March 1945), a job for which he was intellectually and temperamentally unsuited. The outspoken Guderian was again relieved by Hitler after a bitter argument in March 1945 and surrendered to the Western Allies in northern Italy the next month. Later he wrote a book, *Panzer Leader*, which has been translated into many languages. Although a highly valuable historic document, it should be read carefully and not every word should be accepted at face value—especially Guderian's alledged opposition to Hitler and the Nazis. As chief of the General Staff, for example, he did nothing to prevent the spread of Nazi doctrine within the army—in fact, quite the opposite is true. Guderian's first order as chief of the General Staff, for example, was to outlaw the traditional army salute and to order the adoption of the Nazi salute in its place. He also acted to expel anti-Hitler conspirators from the army, so that they could be tried (and usually hanged) by civilian authorities. Despite this, however, Guderian was an outstanding field commander and a brilliant tactician. He died in Schwangau, Bavaria, in 1954.

7. Joachim Lemelsen (1888–1954) had been named acting commander of the 10th Army in Italy (October–December 1943). Later he commanded 1st

Army in France (May–June 5, 1944) and 14th Army in Italy (1944). He was demoted to deputy army commander in Italy in December 1944. A pro-Nazi, Lemelsen was an excellent motorized divisional commander and did well leading panzers in Russia. He was less successful as an army commander.

Chapter 11: The Fall of France

1. Martin Blumenson, *Breakout and Pursuit* (Office of the Chief of Military History, Department of the Army, 1961), 558; Keegan, *Six Armies in Normandy*, 283.

2. Hans Eberbach, "Pz Group Eberbach at Alençon and Its Break through the Encirclement of Falaise," Foreign Military Studies MS # A-922 (unpublished manuscript, Historical Division, Headquarters, U.S. Forces, European Theater, 1946). Zangen (1892–1964) led the 15th Army for the rest of the war. He surrendered it in the Ruhr Pocket on April 18, 1945.

3. Ibid.

Chapter 12: The Fall of Brittany

1. Each grenadier regiment of the 266th had only two battalions instead of the usual three. Blumenson, *Breakout and Pursuit*, 384; Tessin, *Verbände und Truppen*, 8: 281; Ruge, *Rommel in Normandy*, 94.

2. Major General Ulrich Kleemann, the commander of the 90th Light, was wounded on September 8, when his staff car ran over a mine. Ramcke was succeeded by Colonel Hermann Schulte-Heuthaus on September 17.

Chapter 13: What Happened to the Defenders of Fortress Europe?

1. Joachim von Kortzfleisch was sent to the Western Front and was killed in action on April 20, 1945. Baron von Thüngen-Rossbach was arrested on August 7 (the day Witzleben was hanged) and was hanged on October 24. He had previously commanded the 18th Panzer Division on the Eastern Front (1942–43). General Stieff, who was also a member of the conspiracy, was hanged on August 8. Roland Freisler was killed on February 3, 1945. That day, a thousand American B-17s dropped three thousand tons of bombs of Berlin. One of them scored a direct hit on the courthouse, and Freisler was crushed beneath a falling beam.

2. Peter Hoffmann, *The History of the German Resistance, 1933–1945*, trans. Richard Barry (1977), 682.

3. Stauffenberg papers.

4. Ibid.

5. Hans H. Hildebrand and Ernest Henriot, *Deutschlands Admirale, 1849–1945* (1990), 2: 59–60.

6. Mark C. Yerger, *Waffen-SS Commanders: The Army, Corps, and Divisional Leaders of a Legend* (1997), 1: 326–327; and Franz Thomas, *Die Eichenlaubträger, 1940–1945* (1997), 1: 399.

7. "Richard Schimpf," in *D-Day Encyclopedia*, 481–482; Absolon, *Rangliste der Generale der deutschen Luftwaffe*, 41.

8. Luck, *Panzer Commander*, 262–263.

9. "Colonel Hans von Luck," Obituary, *Times* (London), August 1997.

10. Choltitz's daughter, Timo von Choltitz, maintains a website devoted to her father at http://www.choltitz.de/textebilder/index.htm.

11. Berberich, "Gustav Wilke," 596; Absolon, *Rangliste der Generale der deutschen Luftwaffe*, 42.

BIBLIOGRAPHY

Absolon, Rudolf, comp. *Rangliste der Generale der deutschen Luftwaffe nach dem Stand vom 20. April 1945*. 1984.

Barnett, Correlli, ed. *Hitler's Generals*. 1989.

Berberich, Florian. "Gustav Wilke." In *The D-Day Encyclopedia*, edited by David G. Chandler and James Lawton Collins Jr., 596. 1994.

Blumenson, Martin. *Breakout and Pursuit*. Office of the Chief of Military History, Department of the Army, 1961.

———. "Recovery of France." In *A Concise History of World War II*, edited by Vincent J. Esposito. 1964.

Blumentritt, Günther. *Von Rundstedt: The Soldier and the Man*. 1952.

Bradley, Dermot, Karl Friedrich Hildebrand, and Markus Rövekamp. *Die Generale der Heeres, 1921–1945*. 1993–2004.

Breuer, William B. *Death of a Nazi Army: The Falaise Pocket*. 1985.

———. *Hitler's Fortress Cherbourg: The Conquest of a Bastion*. 1984.

Carell, Paul. *Invasion—They're Coming! The German Account of the Allied Landings and the 80 Days' Battle for France*. 1966.

Chandler, David G., and James Lawton Collins Jr., eds. *The D-Day Encyclopedia*. 1994.

Chant, Christopher, ed. *The Marshall Cavendish Illustrated Encyclopedia of World War II: An Objective, Chronological, and Comprehensive History of the Second World War*. 20 vols. 1972.

Choltitz, Dietrich von. *Soldat unter Soldaten*. 1962.

Collins, Larry, and Dominique Lapierre. *Is Paris Burning?* 1965.

Cooper, Matthew. *The German Army, 1933–1945: Its Political and Military Failure*. 1978.

D'Este, Carlo. *Decision in Normandy*. 1983.

Dietrich, Wolfgang. *Die Verbände der Luftwaffe: 1935–1945*. 1976.

Eberbach, Hans. "Pz Group Eberbach at Alencon and Its Break through the Encirclement of Falaise." Foreign Military Studies MS # A-922. Unpublished manuscript, Historical Division, Headquarters, U.S. Forces, European Theater, 1946.

———. "Report on the Fighting of Panzergruppe West (Fifth Pz Army) from 3 July to 9 August 1944." Foreign Military Studies MS # B-840. Unpublished manuscript, Office of the Chief of Military History, 1947.

Ellis, L. F. *Victory in the West.* Vol. 1, *The Battle of Normandy.* With G. R. G. Allen, A. E. Warhurst, and Sir James Robb. 1962.

Essame, H. "Normandy Revisited." *Military Review* 43, no. 12 (December 1963): 76–77.

Florentin, Eddy. *The Battle of Falaise Gap.* Translated by Meryvn Savill. 1965.

Forman, James. *Code Name Valkyrie: Count von Stauffenberg and the Plot to Kill Hitler.* 1975.

Foster, Tony. *Meeting of the Generals.* 1986.

Fürbringer, Herbert. *9.SS-Panzer-Division.* 1984.

Gavin, James M. *On to Berlin: Battles of an Airborne Commander, 1943–1946.* 1978.

Gersdorff, Rudolf-Christoph von. "Avranches Counterattack, Seventh Army (29 Jul–14 Aug 1944)," Foreign Military Studies MS # A-921. Unpublished manuscript, Office of the Chief of Military History, c. 1947.

Geyr von Schweppenburg, Baron Leo. "Panzer Group West (mid-1943–15 July 1944)." Foreign Military Studies MS # B-258. Unpublished manuscript, Office of the Chief of Military History, 1947.

———. "Panzer Group West (mid-1943–15 July 1944)." Foreign Military Studies MS # B-466. Unpublished manuscript, Office of the Chief of Military History, 1947.

———. "Panzer Tactics in Normandy." U.S. Army *ETHINT 3*, an interrogation conducted at Irschenhausen, Germany, December 11, 1947. On file, U.S. National Archives and Records Administration, Washington, DC.

Graber, Gerry S. *Stauffenberg.* 1973.

Greenfield, Kent R., ed. *Command Decisions.* 1960.

Gohlke, Helmut. *Geschichte der 363. Infanterie-/Volksgrenadier-Division.* 1977.

Goralski, Robert. *World War II Almanac, 1931–1945: A Political and Military Record.* 1981.

Guderian, Heinz. *Panzer Leader.* 1967.

Guderian, Heinz Günther. *Das letzte Kriegsjahr im Westen: Die Geschichte der 116. Panzer-Division—Windhunddivision, 1944–1945.* 1993.

Harrison, Gordon A. *Cross-Channel Attack.* Office of the Chief of Military History, Dept. of the Army, 1951.

Hart, B. H. Liddell. *History of the Second World War.* 2 vols. 1972.

———. *The Other Side of the Hill: Germany's Generals, Their Rise and Fall, with Their Own Account of Military Events, 1939–1945.* 1951.

Hartmann, Heinrich. "General der Fallschirmtruppe Ramcke." *Deutsche Soldatenjahrbuch,* 1978, 144–157.

Hastings, Max. *Das Reich: Resistance and the March of the 2nd SS Panzer Division through France, June 1944.* 1981.

Haupt, Werner. *Das Buch der Panzertruppe, 1916–1945.* 1989.

———. *Rückzug im Westen, 1944: von d. Invasion zur Ardennen-Offensive.* 1978.

Hayn, Friedrich. *Die Invasion von Cotentin bid Falaise.* 1954.

Hildebrand, Hans H., and Ernest Henriot. *Deutschlands Admirale, 1849–1945.* 3 vols. 1988–1990.

Hildebrand, Karl-Friedrich. *Die Generale der deutschen Luftwaffe, 1935–1945.* 3 vols. 1992.

Hoffman, Peter. *The History of the German Resistance, 1933–1945.* Translated by Richard Barry. 1977.

Höhne, Heinz. *Canaris.* Translated by J. Maxwell Brownjohn. 1979.

Irving, David. *Hitler's War.* 1977.

———. *The Trail of the Fox.* 1977.

Jacobs, Hans. *General Meindl und seine Fallschirmjäger: Vom Sturmregiment zum II. Fallschirmjägerkorps, 1940–1945.* 1969.

Jacobsen, H. A., and J. Rohwer, eds. *Decisive Battles of World War II: The German View.* 1965.

Jacobsen, Otto. *Erich Marcks, Soldat und Gelehrter.* 1971.

Keilig, Wolf. *Die Generale des Heeres.* 1983.

Kluge, Günther von. "Personnel Record," Air University Archives, Maxwell Air Force Base, Alabama.

Krancke, Theodor. "Invasionabwehrmassnahnen der Kriegsmarine im Kanalgebiet, 1944," *Marine-Rundschau* 66 (1969): 170–187.

Krätschmer, E. G. *Die Ritterkreuzträger der Waffen-SS.* 3rd ed. 1982.

Kriegstagebuch des Oberkommando des Wehrmacht (Führungsstab). 4 vols. 1961.

Kurowski, Franz. *Das Tor zur Festung Europa.* 1966.

Luck, Hans von. *Panzer Commander: The Memoirs of Colonel Hans von Luck.* 1989.

Luther, Craig W. H. *Blood and Honor: The History of the 12th SS Panzer Division "Hitler Youth," 1943–1945.* 1987.

Lüttwitz, Heinrich von. "Avranches." Foreign Military Studies MS # A-904. Unpublished manuscript, Office of the Chief of Military History.

MacDonald, Charles, and Martin Blumenson. "Recovery of France." In *A Concise History of World War II*, edited by Vincent J. Esposito. 1964.

Mason, David. *Breakout: Drive to the Seine*. 1969.

McKee, Alexander. *Last Round against Rommel: Battle of the Normandy Bridgehead*. 1966.

Mehner, Kurt, ed. *Die Geheimen Tagesberichte der deutschen Wehrmachtführung im Zweiten Weltkrieg, 1939–1945*. 12 vols. 1984–90.

Mellenthin, Friedrich Wilhelm von. *Panzer Battles: A Study in the Employment of Armor in the Second World War*. 1976.

Messenger, Charles. *The Last Prussian: A Biography of Field Marshal Gerd von Rundstedt, 1875–1953*. 1991.

Meyer, Hubert. *The 12th SS: The History of the Hitler Youth Panzer Division*. Translated by H. Harri Henschler. 2005.

Meyer, Kurt. *Grenadiers: The Story of Waffen SS General Kurt "Panzer" Meyer*. Translated by Michael Mende and Robert J. Edwards. 2005.

Miller, Robert A. *August 1944: The Campaign for France*. 1989.

Mitcham, Samuel W., Jr. *Men of the Luftwaffe*. 1988.

———. *Rommel's Desert Commanders: The Men Who Served the Desert Fox, North Africa, 1941–1942*. 2007.

Montgomery, Bernard Law. *Normandy to the Baltic*. 1958.

Perger, Mark C. *SS-Oberst-Gruppenführer und Generaloberst der Waffen-SS Paul Hausser*. 1986.

Perrett, Bryan. *Knights of the Black Cross: Hitler's Panzerwaffe and Its Leaders*. 1986.

Playfair, I. S. O., and C. J. C. Molony. *The Mediterranean and Middle East*. Vol. 4, *The Destruction of the Axis in Africa*. 1966.

Preradovich, Nikolaus von. *Die Generale der Waffen-SS*. 1985.

Ritgen, Helmut. *Die Geschichte der Panzer-Lehr-Division im Westen, 1944–1945*. 1979.

Rommel, Erwin. *The Rommel Papers*. Edited by B. H. Liddell Hart. 1953.

Ruge, Friedrich. "The Invasion of Normandy." In *Decisive Battles of World War II: The German View*, edited by H. A. Jacobsen and J. Rohwer. 1965.

———. *Rommel in Normandy: Reminiscences*. Translated by Ursula R. Moessner. 1979.

Ryan, Cornelius. *The Longest Day: June 6, 1944*. 1959.

Scheibert, Horst. *Die Träger des Deutschen Kreuzes in Gold: das Heer*. 1983.

Schneider, Jost W. *Verleihung Genehmigt!* 1977.

Seaton, Albert. *The Battle for Moscow, 1941–1942.* 1981.

———. *The Fall of Fortress Europe, 1943–1945.* 1981.

———. *The Russo-German War, 1941–45.* 1960.

Shulman, Milton. *Defeat in the West.* 1968.

Spayd, P. A. *Bayerlein: From Afrikakorps to Panzer Lehr: The Life of Rommel's Chief-of-Staff Generalleutnant Fritz Bayerlein.* 2003.

Speidel, Hans. *Invasion, 1944: Rommel and the Normandy Campaign.* 1950.

Stacey, C. P. *Official History of the Canadian Army in the Second World War.* Vol. 3, *The Victory Campaign (The Operations in North-West Europe, 1944–1945).* 1960.

Stauffenberg, Friedrich von. "Panzer Commanders of the Western Front." Unpublished manuscript in the author's private collection.

———. Papers. In the author's private collection.

Stoves, Rolf. *Die Gepanzerten und Motorisierten deutschen Grossverbände: Divisionen und selbständige Brigaden, 1935–1945.* 1986.

Stumpf, Richard. "Eugen Meindl." In *The D-Day Encyclopedia,* edited by David G. Chandler and James Lawton Collins Jr. 1994.

———. *Die Wehrmacht-Elite: Rang- und Herkunftsstruktur der deutschen Generale und Admirale, 1933–1945.* 1982.

Tessin, Georg. *Verbände und Truppen der deutschen Wehrmacht und Waffen-SS im Zweiten Weltkrieg, 1939–1945.* 16 vols. 1973–80.

Thomas, Franz. *Die Eichenlaubträger, 1940–1945.* 2 vols. 1997–98.

Tippelskirch, Kurt von. *Geschichte des Zweiten Weltkrieges.* 1951.

Warlimont, Walter. *Inside Hitler's Headquarters, 1939–45.* Translated by R. H. Barry. 1964.

Wilmot, Chester. *The Struggle for Europe.* 1952.

Winterstein, Ernst Martin, and Hans Jacobs. *General Meindl und seine Fallschirmjäger: Vom Sturmregiment zum II. Fallschirmjägerkorps, 1940–1945.* 1976.

Yerger, Mark C. *Waffen-SS Commanders: The Army, Corps, and Divisional Leaders of a Legend.* 2 vols. 1997–99.

Young, Desmond. *Rommel: The Desert Fox.* 1965.

Ziemke, Earl F. *Stalingrad to Berlin: The German Defeat in the East.* Washington, DC: 1966

Zimmermann, Bodo. "OB West: Command Relationships." Foreign Military Studies MS 308. Unpublished manuscript, Office of the Chief of Military History, c. 1947.

Internet Sources:

http://mysite.version.net/cpq2ycqf/. This is the website of Bayerlein biographer P. A. Spayd. Accessed 2008.

http://www.forum.axishistory.com. Accessed 2005 and 2006.

http://www.geocities.com/~orion47/. Axis Bibliographical Research. Accessed 2008.

http://www.islandfarm.fsnet.co.uk. Accessed 2006 and 2007.

INDEX

ABOUT THE AUTHOR

Dr. Samuel W. Mitcham Jr. is an internationally recognized authority on Nazi Germany and World War II and is the author of twenty books on the subjects, including *Panzers in Winter, Rommel's Lieutenants, Crumbling Empire, Retreat to the Reich,* and *The Desert Fox in Normandy*. A former army helicopter pilot and company commander, he is a graduate of the U.S. Army's Command and General Staff College. He has appeared on the History Channel and National Public Radio, among other media outlets. He lives in Louisiana.